the
artist inside

broadway books • *new york*

the
artist inside

A *Spiritual Guide* to Cultivating
Your *Creative Self*

tom crockett

Broadway Books titles may be purchased for business or promotional use or for special sales. For information, please write to: Special Markets Department, Random House, Inc., 1540 Broadway, New York, NY 10036.

BROADWAY BOOKS and its logo, a letter B bisected on the diagonal, are trademarks of Broadway Books, a division of Random House, Inc.

Visit our website at www.broadwaybooks.com

Library of Congress Cataloging-in-Publication Data

Crockett, Thomas W.
    The artist inside: a spiritual guide to cultivating your creative self / Tom Crockett. —1st ed.
        p.   cm.
    Includes bibliographical references.
    1. Art—Psychological aspects. 2. Creation (Literary, artistic, etc.)—Psychological aspects. 3. Inspiration. 4. Spirituality.   I. Title.
N71.C758   2000
701′.15—dc21   99-054388

FIRST EDITION

DESIGNED BY JUDITH STAGNITTO ABBATE/ABBATE DESIGN

ISBN 0-7679-0394-3

00 01 02 03 04 10 9 8 7 6 5 4 3 2 1

To Meredith,

Without whose companionship and love

I might never have found my path.

contents

chapter 8:

chapter 9:

chapter 10:

acknowledgments

This book marks a point on my own journey of exploration. Tracking that journey backward, I can easily find people who influenced me deeply. My grandparents helped fill me with the kind of confidence that led me to believe I could do anything to which I set my mind. My father and grandfather taught me a love of the natural world. Whatever social skills I have surely come from my mother and grandmothers. My family is supportive of my eccentricities, always encouraging me to follow my dreams. My sister, in particular, has become a friend, confidant, and valued proofreader.

I was blessed with what I now understand were true mentors in my youth. I was given the gift of recognition and admiration from older men, including my teachers, Don Cox, David Johnson, Wally Dreyer, and Cass Johnson. As I begin the phase of my life I like to call "being an elder in training," I realize what a great gift it is for elder men to honor younger men and to bring them into adulthood by modeling what it means to be a mature male. I hope that in my work and my new role as an elder, I can be the kind of mentor I experienced in these men.

But as I track what led me to do the work upon which this book is based and to write the book itself, I recognize five people who have had a profound influence on me. Barbara Savage, a true contemporary nomad, was a catalyst for me. My collaboration with her not only awakened a yearning in me to live my life as a dream artist, but also brought me together with Doug Zaruba. Doug is a fellow dream artist and a jeweler of enormous talent. Our collaborations and discussions helped me refine my vision of what being a dream artist means. When I first met David Gordon, I knew that he was a soul brother. He taught me formal dream-work and is the best dreamworker I've ever met. He is both my best friend and my most valued colleague. Every idea expressed in this book has been tested against the sounding board David provides. I also want to recognize the importance of my friendship with Joe Maiorano. Joe is an enigma to me. I've yet to understand how someone who sees the world and processes information so differently from me can be such a valuable mirror and confidant. He just is. Peruvian shaman and ceremonialist Oscar Miro-Quesada has been both a friend and a teacher. We have lived many lives together and share a beautiful healing dream for our planet.

Of course books don't get published without the hard work of agents and editors. Marcella Hague rescued a manuscript of mine from the slush pile and brought it to the attention of my agent, Kevin Lang. Kevin allowed himself to be drawn into my world of signs and symbols with good humor and enthusiasm. He was patient and persistent and believed in this book enough to bring it to the attention of Suzanne Oaks at Broadway Books. Her suggestions helped me shape and refine this book into a package that is far better than my original proposal.

Writing acknowledgments is hard for me because I'm indebted to so many people, it's hard to know where to stop. My dream family, Rita Dwyer, Victoria Rabinowe, Aku, Dona Matera, Bob Van de Castle, and Carol Warner, have inspired me through their lives and their friendship. Robert Moss and Tom Cowan have influenced me through their teaching. Sharon Hill, with Janet Kehlenbeck's able assistance, has given me and three years' worth of high school students a wonderful opportunity to explore being dream artists through the ArtQuest program. I have always learned a lot from my students; this book wouldn't exist without them. And finally I need to thank my dream-sharing group, David, Arleen, Mark, Kelly, Linda, and Karen, for being brave and willing guinea pigs for many of the activities and ideas in this book.

May we travel deep and true in the dreaming.

May we travel with healing power and courage,

wisdom and enchantment.

May the spirits guide our going and guard our safe return.

introduction

Does art matter?

Individual works of art can have monetary value. Art can entertain, decorate, amuse. It can reflect and comment upon life. Some people argue that art can inspire, elevate, and even transform. But does it really matter?

This is not an idle question. I take it very seriously. As a trained artist, an art teacher, even a teacher of art teachers, I've wrestled with this question for nearly two decades. I've debated with those who would cut funding for the arts in education. I've argued with artists for whom the very idea of questioning art is heretical. I've raised the question at art openings and exhibitions among wealthy art patrons and community leaders. I've asked this question of adults tentatively experimenting with allowing themselves to express their creativity for the first time.

And the answer I've decided is no—art doesn't matter.

At least not in the way I think it should matter.

For me, art is a spiritual practice. It was a spiritual practice for our tribal ancestors; it's still a spiritual practice for most of the indigenous world. Making art was, and is still considered by many to be, an activity that puts one in contact with the divine. I'm not talking about religious art, though religious art can be created as a spiritual practice. Art as a path to spirit is a tradition that goes back to the very roots of religion, when direct, unmediated experience of the spirit world was open to every individual. Some scholars believe the word "religion" derives from *religare*, meaning to "bind back"—relinking or reconnecting us with a sacred reality. When art serves this purpose in the life of an individual or a community, it matters. When it doesn't, art shrinks and retreats from our day-to-day experience.

The practice of artistic expression should be something that each of us has access to. For when the making of art is left in the hands of the ordained few, another barrier grows between us and our birthright to access transcendent spiritual experience. When art is disengaged from spirit, all that remains is commodity. We can only buy and sell it, worship and genuflect before it, rationalize and intellectualize it.

Sometimes an artist will tap into divine consciousness for us. He or she will make that perilous journey into the dark underworld or the brilliant firmament and return with images and artifacts still white-hot with the power to transform. We may glimpse in this something that moves us deeply. But, in the end, when we are consumers instead of creators, we allow others to live our spiritual lives for us.

Art should matter.

At the end of each day, every one of us should be able to say that he or she has had a brush with the divine and interconnected nature of the world. There are many ways to experience this aspect of the sacred. We can approach our work, our relationships, and the care of our bodies, minds, and spirits with reverence. We can meditate, exercise, serve others, make love, sing, dance, and even breathe in ways that put us in contact with something larger than ourselves. And it is this "something larger than ourselves" that I use to define spirit. We all perceive spirit differently. For you, spirit may be embodied in a specific deity, represented by a certain symbol, attached to a place, or connected to a religious tradition. But if we can agree that spirit is something sacred, divine, and greater than we are, we have the common ground with which to continue. Art is a path by which we may come to spirit.

Understanding or reconnecting with your own creative energy not only brings you closer to spirit, it helps you feel more confident and more at peace. We allow artists to go a little crazy—a natural by-product of plugging into the powerful energy of creation—so that we won't have to. But what do we lose by never being allowed to go beyond the rules, to experience our own breakdowns and rebirths? Artists know their own souls' territories. They express the music of their souls through the art they create.

To find the artist inside is to find your dream artist. I use the term "dream artist" to distinguish between the more traditional view of an artist that many people have and my definition of artist as someone who works with spirit in material form. The path of the dream artist is a way to spirit through art.

This work is not just about becoming more creative, though that will certainly happen as you exercise your divine right to create. As you discover the dream artist inside, you will realize that you've always had a creative capacity. While I can't guarantee you a prize in the next art show you enter, what you will discover about yourself may be more valuable than any prize. As you walk the path of the dream artist, you will gain a new respect and appreciation for the spiritual life of things. You will want the material objects and images around you to be filled with the energy of spirit. Your sacred power to create—to find, arrange, alter, and make—will begin to transform your life and your community.

Finding the dream artist inside is like finding your breath. Breath, like creativity, is with us all the time, but we are most aware of it when we experience difficulty with it. To find our creative souls, we must attend to that creative part of ourselves in much the same way that an actor or singer or one who meditates attends to breath. The dream artist inside understands that, as with breath, there are two equally important phases that make up the sacred creative cycle: inspiration and expression.

Inspiration is our contact with the divine, our ability to access the interconnected and energetic nature of life. Expression is our desire to give form to our experience of the divine. Not paying enough attention to inspiration leads to art that is shallow and inconsequential. Not giving enough attention to expression leads to frustration and unrealized dreams. This corresponds to one of the most common complaints about creativity. Artists experience this as artist's block, while nonartists suffer from a sense of creative impotence. Artists become blocked when they lose touch with divine inspiration. Nonartists wall themselves off from creative endeavors because they doubt or deny their powers of expression.

The Artist Inside: A Spiritual Guide to Cultivating Your Creative Self is the expression of the work I've been doing for nearly fifteen years— helping people reconnect with their creative souls. This is a twofold process that reflects the sacred creative cycle of inspiration and expression. By practicing the exercises in this book, you will discover your own sources of inspiration. You will learn three ways to access nonordinary states of consciousness:

- Vision-shifting
- Dreamwork
- Shamanic journeying or self-induced trance states.

Vision-shifting is an energetic way of seeing that you can use at any moment to turn on your intuitive ability and see with new clarity. Dreamwork is the purposeful exploration of night dreams in search of imagery with which to express your soul. Trance states induced through guided visualization, ceremony, or the rhythmic induction of the shaman's drum or rattle take you on journeys deep into imaginal realms, allowing you to seek artistic and creative guidance and to explore the landscape of the spirit world. These nonordinary states of consciousness are where your inspiration will come from. Accessing them will put you in contact with the divine and interconnected nature of the universe.

The second half of the sacred creative cycle is expression. In my experience as a teacher, I've found that some people do well leaping into a new creative process. They can utilize the act of creation itself to find their way to spirit. If you are one of these people, you will find plenty of ideas for ways of making art that will put you in touch with spirit. But most of my students have tended to be at the other end of the spectrum, best represented by my friend Kelly's comment, "You know Tom, I *want* to think I can make art, but the thought of doing it makes me physically ill." For Kelly and all those others who see themselves as creatively disabled, I've developed a series of steps designed to move you from a place of comfort and confidence to new and unknown territory. These steps are both as simple and as profound as they sound. They are finding, arranging, altering, and making.

In helping people find the dream artists inside themselves, I find it useful to share these steps as ways of working. While some travelers new to the path of the dream artist may be anxious about actually starting from raw materials and painting or sculpting, most would gladly play at arranging or altering found objects. In fact, the notion that one can be a dream artist by following the path of finding and collecting is a liberating idea to most adults.

As a finder, a dream artist is a hunter. Hunters have courage and patience and stamina. They attend to their environment. Imagine yourself, journal in hand, walking softly and silently through the jungles of your next yard sale or flea market. I notice that whenever I've dreamed of an object, an animal, a character, or place in a strong and clear way, or in several dreams in a row, what I've dreamed of shows up in my waking life. It might only be an image of what I've dreamed of or a verbal reference to it, but many times the actual subject of my dream manifests itself. This has happened so often that when it doesn't happen, I assume it's my fault—that I wasn't paying enough attention to my environment. My job as a finder is to leave myself open to the possibility of finding my dreams already in physical form in the waking world. I might hunt them with a camera, a sketchbook, or collecting bag, but I know they are out there.

Arrangers are altar builders. They may not call their arrangements altars or shrines, but they create sacred or magical space all the same. An altar can be as simple as three pebbles arranged in careful order on a shelf, or as complex as a corner of a room draped with photographs, fabric, vessels, found objects, dolls, gifts, and religious icons. Most of us create altars all the time without realizing it, but the act of conscious altar-making will increase the power of the altars we build. When you make an altar, think of yourself as a teacher. I've realized over the years that one of the most important roles a teacher plays is that he or she creates a space where learning, an exchange of information or energy, can occur. An arranger is a space artist. Imagine your home filled with special places for your collections—tabletops, shelves, cabinets. Imagine cleaning, shifting, and rearranging your altars to reflect your journeys into the dreaming.

To work as a dream artist who alters you must think of yourself as a healer, taking what comes to you and shifting its energy. This is a subtle process. You must first get inside the object you find. You merge with it, feeling as it feels, sensing as it senses. You must listen with compassion and nonattachment. When you understand what will build and strengthen the energy of this object, you must act upon it. You might bind together two objects as carefully and meticulously as a doctor setting a bone or a surgeon grafting skin. You might mark a stone or shell with paint, ink, or metallic leaf. You might press a design into a piece of wet clay. You might wrap a leaf around a bone and tie it with braided grass twine. Each action, each alteration strengthens, or shifts, or forges a new energetic connection. This is talismanic work.

Those who choose to make imagery or artifacts are the magicians of the dream artist's path. Can you see yourself painting that magic circle on canvas or panel? Can you see yourself filling in the painting with the colors that you brought back from the dreaming? Can you see yourself breathing life into a little ceramic figure, weaving or embroidering an altar cloth that maps your journeys, or throwing spirit vessels on a potter's wheel? Maybe not, but perhaps you will after you fully awaken the artist inside you.

Accessing dreams for inspiration through vision-shifting, dreaming, and journeying in trance states and then expressing and manifesting those experiences in the material world through finding, arranging, altering, and making is shamanic work. A dream artist is also a kind of shaman.

While the title of shaman might be the simpler term, dream artist is more specific—one who does the work of a shaman through the arts. While this may sound like an unfamiliar and inaccessible term, a shaman is simply someone who accesses the spirit world or divine energetic pattern behind life itself to affect change, maintain balance, communicate with spirit, and honor creation. Through your chosen path of finding, arranging, altering, or making, you will learn to perform these same tasks. Sometimes this work is done for personal benefit. More often it is done on behalf of others. The work of a shaman is healing, empowering, enlightening, enchanting. The shaman-as-artist, or dream artist, does this work through images and artifacts. This is the communal aspect of what a dream artist does. When you manifest spirit in material form, you bind your community together and weave yourself inextricably into it.

Dream artists invite magic and enchantment into their lives and the lives of those around them through their work with dream images and dream artifacts. They fill the world with the art of their dreaming lives. Their art is akin to that of tribal cultures that possess no word for art, although their work may not look primitive or borrow from the traditions of any culture. Dream art is not an art of appearance; it's an art of real power. Its source is the dreaming. And, because everyone dreams, becoming a dream artist is within the grasp of everyone.

I believe that art as a path to spirit does matter, but it's taken *me* half a lifetime to fully embrace what it means to believe in the reality of the dreaming—to fully live as a dream artist. It needn't take you so long. *The Artist Inside: A Spiritual Guide to Cultivating Your Creative Self* is an invitation to the shamanic path of enchantment and the soulful expression of spirit through art. It's a guide to using art as a spiritual practice.

• • •

Let me tell you a bit about how I came to be a dream artist. I was blessed with a magical childhood. I had a rich connection to the dream world, which I was allowed to nurture through creative endeavors, and I had a family which was supportive of my eccentricities. As a young adult, I discovered spirit in another, more communal calling: the arts. I first fell in love with theater, especially the raw and ritualistic theater of the sixties and seventies, which seemed to offer a path of transcendence. I acted in, wrote, and directed experimental theater pieces. Later, in college, I had a series of gifted teachers who opened the world of fine art for me. I lost myself in the mind-expanding freedom of a university art department, earning a bachelor's of fine arts with honors in the process. The world of art drew me almost as strongly as the dreaming world.

As I completed my undergraduate degree and went on to earn a master of fine arts degree from the School of the Art Institute of Chicago, I learned to utilize my dream imagery more and more frequently in my art. By the time I completed my formal training as an artist, however, I realized that what I most wanted to be was a primitive artist: a naif, a visionary, a folk artist. I wanted magic, real power, enchantment. I studied prehistoric art and the art of native tribal peoples. I was fascinated by the relationship between their stories and their artifacts. I looked at fetish objects, magical and ceremonial tools, and maps and illustrations for their cosmologies. I wanted to create magical, sacred artifacts. I wanted to be one of a long line of shaman-artists with a deep cultural well from which to draw. But, at the same time, I didn't want to simply appropriate the cultural icons and patterns of different indigenous and tribal peoples, so I did the next best thing. I traveled inward and explored the landscape of dreaming. I learned from the spirit guides I met in the dreaming. I tapped the wisdom of nonordinary reality. I began returning from my dream journeys with stories of whole cultures. I recreated their artifacts, wrote down their myths and legends, and documented them as if I was an anthropologist.

Actually, I've come to see myself as a kind of archaeologist of alternate realities. Just as archaeologists of the waking world travel across physical space and back through chronological time to unearth the artifacts of ancient civilizations and cultures, I can return with the essence of the artifacts of my dreams. By creating—by manifesting—those artifacts in the waking world, I enter more fully into the sacred creative cycle. By bringing back information about the artifacts from my night dreams and my shamanic journeys, I come closer to spirit. This information from the dreaming constantly encourages me to not only observe and quote from the spiritual essence of the world, but to become an active participant in it.

As an art teacher, I've always been most interested in helping amateurs—those who make art for the love of it. Bringing the joy and fulfillment of creative expression into the lives of people who have been persuaded that art is only for the gifted (those blessed by the art gods) has been a passion for me. This book is written from that experience and that perspective. I don't intend for this book to dictate what your art should look like, though you will find exercises and suggestions for bringing spirit into your life through art. I hope that I can set you on a journey to a new world, giving you the guidance and tools to explore your own inner landscape.

Because this is a journey we will take through the magic of the written word, it might help you to have a sense of the territory we will cover. The first part of this journey will be to discover your inner resources. In chapter 1, Art as Sacred Practice: Recovering the Creative Soul, you will learn to jettison some of the baggage that keeps you from claiming your creative legacy and to look at a new model for living a more creative life. Moving more deeply inward in chapter 2, you will discover the power of creative trance and begin to meet and listen to the guidance of the artist inside. Chapters 3, 4, and 5 provide specific instruction for accessing altered states of reality and cultivating new ways of seeing through vision-shifting, dreamwork, and shamanic journeying. Chapter 6 will help you design and create your own sacred space—your studio—for the work you will do as a dream artist. Chapters 7 and 8 offer specific guidance for the techniques of finding, arranging, altering, and making. Chapter 9 is about returning to your community with the new gifts you've acquired. It offers suggestions for giving art to others and using art in ceremony. The final chapter is an invitation to expand the practice of being a dream artist into all aspects of your life.

Each chapter contains some background information that weaves together shamanic tradition and the "work" of the dream artist. I also discuss outfitting—the supplies, materials, and specific techniques you will need for your journey. In addition, each chapter contains exercises and suggestions for discovering the dream artist inside you and developing a spiritually rich creative practice. Each exercise in this book begins with a short reminder of why I recommend this exercise and what you will gain from doing it. Woven throughout are my own personal experiences as well as the experiences of other dream artists who have shared with me their stories.

I've discovered that becoming a dream artist is a path that is open to anyone with a desire to explore and the discipline to practice. My primary task is to provide you with information and techniques that you can use on your quest to discover the dream artist inside of you, but I also want to help you imagine yourself as a dream artist, because if you can imagine it, you can live it.

Your work as a dream artist is alchemical. It involves translation and transformation, manifestation and realization. The task a dream artist takes on is as simple as turning lead into gold and as complex as picking up a pebble. As a dream artist you will translate the images, artifacts, events, and characters of the dreaming states of consciousness into another language—that of physical materials. The insubstantial will be transformed into the substantial. This practice will help you become a master at manifesting reality.

Your view of the artifacts you work with will be different, more energetic, and more animate. You may appreciate the surface qualities, the formal elements of construction and composition, but you are more likely to be drawn to the hidden energetic power of the object or image. The source of your creative energy will be the dream world. You may use different pathways into this state of consciousness, but you will return to and work from this magical place. You may not think of yourself as an artist in the traditional sense. You may choose to express spirit as a collector or by making a ritual out of arrangement, balance, and combination. You may find and alter, or you may actually make images and artifacts with paint, clay, charcoal, wood, stone. But, however your practice evolves, it will be the practice of a dream artist. Can you imagine this?

So now, if you're ready, I'd like to invite you on a journey that begins in the Paleolithic era and stretches into the new millennium—the path of the dream artist.

The gift of this first chapter is a

new awareness.

If you practice these exercises, you should have a

new understanding of what is interfering with your

own creative expression. You should also have

the feeling that you've put some of those fears

and creative curses behind you.

Your creative spirit should feel lighter and

more empowered to emerge in your life.

chapter 1

Art as *Sacred Practice:*
Recovering the *Creative Soul*

*The artist and the shaman were probably one in the same, as artists have ever
since claimed. Through their magical power to recreate the animals on the
walls of the temple caves, they—the artist-shamans—connected the tribe with
the source of life that animated both human and animal, becoming themselves
vehicles of that source, creators of the living form like the source itself.*

—ANNE BARING AND JULES CASHFORD
The Myth of the Goddess: Evolution of an Image

When was the last time you made music? When did you last
dance? What was the last story you told? When was the last time you
engaged in the "work" of art?

These are the questions a shaman or indigenous healer might ask if
you came seeking help or guidance. It wouldn't matter whether your
condition was physical, emotional, spiritual, or emotional. The answers
to these questions would still be of vital interest. If your answer to any of
these questions is "not within the past six months," you might be

instructed to go home and sing, dance, perform, or express your creative spirit. This recommendation alone is often considered sufficient to cure an illness. But even if a return visit to the healer is required, this first step of entering into communion with the spirit world through creative expression is critically important.

There is a connection between artistic expression and spirit that resides deep in our ancestral memory. The native and indigenous cultures from which we all descend understand this connection. It is only our contemporary, Western view of art that de-emphasizes the connection between the material and the spirit. In his book, *The Strong Eye of Shamanism: A Journey Into the Caves of Consciousness*, Robert E. Ryan describes how a well-known aboriginal "shamanic ecstatic dream artist" named Allan Balbungu was able to separate his soul from his body, and, with the aid of his spirit helpers, enter the otherworld of the ancestors to find songs and dances for the tribe. "Allan translates his visionary experience onto the corroboree ground. The poet has delved deeply into the creative source, the world of the spirit, and touched its deepest source. This art not only represents his reception of the songs and dances he has received in the Otherworld but also the very structure of the creative visionary experience itself."

For tribal peoples, the "work" of art is the manifestation of spirit in material form. The tribal individual engaging in artistic expression first accesses the realm of spirit, seeking what we might call inspiration or the breath of the divine. This divine inspiration is then translated into material form with words, images, music, dance, or artifacts. Engaging the spirit, now in material form, through ritual completes the cycle. This ritual releases that spirit and draws artist and community alike back into sacred communion with the divine. This is the sacred creative cycle. It is a cycle of transformation. In his book, *Voices of the First Day: Awakening in the Aboriginal Dreamtime*, Robert Lawlor writes, "Sacred art always implies transformation: the transformation of pure energy into form, the transformation of ancestral powers into animals, animals into humans, and humans, through ritual costume and body painting, into the ancestral beings and their animal powers." When art is about transformation, it is a sacred practice.

But we needn't look far afield to find examples of artists engaging this sacred creative cycle. When dream artist Dan Raven finds a piece of stone, he studies it energetically, vision-shifting to look and listen to what the stone has to share. He slips momentarily into divine space to seek the animal spirit waiting to be released from the stone. Carving the stone is a careful process. He carves until just enough of the animal is visible. This is what is required to release the spirit into the world. More than this and he would be imposing form rather than revealing it. His carvings then become ritual offerings to the elements and power connections between the people who purchase them and the primal spirit. Dan hasn't done this work all his life. He just reached a point where he couldn't "not do it" any longer.

So why is this important? Most of us don't consider ourselves artists. Even if we secretly enjoy expressing ourselves creatively, we may still be frightened of claiming that we are artists. It may seem pretentious to label oneself as an artist, and identifying oneself as an artist might mean being judged. We remember how competitive the arts were in school. Someone else's work was always better than our own. Who needs that pressure?

The point is that being an artist, expressing oneself artistically, is a birthright, not a career path. It's part of what makes us whole and fulfilled. It's one of the primary ways we can connect with spirit in our lives.

The complaints that are most often expressed by members of Western, materialist cultures include a vague sense of unease and insecurity, a deep loneliness or emptiness, and, despite material abundance and prosperity, a sense of being unfulfilled. Sometimes our emotional and spiritual states of dis-ease end up manifesting in physical form within our bodies. But even emotional and spiritual distress can keep us from living our lives fully. A shaman or indigenous healer would identify our condition as growing from a lack of connection to community and spirit.

Engaging in the soulful expression of spirit through art is a way each of us can reconnect to spirit and find a place in a greater community. Organized religions can provide a connection to community and spirit, but many of us are simultaneously evolving beyond the need for institutions and authority figures that interpret the divine for us. We want direct experience. We no longer want to believe in a thing, we want to know it.

In the same way that we've come to rely upon gurus, spiritual leaders, and churches to experience the divine for us, we've also abrogated our right to engage in the "work" of art. We allow artists to make our art for us, as though it was nothing more than a craft or trade—a commodity to be produced by the most efficient means possible. This is as deadening to our creative soul as our reliance on organized religion has been to our spirit. This is not to suggest that powerful artists who dedicate a greater portion of their energy to manifesting spirit in material form will not bring us important visions through their work. In a small ideal community, we might have regular intimate contact with several individuals who engage in the work of art on behalf of their community. We would benefit immensely from such an arrangement, but our role would then be to reflect upon that vision in our lives, to manifest it and translate it through our own creative processes. There is no way around our own individual obligation and responsibility to honor spirit through creative expression.

This is what I call the work of the dream artist. It's a practice that's as old as the painted caves of Lascaux and Altamira. It draws inspiration from the idea that the first artist, the first healer, and the first spiritual caretaker were one in the same—the shaman.

To practice art as a shaman is to see the world as interconnected and alive with spirit. As we journey inside to meet our own dream artists, we undergo a kind of initiation and apprenticeship to open ourselves to the creative world of spirit. I can provide some navigational aids and some tools for embarking on this journey of personal discovery, but this is your heart-path. It will, in the end, be your quest, your manifestation of the beauty and truth you perceive.

Outfitting:
The Dream Artist's Journal

As WITH ANY JOURNEY, there are tools and materials you will need to have at hand. The first and most important of these tools is a journal. Your journal will, in the end, be a better guide to the dream artist's path than anything I could write. You are becoming a shamanic artist, and, like all shamans, your training will come both from without and from within. Your outer guidance will be in the form of this book, your inner guidance will be reflected in the pages of your own journal. I'm hoping to suggest a path rather than provide a detailed itinerary, so I will be setting up experiences that test, challenge, and illuminate. I will periodically ask you to record experiences in your journal. Don't avoid this step. Your own journal can become one of your most profound resources.

So, before going on, find yourself a nice journal. Take some time to select a journal that pleases you aesthetically—one to which you are drawn. I like wire-bound artist's sketchbooks, but I also use scientific lab notebooks with grid patterns printed on each page. As an alternative, you could make your own journal by designing interesting pages on a computer and having them bound at a print shop, or by doing a simple sewn binding of interesting and exotic papers. Gift stores often carry beautiful handmade journals that can be wonderfully evocative. Bigger is better than tiny, but if you travel or choose to carry it with you during the day, get one you can transport easily.

What kind of pages do you want in your journal? Do you like pages with lines? You will be doing some writing, but you'll also draw and paste in pictures. Pay attention to the quality of the paper. Is it heavy enough? Does it have a pleasing texture? Do you like to work on white pages or would you prefer color? How about the cover for the journal— is it stiff enough to support your writing on your lap when a thought occurs to you away from your studio? Test how easy it is to write or draw in. Do you have to forcibly hold the pages open while you write? Is the cover suggestive of what is on the pages? Does it inspire you, or would you prefer something nondescript to keep secret the magical work it contains? The most important thing is to get one you will use. Leave the inside cover and first page blank for the activity described in chapter 2.

Find a pen or a small set of colored markers (black, blue, red, and green are fine). Keep these items together and get in the habit of traveling with them. In a separate pouch or box, keep a pencil and sharpener and a pair of scissors or an X-Acto knife for cutting images out of magazines. It can also help to have a glue stick handy for attaching pictures and found elements to your journal.

In addition to the exercises I will ask you to specifically record or process in your journal, you might also use it to:

1. Sketch objects or patterns
2. Document what you see when practicing vision-shifting
3. Record your dreams
4. Log your shamanic journeys
5. Document images that show up in your life
6. Sketch or design charms, talismans, or amulets
7. Plan ceremonies and rituals.

Carrying a journal or sketchbook will also make you feel more like an artist. It will actually enhance your creativity. A journal or sketchbook is one of those signs by which we recognize creative people. In *The Wizard of Oz*, if the Tin Man had wanted to be an Artist instead of a person with a heart, perhaps the Wizard would have given him a sketchbook.

There are also some ceremonial objects you will want to have for this chapter. Don't spend too much time worrying about these items. You will have plenty of time to replace what you use now with more aesthetically or spiritually satisfying choices later. For now, find a fist-size stone, a bowl of water, a candle, and an incense burner with natural incense. These represent the four elements—earth, water, fire, and air. You may also want a cloth to use as the base for an altar and to have matches or a lighter handy.

To warm up your ceremonial items and dedicate your new journal, set the stone, bowl of water, candle, and incense burner on a table or place where you can easily see them. Light the candle and the incense. Fill the bowl with water. Sit in a comfortable position and breathe deeply from your belly. Honor each of the elements by touching the journal to the symbols before you. Pass the journal through the incense to represent air. Pass it over the candle flame. Touch the cover with a drop of water and press it against the stone. Give thanks to those elements of the earth that give us raw materials like pigment, stone, and the cotton from which our canvas is woven. Give thanks to the transforming power of fire from which we have light to see and heat to forge our tools and harden our clay. Give thanks to the spirit of water that rounds our river stones and gives us paint, dye, and ink. Give thanks to the element of air which dries and cures and carries sound. Create your own dedication, or repeat this one:

> *When I open these pages, I'm calling forth my own dream artist.*
> *Let me be filled with the power of creation.*

Now that you have your first and most important tool—your dream artist's journal—it's time to begin our journey—the journey of developing a personal spiritual practice around art.

In some cultures, shamans select themselves, choosing to study and practice with an elder. In other cultures, the elder shaman identifies his or her apprentice. But one of the most common ways of being called to a shamanic path is through a near-death experience. There is a mythic quality to the shamanic stories of near-death experiences. They symbolize a shedding of old, unproductive ways of thinking to make room for new possibilities.

While I'm not advocating high-risk behavior or telling you to seek out a near-death experience, I think there is something to be gained from cutting loose some of our old ways of being. Most of us have distorted relationships to creativity and the idea of creative expression. This distortion can result in both blockage and disconnection. The artist inside each of us may be buried or submerged in layers we've unconsciously laid down over the years. Before we can establish a healthy relationship with our own creative souls, we need to do some excavation.

Creative Soul Recovery

"*CREATIVITY IS A GIFT. Some people have it, some don't.*"

Is this how you feel about creativity? You're not alone. You're also not ignorant or backward in your thinking. I've heard this same sentiment expressed by university professors with advanced degrees and, even, well-known artists.

But you *are* wrong.

When I teach and lecture to adults, encouraging them to explore their own creativity, I almost always encounter vocal minorities who claim to be without any creativity. I suspect that this vocal minority is actually speaking for an even larger group within any gathering—those who don't feel creative and are too timid to admit it. When I hear a statement like this, rather than dismiss it as foolish, I try to think like a shaman. And as a shaman, I've learned that creativity is, after all, a form of energy to which we all have access. It's a part of our soul that needs to be present for each of us to be whole. When people say that they aren't creative, they are telling me the truth in their own way. Creativity is an energy that, for whatever reason, they do not feel they can access. But that can change, through learning to become a dream artist.

In the traditional sense, a shaman is a healer who accesses and works in nonordinary reality with spirit helpers and guides to identify energy that is either foreign to a person's energy field (unwanted) or missing and depleted (lost, stolen, sacrificed). A diagnosis of foreign energy might suggest an extraction process—the removal of unwanted energy. A diagnosis of missing or depleted energy would suggest the need for a retrieval or recovery process. (At this point it doesn't matter if you believe or accept any of this. Even if only as a metaphor for reality, it makes for a useful way of thinking about a person's relationship to his or her own creativity.)

When a shaman speaks of doing a kind of soul retrieval, you may understand this as the building of a new bridge. It's a reconnection to a kind of energy with which an individual has lost touch or to which he or she has lost access. So, in a workshop or class, my job as an artist/teacher working shamanically is to help as many people as possible rebuild the links to their own creative energy. Facilitating the return of the creative soul is one of the most healing things you can do for another person. Recovering your own creative soul is one of the most empowering things you can do for yourself.

The first step in this creative soul-recovery process is sometimes the hardest. It's amazing to me how many people in our culture can't or won't identify with any of their talents or abilities. We seem to suppress even an honest appraisal of our gifts, as if we are teetering at the edge of some egomaniacal canyon. One positive assessment in our favor and we fear we will plunge headlong into some kind of preening, boastful, self-obsessed madness.

Venture into any preschool and ask children about their gifts. They will unabashedly admit to being dancers, singers, artists, and athletes. Visit the same set of children three or four years later, and the talent inventory will be seriously depleted. What's happened? Did these children suddenly become ungifted, or did we somehow convince them that it was not acceptable to have gifts? As adults, I believe we send mixed signals to our children and students. We encourage them in the belief that they are gifted and talented while socially suppressing our own giftedness. Since children learn first and foremost by example, it's not surprising that the behaviors we model win out over the behaviors we advocate. In tribal cultures, such as the Dagara of Burkina Faso on Africa's western coast, it is the responsibility of the village to see that each adolescent's genius is recognized and brought out into the world. By contrast, we in the West have a very ambivalent relationship to talent, genius, and giftedness. So for many of us, our giftedness has never been formerly recognized by a mentor or by our community.

To begin to address the issue of your own relationship to giftedness, try your hand at identifying your own gifts—by listing them in the shamanic technique of doing an inventory. This inventory will serve as a systematic catalog of your beliefs about yourself and the world.

—— ·ᘏᘏᘏ· ——

THE INVENTORY OF GIFTS

*This exercise will allow you to develop a more
balanced sense of yourself and your potential by
admitting and honoring your gifts and talents.*

Using your journal, make a list of seven things you're good at. Don't be overly concerned with qualifying what "good at" means. You needn't have won prizes to claim to be good at gardening. Don't be surprised if this is difficult at first. We're not encouraged to think about or admit our gifts out loud. There is a great deal of social pressure for us not to stand out in any way. Without even thinking about it, most of us have internalized these constraints. We come to restrict ourselves from admitting giftedness far better than any external critic could.

The gifts you identify should be ones that you are proud of and that make you feel good about yourself. Some of the items you write down may be big gifts or talents, others on your list may seem to be of lesser importance. Don't judge your gifts or evaluate them. Simply claim them. If you run out of talents before you get to seven, go back to your childhood. Remember what you were once good at and proud of. Try to remember if others have commented positively on any of your qualities. Stay with it until you can identify at least seven. If you have more than seven, feel free to skip this exercise and move on. You clearly already have a healthy relationship to your own gifts.

Now, with each of the gifts you identified, describe what it is that makes you good at exercising that gift. Be as specific as possible in listing these elements. For instance, some people may be good cooks because of an ability to follow directions. Others may have an intuitive sense for combining ingredients. Still others might arrange food on a plate or table as carefully and creatively as an artist composing on canvas. Imagine yourself in conversation with a young person who looks up to you. If that young person genuinely wanted to know what it is that makes you good at what you do, what would you say?

Next, name each of the gifts you claimed as your own. Give each gift a title as if it were a kind of energy that you could bring to a situation. For instance, if you identify that you're good with people because you listen well to others, you might name your gift "The Energy of Attentiveness," or "The Gift of Deep Listening."

Rewrite your list of gifts by title in your journal. You should have seven. Find a small object to represent each of the seven gifts. This could be as simple as a shell to represent listening or something more elaborate like a small statue of the Buddha to represent your ability to remain calm.

Give yourself the time to do a small ceremony with these objects. In addition to your objects, gather the following items: a candle, a stone, a bowl of water, and some incense in a burner to represent the elements of fire, earth, water, and air. Place these objects together on a table or shelf in front of you and sit in a comfortable position. Light the candle and the incense. Take seven long, slow, deep breaths. With each exhalation, release self-criticism and judgment. With each inhalation, imagine yourself being filled with spirit. Relax. Slowly and deliberately, one at a time, pick up each of the objects representing your gifts. Pass each object over the candle flame and through the smoke. Touch it to the stone and sprinkle it with a drop of water from the bowl. As you hold each object, state out loud what gift in you it represents. Remember that the gift is in you, not in the object. Once you have stated what the object represents, take a deep breath and retain for the count of three beats. Then bring the object to your lips and blow softly into it, transferring your intention to let that object hold the power of that gift.

Now the objects are filled with the spirit of your individual gifts. When you forget the gifts or need to be reminded of them, picking up the objects will allow the spirit of that gift to flow back into you. Every so often pick up and handle each object. Remember what it stands for. Let the power you've stored in these objects recharge you.

To further deepen your relationship with your gifts over the next seven months, select one gift each month to celebrate. Share this gift with others in as many ways as you can, and with as much drama as you need, to honor your gift publicly. Work this gift into conversation in such a way that you can own it as being yours. Make each month a time to celebrate and honor one gift by exercising it. Don't neglect the act of going public with your gifts. Who knows? You might even encourage others to admit their gifts.

Being proud of our gifts does not necessarily mean that ego must rule our lives, though it is just this fear that is often used by others to discourage or suppress our creativity. We all know the stories and contemporary myths of artists' inflated egos, but there's a real benefit to having a healthy relationship with your gifts. All too often our gifts are hidden or are inaccessible because of the layers of societal control that shroud them.

In the world of the shaman, there is a parallel to this act of identifying gifts and abilities. That is the journey of initiation. This journey, or experience, often involves some form of symbolic or actual wounding or near-death experience, but it also involves the identification of a shaman's medicine or power. In many of the heroic journey myths, there is an external goal or treasure to find or recover, but this is usually symbolic of acquiring some spiritual enlightenment or activating some internal gift lying dormant within the hero. In *The Wizard of Oz*, even children understand that, from the very beginning of their quest, the Scarecrow was smart, the Tin Man compassionate, the Lion brave, and Dorothy could have found her heart's desire all along. What their quest was about was realizing their gifts, claiming them, and living them.

To early anthropological researchers, shamans in many cultures seemed flamboyant and egocentric, proudly displaying the symbols of their power and the records of their achievements, even when the culture at large was more reticent about such behavior. This aggressive self-promotion was sometimes dismissed as a kind of Paleolithic marketing campaign, intended to drum up more business. But this simple explanation missed two key points.

First, for the shaman, everything is done in relationship. There is always collaboration between the healer/teacher/artist and the client/ student/audience. Recent research in learning indicates that we learn more and learn better from people we believe are well qualified. In other words, we agree to learn when we are convinced of our teacher's qualifications. I believe we prepare ourselves to heal in the same way—based on our confidence in the doctor. A young doctor, fresh out of medical school, may actually have better information and more knowledge of advanced techniques and procedures, but patients invariably want an older doctor. We want to see the signs of our doctor's expertise and status. We want the white coat and stethoscope. In the same way, we believe in the work of an artist, if he or she exhibits the behavior and trappings of an artist. Even in the case of creativity, a business may accept creative input from a consultant hired to be creative when it would reject the very same idea when presented from its own staff.

The second benefit the shaman or anyone draws from openly claiming his or her power, medicine, gifts, or abilities, is the increase in self-confidence that allows the energy to build up within and be directed more clearly. When I hang my diplomas on the wall or surround myself with symbols of my achievement, I'm reminding myself of my capabilities more than trying to impress others. If I couple sensitivity with self-confidence, I'm able to act decisively when necessary and eliminate the distraction of self-doubt. A dream artist works with energy as seriously as any healer. If I face a blank canvas plagued with self-doubt, my painting, if I complete it at all, will be timid and lack clarity. Being confident in my creative gifts and skills does not guarantee a great painting, nor does it preclude honest self-challenge or exploration. It does mean that I begin the journey well prepared to do the work to which I'm called.

The ability to claim access to beneficial energies is an important first step in the return of the creative soul, but sometimes there is a deep resistance to engaging the world creatively and expressing the soul's music. I think of this resistance as a curse and, in my experience, have found that it can be linked back in the lives of most people to events and interactions that were indeed very much like curses.

LIFTING A CREATIVITY CURSE

*This exercise will allow you to confront the beliefs
that suppress the dream artist inside and
keep you from living to your full
creative potential.*

Okay, it's time to return to your journal. This is another inventory. This time I'd like you to list the creative things you *can't* do. I'm not talking about creative endeavors you've never tried, but endeavors you believe you have no talent for or at which you think you are particularly inept. Leave some space next to or below each item for additional notes. If you're having a hard time thinking of creative areas, just compare your own sense of your creative ability against the following list:

- Drawing
- Painting
- Sculpting
- Modeling with clay
- Photographing
- Singing
- Dancing
- Playing a musical instrument
- Storytelling
- Performing
- Telling a joke
- Arranging
- Crafting
- Designing
- Planning
- Organizing
- Writing
- Building.

Next to each item in your list, explain why you believe you don't have a talent for this. Be as specific and go as far into your past as necessary. Identify what feedback convinced you that you were untalented in this area. It may have been a deliberately mean or hurtful comment by a friend, a teacher, or a family member, like in the case of my friend Mark, whose family made deliberate sport of his early experimentation with dancing. To this day he holds himself rigidly. It may have been an accidental comment that was not meant to hurt, but stifled you nonetheless, as with my wife, Meredith, who finds it painfully hard to sing out loud. When she was a child at choir practice, the choir leader asked her to just move her lips and not let any sound come out. It may also have been expectations you set for yourself that were not met. Sometimes we can be our own harshest critics. As a young adult, I set up tests for myself to find out if I was talented in certain areas. If I didn't win some prize or receive some external reinforcement, I decided that I was not talented in those areas. Sometimes our curses aren't connected to our sense of talent but our sense of expression. For example, I've heard people say, "Even if I was expressive, I wouldn't have anything to say."

All of these are curses. A curse, as I define it, is a belief that keeps you from living to your potential. We can curse ourselves as easily as we can be cursed by others. Those closest to us have the greatest capacity to curse us, but sometimes strangers can reinforce or resurrect a long-forgotten curse. The first step in lifting a curse is acknowledging it. We have to turn and face the curse and the source of the curse. Sometimes this means examining some of our earliest childhood experiences.

Next, I'd like you to write out each curse individually on a small piece of colored paper. Get a fireproof bowl or container (an ovenproof glass dish or a clay flowerpot with some sand in it) and a candle. Set aside some time in which to perform a ceremony of release. Play some somber and relaxing music and sit in a comfortable position in front of your candle and bowl. Light the candle and do some deep breathing to relax. Read your curses out loud one at a time in this format:

I once believed . . . (insert your curse) . . . but now I believe . . .
(refute your curse by stating the opposite)

Light the paper and hold onto it as long as possible without burning yourself. Drop it into the bowl and watch the smoke rise up, carrying your curse with it. Feel yourself growing physically lighter with the lifting of each curse. Even if you don't feel anything, make an effort to sit up straighter and imagine yourself getting lighter. When you are done, make sure the ashes are completely out. Mix them with sand and take it outside to a place where you can sprinkle the remains. Let the wind or the current or the earth itself take the remains of your creativity curses.

These are your major curses—the ones that reflect your specific beliefs about your talent in areas of expression. You should be feeling lighter and energetically more open already.

To complete this lifting and clearing, you also need to address some lingering minor curses. These are the beliefs you hold about creativity, art, and expression in general. Use your journal to complete the following statements:

- To be an artist, I'd have to give up . . .
- All artists are alike, they're . . .
- I can't be creative until . . .
- If I really expressed my soul's music . . .
- Creative people are never very good at . . .
- I had a friend who was real artistic and now she's (he's) . . .

Do the sentences you've completed betray negative beliefs or fears about being artistic? Do they seem silly when you write them out or do they seem like statements of common sense? If they seem both negative and justified, try to find out why you believe this. Have you ever felt betrayed by or jealous of someone's creative expression?

These are the scripts we carry about the relative value of creative and expressive individuals to society, community, or family. Another set of beliefs goes like this:

- Artists are emotional.
- Artists are unrealistic.
- Artists are just children who won't grow up.

- Artists are egomaniacs.
- Artists tend to abuse drugs and alcohol.
- Artists are difficult to live with.
- Artists must starve for their art.
- Artists must suffer to be great.

Again, try to track the origin of these beliefs. From whom did you first hear them? Sometimes these beliefs come from family; sometimes they come from society. After you've explored each of your curses, examine them in the light of reason. Are there exceptions to the blanket rules of these statements? If so, write those exceptions down. Turn these limiting beliefs around. Restate them in a more positive fashion.

- Artists are often more in touch with their emotions.
- Artists sometimes don't accept the "real" world as it is.
- Artists are able to experience the world with childlike wonder.
- It helps an artist to have a healthy and strong sense of self.

The minor curses are easier to lift because they don't directly relate to your sense of self at this point. Often all it takes is to face them, acknowledge them, and reframe them.

The work of creative soul recovery never really ends. The exercises you've just practiced are a way of opening the door for the creative soul recovery process to begin to occur. But the real return of your creative soul will occur as you begin to do creative work.

I taught a workshop once in which I used instant photography to help the participants open up to their own creativity. An older woman came with her daughter and made it clear from the start that she should not have been there because of her creative shortcomings. After some preliminary work, I sent the participants out with an assignment to photograph objects that could serve as metaphors or symbols for themselves. I was not so interested in what they intended to photograph as I was in what ended up in their photographs, for I have found that there is always a fascinating dichotomy that emerges through the conflict between waking and dreaming (or conscious and subconscious) minds. Upon returning, the skeptical woman tossed her first bunch of photographs down in front of me as a challenge. I focused on one image of a thick gnarled wisteria vine growing up a brick garden wall. "That's me," she said, "old and bent." I called her attention to the light streaming through the open gate at the edge of the image. "I didn't mean to include that," she argued.

"But you did include it," I continued. "What does that part of the image say about you?"

She thought about it a moment and then observed that the vine was actually growing around the wall into the light. She smiled despite herself, and her whole demeanor shifted. Her body lifted and straightened. Her eyes brightened.

"Maybe there's hope for me yet," she laughed.

I haven't seen this woman since the workshop, and I have no way of knowing how lasting her experience was, but in that moment she had access to something she had long ago lost. A gateway opened up just like the one she had subconsciously photographed, and through that opening she caught a glimpse of her creative soul.

Now that we've opened up the possibility that you have a creative soul, it's time to get to know that artist inside. Through a series of inner and outer directed exercises in the next chapter, you will learn to draw out the dream artist that lives inside of you. But before we leave this chapter, think back to the questions I asked at the beginning of the chapter. Answer these questions for yourself in your journal.

1. When was the last time you made music?
2. When did you last dance?

3. What was the last story you told?
4. When was the last time you engaged in the "work" of art?

Think about—and describe in your journal if you wish—the last time you engaged in these activities, how you felt doing them, and why you haven't done them more recently.

———— ʊʊʊʊʊ ————

The gift of this second chapter is

confidence

—the confidence that comes from an introduction—a formal

meeting with your own dream artist. The exercises in this

chapter will help you create an image of the potential and

possibility of your own creative spirit. Also, you will be

introduced to some of the internal and external techniques

that the dream artist uses to make art a spiritual practice.

chapter 2

Meeting the *Artist Inside:*
The Creative *Trance*

As mediators between the sacred and the profane, shamans may also become
"image makers." This does not necessarily mean that they create images of
spirits and deities. Images themselves, if not activated during ritual, are
ineffective. Because sacred messages are formless and ineffable, shamans have
to provide symbolic representations of the sacred in the material world, and
they achieve this, for example, non-verbally during their rituals and through
their paraphernalia and the objects they use during their sessions.

—RUTH-INGE HEINZE
Shamans of the 20th Century

Do you know what sends you into a trance? What kind of stimulation relaxes you deeply, allowing your mind to fill with images, sounds,
and feelings? What takes you out of your body? Is it imagery—a colorful
mandala, a beautiful sunset, a painting, an intricate pattern, the sensual
curve of a body in repose? Is it sound—a droning background noise
like waves, wind, or water splashing; a symphony; ethereal new age

compositions; rhythmic drumming; or the human voice? Is it a kines-thetic experience—holding a yoga posture, running, floating in warm water, dancing, making love, giving or receiving a massage?

A shaman knows these things. The anthropologist Mercea Eliade described shamans as "technicians of ecstasy." As a dream artist you will need to be aware of your own triggers—the kind of things that allow you to slip into a nonordinary state of consciousness. This dreaming state is where you will first meet your artist inside, and it is the place to which you'll return again and again to access the vision that will inspire your creative work.

The need for regular contact with the dreaming states of conscious-ness is important. Without it we cannot see pattern, or connection, or our deep relationship to the world. We become deaf to the song of our soul. When we lived lives defined by village and tribe, we would have had regular access to a shaman—someone fluent in the language of the dreaming world, someone with direct access to it. Now, unless we seek out a therapist or counselor of a particular school of thought, no one fa-cilitates our dreamwork. No one helps us re-imagine the world.

Most of us live cut off from the wisdom of the dreaming world and the joy of creative expression. Even if we feel a calling in this direction, there are few shaman artists to whom we can turn for information and in-spiration. We are left to seek guidance from artists who teach us tech-niques for manipulating materials without addressing the spirit. Or we turn to spiritual advisors who are sometimes ambivalent about their own creative energies or, worse, are dismissive of anything existing on the material plane. The truth is that you don't need to consult an expert. Ac-cess to the dreaming is a natural birthright. It's a world you were made to visit.

Meeting your own dream artist is a process of going inside. How to best make that journey will depend on your own preferred method of shifting your consciousness. You may already know what sends you into a trance, or you may discover the answer through the exercises in this chapter. Some people prefer to make their inner journeys first, in a more open, receptive state, perhaps triggered by internal visualization or ex-ternal sound. The expressive act comes second as they return inspired and ready to work. For other people, however, the very act of drawing, painting, or working with their hands in a steady focused manner is enough to alter their consciousness. They move into the flow of the work and integrate the visionary with the manifestation of that vision in real time. For still other people, the distinctions are blurred, and they find themselves shifting back and forth between passive, receptive trance states and active, expressive ones.

But no amount of description will convey this idea as effectively as experiencing it yourself. This is the shamanic way of learning—to put it into practice. You will have a chance to practice an inside-out method, an outside-in method, and a hybrid. What's most important is that you find the way that's most comfortable for you.

Outfitting: Guided Visualization

You already have your most important tool for this chapter, and that's your dream artist's journal. For the exercises in this chapter, you will also need a box of crayons (or charcoal sticks), a fine-tipped paintbrush, some black ink (water-based is fine), and a pad of inexpensive paper, such as newsprint. Inexpensive unlined computer printer paper will also work. You don't need a big box of crayons, and it doesn't even need to be a new box (though I must confess to being a sucker for a new box of crayons). If you don't have them already, you will need a glue stick and a pair of scissors. You should also have some magazines that you don't mind cutting up.

Though it isn't actually in the category of supplies, there is a technique we will be using in this chapter that you may not be familiar with, so I'm going to offer some guidelines for working with guided visualizations.

Guided visualization is a kind of internal journey. It's like listening to a story in which you are the main character. You will be guided on a semi-structured journey, filling in the blanks from your own imagination. A good guided visualization can be as powerful as a night dream.

In addition to being useful experiences on their own, guided visualizations are also a good preparation for the more free-form shamanic journeying technique we will be practicing in chapter 7.

The best way to experience the guided visualizations in this book is to have someone read them aloud to you or to tape record yourself reading them. If you are recording your own voice, remember to speak in low, soft tones. Speak slowly and clearly. Leave pauses in the tape where they are indicated by this sign in the script: >>. The symbol >> indicates a short pause and >>>> indicates a longer pause. An alternative is to read the guided visualization script through several times until you are comfortable with what you will be asked to visualize, and then to trust your memory and imagination.

To prepare for doing a guided visualization, either read the script into a tape recorder or read it through several times. Give yourself twenty minutes of undisturbed time. Turn off the ringer on the phone and do your best to eliminate distractions. It's best not to attempt this when you are really tired. Though you may find this very relaxing and helpful for falling asleep at night, the point here is not to fall asleep. Adjust the room temperature to a comfortable level and have a blanket available. As you relax, your body temperature will drop and you may become uncomfortably cool. It needn't be dark in the room, but low light seems to work better. A blindfold or cloth to lay over your eyes can help reduce distractions from the light.

You can do guided visualizations sitting in a comfortable position on the floor or in a chair, but the best way to start out is by lying on your back. The only concern here is that it's also the easiest position from which to fall asleep. When lying on your back, make sure to support your lower back with a cushion under the back of your knees.

Select some relaxing music and play it at a background level. The best kind of music will have a dreamy, spacey sound. There are recommendations in Sources of Music (page 237), or you can sample some new age music at your local record store. The music you choose should not have words or familiar melodies. Pick something you like and work with the same piece often. After a while you will find that you begin to slip into an altered state of consciousness as soon as you hear the music.

Next take yourself through a relaxation sequence. These are two that I find most useful.

1. If you are very physical and/or tense, try systematically relaxing your body beginning at your toes. Tense your feet, spreading your toes wide and flexing your arches. Hold this for the count of three and relax. Tense and relax your calves, thighs, buttocks, pelvis, abdomen, chest, fingers, hands, forearms, upper arms, shoulders, neck, and face.

2. Another technique is to imagine a golden wave of relaxing energy that washes over your body each time you exhale. With each inhalation, draw that relaxing energy in. On the first exhalation, direct it down to your feet. Feel it wash over your feet. Feel them tingle and relax. Repeat this process with your legs, torso, arms, neck, and head.

After you've relaxed, begin the guided visualization. Ten to fifteen minutes is plenty long enough to do a guided visualization. After twenty minutes, you will be in danger of falling asleep, and you may find that imagery begins to repeat and recycle.

When you finish your session, allow yourself to come out of it slowly. Before you move about much, replay the experience of the visualization once or twice in your head to make certain you remember it fully. After you roll over or sit up, log what you remember about your experience in your dream artist's journal.

INSIDE OUT: PICTURING THE
DREAM ARTIST INSIDE

With this exercise, you will use the guided
visualization techniques you just practiced to
learn to access your own deep image-generating
potential and to translate that into the waking world,
through finding, arranging, and recombining
preexisting images.

THE sacred creative cycle has two arcs. The descending arc is external. It is the work of our hands as we manifest spirit in material form. The ascending arc is internal. It is the journey for inspiration and direct contact with spirit. Both are necessary, and both can lead us into art as a spiritual practice. People tend to have an affinity for engaging the sacred creative cycle in either its descending or ascending arcs. This first exercise is designed to take you on an inner journey first. It uses the guided visualization technique described above as a starting point. Reread the instructions above. Complete the relaxation phase and have soft music playing as you begin this visualization.

> *Softly, slowly, let your awareness sink inside your body. Turn your attention inward. Feel yourself sinking gently back to a place where you once felt relaxed and peaceful. This may be a place you've visited or it may be a place you've only imagined. Experience it now as richly as your imagination will allow. Feel the temperature and the environment. >> Smell the scent of this place. >> Taste the air. >> Listen for the sounds that are special to this place. >> Look at the colors and shapes and patterns around you. >> Move around in this environment. Feel your body moving in this place. Experience how you move so gracefully, effortlessly, without pain or awkwardness. Experience your own lightness.*
>
> *Now look around your sacred and secret sanctuary. Find a*

door, a cave, a gate, an arbor, some narrow gap between trees, or an opening of some sort. Don't force or rush yourself to find this opening. Allow it to call you with gentle sound or sparkling light. Allow it to attract you. >>>>

Now, move to this opening and stand before it. See the shimmering curtain of light that hovers between inside and outside. Hear the sound of music coming from the other side. Smell wonderful fragrances. Through this opening is the place where your dream artist lives. Remember that you once knew your dream artist well. This is not an introduction but a reunion. Know that you are invited to cross this threshold. You will be embraced and welcomed.

When the time is right for you, step across the threshold. You pass easily through the shimmering curtain of light. Experience its feeling against your skin. Before you is your dream artist twin. He or she may look like you, or the person you wish you were. Your dream artist is a kind of soul mirror for you. Look for the ways you are alike and the ways you are different. >> Notice how your dream artist is dressed. >> Observe jewelry, hairstyle, and accessories. >> Look closely at your dream artist's face. Remember the expression.

Greet your dream artist and allow yourself to be greeted. Speak to your dream artist. Listen to what he or she has to say. >>>> Allow yourself to be shown around. Look at what your dream artist has around him or her. >>>> Experience the space in which your dream artist feels most comfortable. Ask how you might bring your dream artist back to the waking world. >>>>

(Pause here to give yourself time to experience.)

Now it's time to return to the waking world. Thank your dream artist for waiting for you. Ask if you might return again. Embrace your dream artist and feel the creative surge of energy flow into your own body. >>>> Take one last look around. Pass back through the shimmering curtain of light and find yourself in your own special place once again.

Gradually expand your consciousness out and up. >> Fill the space of your body with your own awareness. >> As you

*return, feel the creative energy and the relaxed peaceful feeling
stay with you. Bring that feeling back into your body. >>>>
Wiggle your fingers and toes. Feel your presence return to your
whole body. Recall as much of what you saw as possible.*

*When you are ready, open your eyes. Stretch, but don't move
too much. Record what you experienced in words or pictures in
your dream artist's journal.*

Use the inside front cover and first page of your journal to create a
collage image of your dream artist. Gather scissors, a metal straight
edge, and a glue stick or rubber cement. Use magazines to cut out images. You can begin with a photograph of you that you've decorated and
enhanced, or use a picture that symbolizes your feelings and desires
about recovering your creative soul and living as a dream artist. Remember that your dream artist may look like you or the way you wish
you looked. Go wild! Be as colorful and flamboyant as you want. Be
playful. Make this page magical. Remember to include jewelry, clothing, accessories, patterns, designs, tools, and other items you saw on or
around your dream artist. If you can't find the perfect image, don't ob-
sess. Work with what you find. Have fun.

If your dream artist shared thoughts or words with you, find a way to
incorporate them into your picture. Handwriting or applying found
words and phrases with glue can work equally well. Did you receive
specific instructions or guidelines? Include them. What did the background look like? Can you find images that represent that?

As you work, remain open to intuition. If you find an image that
speaks to you, even though you don't specifically recall it from your experience, trust this as the voice of your dream artist. Use it. Overlap
your images or cut them to interpenetrate in interesting ways. Consider
using acrylic paints to fill in blank spots between images. Apply glitter
to the wet paint. Use gold or silver foil or paint to highlight areas.

By creating this image, you are giving the essence of your dream
artist a place to live in the waking world. You are preparing a home for
an important part of yourself. You are also setting an intention to live
creatively. You will see this inside front cover more than any other page

of your journal. Every time you open it up and see this, you will be affirming your intention and manifesting your own destiny.

After you've completed your dream artist's portrait, it will be much easier to engage him or her in dialogue. Simply opening your journal to this image will put you in contact with your dream artist as a source of guidance.

Don't be surprised if a certain synchronicity seems to occur around the images you find for your collage. One of my students, Lisa, was both elated and frustrated after her guided visualization. Her dream artist appeared to her as a mirror of herself, but with the most incredible and unusual wings. She described them as being not completely a bird's wings, but some odd combination. She felt intuitively that it was important to get the wings right, but she didn't know how she could. We took a photo of Lisa to use as a starting point. Among the magazines I had available for cutting and pasting was a set of *National Geographic* magazines and other science magazines. In the first magazine she picked up, Lisa found an image of a seagull's outspread wings. In the second, she found the tiny wings of a hummingbird frozen by stop-action photography. In the third, she found a pair of butterfly wings. Working with elements of all three, she gasped in amazement at how close this was to her vision.

The choice of wings also helped her illuminate the meaning of the configuration in the guided visualization. "As a dream artist," she explained, "I will need the strong wide wings of a gull to travel the distance I will need to travel. I will need the delicate acrobatic wings of the hummingbird to hover in one place and stay focused. And, finally, I will need the butterfly's wings to go with the flow and be sensitive to the subtlest of wind currents."

Don't be surprised if you continue to discover meaning and relevance in the image you create of your dream artist long after you've finished it. To this day I continue to see things that I don't remember being conscious of adding to my dream artist's image.

OUTSIDE IN: ENERGETIC DRAWING

With this exercise, you will learn to enter a simple
trance state to access your dream artist while
expressing that connection through
nonrepresentational drawing.
Make doodling a spiritual practice.

IN this next exercise, we will explore how the physical act of drawing can take you into a trance state and help you access intuitive guidance. When an Aboriginal painter sits down to place the thousands of minute dots of color on canvas that will become his or her dreaming, it is a form of meditation. The same can be said for the Tibetan Buddhist monks who create elaborate mandalas with colored sand. The combination of being fully present and in touch with the moment and the repetitive nature of the activity serves to carry the meditator into a light trance.

To see if this kind of repetitive but attentive activity is a good trigger for shifting your consciousness, you will need the following items: a pad of inexpensive newsprint or drawing paper (even recycled computer printer paper will work—use the backside) and a box of crayons or soft charcoal sticks. Use inexpensive materials for this so that you will not concern yourself with using them so freely. If you use large paper, you can involve more of your upper body in the act of drawing. Smaller sheets of paper put more emphasis on expression through the hand and wrist.

Put on a piece of music that will play for between twenty and forty minutes. It should be music without words, but it may be more emotionally evocative than the music used for your guided visualization. The music will be your timer so that you won't need to check a clock to see how long you've been working. Sit at a table or desk with plenty of room around you. Your chair should offer good support for your back, as you will want to be sitting up straight. To one side, place your supply of paper. Put one sheet in front of you and select a crayon or stick of charcoal.

Close your eyes for a moment and do a series of ten long, slow, deep breaths. Feel your shoulders, neck, and arms relax. Invite your dream artist to work through you. Remember: Your dream artist is really a part of you, so this is not like channeling or possession. You aren't surrendering control.

Begin with your crayon or charcoal resting lightly on the page. Let your gaze soften and blur. Follow your breath. Inhale and draw energy in with your breath. Exhale and let it flow down your arm to your hand. Begin to draw by letting your crayon trace flowing shapes on the page. Don't try to control what you put on paper. Just let it happen. Allow yourself to respond to the music, to your own moods, to images that pop into your mind, or to the flow of energy you feel. Don't try to draw realistically. Stick with shapes, lines, and patterns.

Pay attention to the inner voice that tells you when your page feels full. When you hear this voice, take another sheet and continue drawing. You don't need to feel obligated to fill a page before starting on another one. You can repeat lines and forms on top of each other, extending or reinforcing them. Feel the energy you are tracing. Remember that you needn't do anything. The creative moment occurs between the moments when you are thinking about it. If your mind wanders, gently bring it back to the page. Don't evaluate what you are doing. An "Oh, that looks good," can interfere with your creative trance as seriously as an "Oh, that looks terrible."

How do you know if you've moved into an altered state of consciousness from this activity? Look for experiences or moments like this:

- Time has passed more quickly than you thought.
- Time is moving far more slowly than you perceived.
- You lose the definite distinction between where your hand or crayon ends and the line begins.
- Your hand feels pulled along by external forces.
- You feel a deep sense of peace.
- Images appear in your imagination that seem unusual.
- You hear overtones, harmonies, or polyrhythms that aren't part of your recorded music.
- You experience temperature shifts or odd physical sensations.
- You hear voices singing or speaking.

Stop drawing when the music stops. Spread your drawings out on the floor so that you can see all of them or most of them at once. Look for patterns that repeat or that call your attention. Pull out the ones that feel meaningful to you. You don't need to save every drawing in the series, but treat all of them with respect. Even if you decide to throw some away, do it with a sense that you are making room for new energy. Regardless of what your critical waking mind might think of them, these drawings are the evidence of your energetic awareness. In those moments when you manage to surrender your waking control and enter the trance state, you reflect in your drawings the direct expression of your dream artist.

To take this one step further, think about a key issue or problem that has engaged you. Look at the drawings that attracted your attention. Imagine that they were meant to be encoded or symbolic answers to the question that is on your mind. What would a shape that suggests a bird taking flight mean to you? What would a river or a snake or a tree mean as an answer to your question? If an answer suggests itself from one of your drawings, save that drawing and put it on display for awhile in a place where you can look at it. If you are engaged in other artwork, ask yourself how some of these basic shapes might be integrated with your other projects.

When Michael, a man in his mid-thirties, did this exercise, asking to get in touch with the intuitive guidance of his dream artist, he drew circular shapes repeatedly. When he confessed that his most pressing concern of late was what to do about his career, I inquired further and learned that he had left the field he knew and loved to work in increasingly unrelated fields with the incentive of higher salary. He was unhappy and trying to decide what his next career move should be. None of the options he outlined for himself seemed exciting. We looked again at his drawings. I asked him what they had in common. Some were oval, he observed, some more like perfect circles, but all of his drawings began and ended in the same place. I didn't need to say anything as the wisdom of this hit him. "I need to go back to what I love doing," he said. "The money is not as important as I once thought it was."

When you relax and open up to possibility, whether you do this through internal or external techniques, you will find your dream artist. What you will most likely discover, however, is that your best way of working is some dynamic combination of internal and external techniques.

INSIDE OUTSIDE IN: THE DREAM ARTIST'S SONG OF POWER

In this exercise, you will learn to move in and out of various levels of creative trance while you work. Access intuitive guidance while you work. Understand the power of dynamic translation in art.

THIS exercise moves us inside ourselves, leads us back out into the waking world, and engages us in work that ultimately guides us back inside again, like the pattern of a Celtic knot. In the Celtic tradition, the bards and mystics sang songs in which they not only fused themselves with the spirits and energies of the natural world, but also identified themselves with the powers of those spirits. This activity is a chance to move back and forth between external and internal methods of getting to know our dream artists. It also allows us to practice dynamic translation—the idea that the greater the variety of ways we express an idea, the more deeply and completely we know that idea.

For this activity, you will need your dream artist's journal, a pen, some large sheets of paper, crayons, colored chalks, or charcoal sticks, a fine brush, and some acrylic paint or ink. It is best to do this activity all at one time. You will want a desk or writing surface and some room to move about. Play some instrumental music that you like.

Begin by writing your own song of power. Number a page in your journal from one to twenty-four. Answer the following questions quickly, without spending too much time thinking about each answer. Give yourself three minutes to complete the whole list.

1. If I was a season, I would be_____

2. If I was a gemstone, I would be_____

3. If I was an emotion, I would be_____

4. If I was a musical instrument, I would be_____

5. If I was an animal, I would be_____

6. If I was a fairy-tale character, I would be_____

7. If I was an historical period, I would be_____

8. If I was a kind of water, I would be_____

9. If I was a color, I would be_____

10. If I was a time of day, I would be _____

11. If I was a kind of weather, I would be_____

12. If I was a sport or game, I would be_____

13. If I was a piece of clothing, I would be_____

14. If I was a mythical creature, I would be_____

15. If I was a tool, I would be_____

16. If I was a physical sensation, I would be_____

17. If I was a kind of tree, I would be_____

18. If I was a scent, I would be_____

19. If I was a geographical feature, I would be_____

20. If I was a way of moving, I would be_____

21. If I was a piece of furniture, I would be_____

22. If I was an art form, I would be_____

23. If I was a body part, I would be_____

24. If I was a flavor, I would be_____

Now take eleven of the answers to the questions from above and weave them together into a poem or short paragraph that begins with the statement "I am." You can add connecting, amplifying, or descriptive words. You can also use more of the answers if you choose. It's okay to write long sentences. Some people write their song of power as one long sentence. If you start new sentences or write a series of short sentences, consider referring back to yourself by putting "I am" at the beginning of each one. Here're two examples:

I am an island of shivering gardenias where a princess rolls down silk stockings to touch vanilla to the hollow behind each knee with the sun setting on a day between spring and summer beckoning her to dance recklessly into the obsidian night.

Or

I am a strong oak, having stood against every storm
I am the rainwater that slides from leaf to trunk to roots
I am the autumn sun that turns green to crimson
I am the wind sounding like flutes weaving past tangled branches
I am the mountainside cloaked in bittersweet colors that cannot last
I am the hand of the little boy caressing the rough bark coat

This is a description of your dream artist. This is a song of power that will invoke the dream artist. The next step is to repeat the piece you've written until you can recite it from memory. Once you are comfortable doing this, recite it aloud several times. Do this standing up and add movement to your recitation. The movements can be abstract or they can be a pantomime of the elements of your writing. Repeat these movements and time them to the music you have playing in the background. Do this until the pantomime begins to feel dancelike. You can stop reciting whenever you feel you don't need to hear the words out loud to drive the movements. If you've been making small gestures, expand them. Use your whole body. Flow one movement into the next. If other movements evolve from or are suggested by your first movements, add them. You can think of this as dancing your dream artist or dancing your dream artist's song of power. This process begins to internalize and transform your writing. Your body understands what you have been writing in a new way. Often this movement will have a meditative quality to it. If done fast, it may feel like the devotional movement of a Sufi dervish. Done slowly, it can feel like tai chi or the sun salutation exercise in yoga. Allow yourself to experience this movement fully.

For the next step, select three discrete movements from your dance of power. Return to your large sheets of drawing paper. You can draw on paper on a table, on the floor, on an easel, or taped to the wall. Translate the first of your three movements into large hand and arm gestures. Using charcoal sticks, colored chalks, or crayons, draw this gesture repeatedly on the paper. Use the whole sheet of paper. Draw with as much of your body as you can. Simply repeat this gesture again and again. Don't intellectualize it. Don't think about what it looks like. Don't evaluate it. Just draw. When the time feels right, move on to a fresh sheet of paper and the next movement of the three you've selected. Then complete the third movement drawing.

This drawing is now at a kind of primal level. You should have been able to shift from the standing movements to the drawing without losing the trance state. As you allow the energy of your third movement to expend itself on paper, allow yourself to slow down as well. Stop drawing and come to a resting point. Close your eyes and ask your dream artist to come to you. Ask how the three gestures might be incorporated into a single symbol. Look for images that appear or listen for advice. If you receive specific guidance, open your eyes and, using a brush and black ink, paint the symbol into your journal. If you did not receive specific guidance, know that your dream artist is inside you, acting through you. Begin to play with possibilities. Try different symbol designs that incorporate your movements and gestural drawings. In either case, feel free to modify what you're working on based on your own intuitive sense of the moment.

When you have a symbol that captures the energy of the three movements, sit with it awhile. This symbol is a distillation, a refined version of the energy of your own dream artist. Paint a finished version of it. It is your special symbol. Add it to your dream artist collage image in the front of your journal.

You may find yourself sketching this symbol without realizing it. Or, as in the case of some of my fellow dream artists, you may mark the things around you with this symbol as a way of formally honoring those items that seem important.

W e are all meant to express ourselves creatively. For some people it comes easy, for others it takes practice. Most of the exercises you've done up to this point would be useful for any artist, but developing the spiritual practice of a dream artist requires a shift in perspective. As my journey has progressed and my practice evolved over the years, I've come slowly to accept and believe in four basic premises that define the work and worldview of a dream artist:

1. Objects can have spirit, and working with this spirit is a sacred practice.

2. To work with the spirit or energetic aspect of objects and images requires that one access the dreaming world. This dreaming state of consciousness is the true source for sacred creativity.

3. The practice of making art in a spiritually or energetically conscious way can affect the practitioner.

4. The artifacts and images of this process can affect others.

In practical terms, this means that to be a dream artist you must begin to see the spirit in the material. You must learn to access that spirit at its source in the dreaming world. You must understand that the process of manifesting dream images and artifacts in the world can be healing, instructional, empowering, and enchanting to the practitioner. And, finally, you must understand that the images and artifacts themselves can have an effect upon others.

Accepting these premises seems to suggest that not only is a dream artist different from those we traditionally call artists, but that dream art is somehow fundamentally different as well. So how is the shamanic art of a dream artist different from what we usually think of as art?

I was in Minneapolis, Minnesota, to present a workshop and was thinking about that very question. I wondered how I might convey the difference between the Western conception of art and the more tribal, shamanic conception of art.

I had been playing with the idea for several days and had lots of ideas, but couldn't express them succinctly. So I decided to pose the question to my dreaming consciousness. To do this, I asked myself the question before going to sleep in a process called dream incubation, which you will learn about in chapter 4. This means that I wrote my question down on the top of the next blank page in my dream artist's journal. I fully prepared myself to receive an answer. As I fell asleep, I repeated the question to myself several times. I intended to dream an answer.

I woke the next morning without remembering a single dream.

This was surprising.

I always remember at least one dream, but this morning I had nothing. Perhaps it was sleeping in a strange place, I told myself, or the fact that it was one of those hotels where the windows don't open (sometimes I feel that some connection with the natural world, even if it is only fresh air, is essential for my dreaming). But, whatever the reason, I found myself with a few extra minutes of time. I didn't have anything to write in my dream journal. So I sat down with one of those city guide magazines that one finds in hotel rooms in bigger cities and flipped through it. As I browsed, my attention was drawn to a beautiful African sculpture of a black panther. It was an advertisement for a show of African sculpture to be held at the Minneapolis Art Center. I laughed out loud as I read the text to the advertisement. Here was the answer I had sought in my dream. In big, bold letters it read, **"The difference between western art and African art is that western artists don't have to worry about being eaten by their models."**

The dream artist and the indigenous artist view the world and their art in a similar fashion. Malidoma Patrice Somé describes this view in his book *The Healing Wisdom of Africa: Finding Life Purpose Through*

Nature, Ritual, and Community. "In some stores and museums, it is often frightening to view live ancestral masks displayed as if their purpose and function were to be looked at. These objects emit powerful energies because they are alive. Westerners do not realize that they are being affected by the energy put out by these live sacred objects. In Africa, a person who knows and understands the dynamic between art and culture will run away when he confronts living but displaced masks." Somé goes on to say that, "In the indigenous view, a mask of an ancestor is not a symbol of the ancestor, it *is* the ancestor."

For a dream artist, the process and product of art making is just that real, that vital, and that important.

Returning to the first premise I suggested above, there is no way I can convince you logically and rationally that objects can have spirit or energetic consciousness. What I can do, on the road to helping you develop a spiritual practice around art, is to help you shift to an energetic way of perceiving the world. It is through the technique of vision-shifting that I believe you will come to agree with me that objects can, indeed, have spirit.

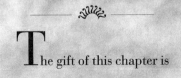

The gift of this chapter is

openness.

To create a spiritual practice out of the work you do in the

material world requires that you find in the material world a

spirit of energetic consciousness. The exercises in this chapter

will help you open up to seeing or sensing the invisible world

and to finding a way to express that perception.

chapter 3

Vision-Shifting:
Developing *Energetic* Awareness

Typically a shaman would find an object, previously unknown to him, exactly like one seen in a dream. Maybe a song or a prayer would come back to him from a forgotten dream upon cradling this object in his hands. These objects are said to speak, because it is through them that shamans retain the special mysterious language of their power in the dreams. Such found objects become the throne or client for one's spirit. One's power would then have an actual physical place to sit, as the Tzutujil say.

—MARTIN PRECHTEL
Secrets of the Talking Jaguar:
A Mayan Shaman's Journey to the Heart of the Indigenous Soul

W hat speaks to you?

When I hold an object in my hand, I see pictures and hear stories. A stone turns into a novel, a feather into a photograph, and a tree branch into a work of art. This is something I've always been able to do, though the more I practice it—the more I use this gift—the more powerful it becomes. There is an energy or spirit in materials—a consciousness.

The quantity and quality of consciousness varies, but there is always some exchange of conscious energy between two things. Being aware of this exchange is what vision-shifting is all about. The importance of learning to vision-shift comes from the fact that a dream artist is always a dream artist—twenty-four hours a day, seven days a week. We may not always be arranging, altering, or making, but we are always in the process of finding—connecting with spirit and divine inspiration. We don't need to make the time to sleep and to dream, but we do need to allow ourselves time to process our dream imagery. We need to arrange protected and sacred time for ritual journeys into the spirit world, and we must give ourselves the gift of time in order to express our visions through creative work. With vision-shifting, we can learn to walk in two worlds simultaneously.

We all have the ability to shift the way we perceive to a more energetic level. Though I call it vision-shifting, it does not necessarily manifest in sight. Some people see this energetic reality as aura, or hear it as a vibratory hum. For me, that spirit speaks in both image and tale. Though I was not aware of this at the time, I think I became an artist for the express purpose of creating objects and images that would house spirit. I began to write as a way of telling the tales I heard when I touched something. I stumbled onto my ability to vision-shift, refining it through practice, but anyone can learn to do it. If you can attend (really look and listen) to a person or thing, open yourself up to it, and maintain some sense of self in the process, you can vision-shift.

Shamans speak of three worlds: the lower, the middle, and the upper. While we may explore the upper and lower realms of spirit through night dreams and shamanic journeys, vision-shifting is the best way to explore the middle world. Where the lower and upper worlds often contain mythic and primeval landscapes and fantastic architecture, the middle world looks like this world, only seen through energetic eyes. An awareness of the middle world means to see not only the shadows (the physical form of things), but the pattern which casts the shadows. Some people come to see this pattern, some hear it. You may find that you feel it in things or that you have a clear knowing of this spirit pattern. The exercise of this faculty, the ability to shift to an energetic way of seeing, requires that we first learn to pay attention to the world around us, to see it not just as the mundane world, but as a magical middle world. Then we open our intuition to understand the pattern and exchange of spirit. Finally, we direct our intention to see what we need to see.

Outfitting: Ceremony and Practice

You WILL NEED your dream artist's journal for the activities in this chapter. You will also need paper, though you may choose to do all the activities in your journal. In addition to a pencil and pen, you might want to invest in a set of colored pencils. If money is an issue, get a small set of high-quality colored pencils instead of a large set of cheap ones. Better quality pencils flow onto the page more smoothly and lay down richer color. Your dream artist will appreciate that. You will also need the brush and black ink you used in the last chapter.

So far the activities I've described can be done by themselves as one-time experiments. While there is a benefit to doing them even this way, they are much more effective as part of a regular practice. Now that you've had a chance to meet your dream artist, you need to regularly invite that energy to be a part of your life. You do this through practice and through ceremony.

I'd like to encourage you to set aside a time and a place each day where you can formally work with your dream artist. Later we will discuss creating a sacred studio space, but for the time being all you'll need are your symbols of the elements: a candle for fire, a stone for earth, a bowl of water for water, and some incense or sage leaves and a burner for air. (If you don't want to burn incense, a feather can represent the element of air.) Set these items where they will be easy to see and reach when you're sitting before them. Have your dream artist's journal at hand. Gather the other supplies you will be using for this exercise as well. You can use the following opening ceremony before practicing any of the activities described so far or for the activities coming up in this chapter. You can also use this ceremony when simply making time to write or sketch in your journal each day.

1. Wash your hands and dry them. Let the water pull any heavy energy out of your hands.

2. Put on some soothing instrumental music that is conducive to moving into a meditative state.

3. Take a moment to center yourself. Close your eyes. Breathe deeply and focus on releasing the tension you are carrying or any negativity that may be lingering about you.

4. Light the candle and say: *Thank you for the light by which I see and the clarity with which I work.*

5. Touch the stone and say: *Thank you for keeping me grounded and strong and connected to the earth.*

6. Dip your finger in water and touch it to your heart and to your third eye (the point between your eyebrows) and say: *Thank you for the guidance of my higher heart and the vision of my inner spirit.*

7. Touch the feather or pass your hand over the candle and say: *Thank you for the inspiration you bring with each breath.*

8. Open your dream artist's journal to the inside front cover where you have the image of your dream artist spirit and say: *Thank you for being with me. I welcome you into my life.*

Feel free to translate this into your own words. In time you may find a simpler and quicker ceremonial opening that works to create a sacred container for your work, but for now practice what I've suggested as a way of inviting spirit to be with you when you create. At the very least, get in the habit of lighting a candle before you work. This simple physical act of ceremony sets your intention and defines the way you will work—safely held and yet open to spirit.

Consider doing the following vision-shifting activities as a morning or evening practice within the framework of ceremony. When you have finished your session, respectfully and mindfully blow out the candle, touch each of the elements, thanking them again, and offer your gratitude to your dream artist spirit.

The Soul of a Stone

THE FIRST AND MOST difficult transition for most people to make is to begin to see or sense spirit and energy in the objects around them. It may come easily to you, but even if it seems difficult at first act as if it will be easy. It's much more useful to prepare yourself for success than to prepare yourself for failure. Making this shift is actually a two-step process. There is a philosophical/intellectual leap—allowing that it might be possible—and a sensitization that enables you to experience it for yourself.

Actually the idea that the objects around us have spirit is much older and has been with us much longer than the idea that they are mere lifeless stuff. The memory of this is still with us, for all our rationality and science. We swear at our computer when it crashes and talk to it soothingly as we coax it back into operation. We curse the piece of furniture on which we stub our toe or bump our head. We name our boats and our appliances. We fall into despair at the loss of a special ring or lucky piece, even though the monetary value of these things may be insignificant. We make pilgrimages to see and touch relics and walls and sacred sites.

When a dream artist creates an artifact or paints an image, it is first and foremost a living thing. It's not about spirit, it is spirit. While it may depict a scene or event, it's no less real for being a depiction. A dream artist fully expects to effect change in the waking world by illustrating an event from a dream. A carved piece of bone might actually contain a soul. A branch woven with a net of sinew and feathers has the power to actually catch dreams. A fetish doll can kill or cure. The painted geometric pattern on the wall of an aboriginal cave is not a representation of power—it is power. A bundle of found objects can empower its owner. Shamanic art is both material and energy. The ability to see objects as being both physical things and the embodiment of spirit and energy is an aspect of the shaman's way of viewing the world.

It's easy to see this view of the world as being superstitious. For most contemporary Westerners, this shift in awareness flies in the face of our entire cultural conditioning. Our rational and supposedly enlightened worldview holds that a thing is a thing and nothing more. This scientific and materialistic worldview has lead to incredible advances in science and technology. It has also allowed us to consume and destroy our environment at a phenomenal rate, to treat fellow living creatures—plants, animals, humans—as if they had no soul or spirit, to live lives without the possibility of magic, wonder, and enchantment. So, even if I can't prove my premise about the spiritual or soul life of things, how would the world be different if we acted as if this were a true picture? It might mean that we were kinder to our environment. It might mean that we were more careful of and sensitive to the things we chose to have around us. We might attend to beauty and pattern not as an afterthought, but as an essential element in our lives. We might live more simply—more in balance. Consider how your day would be different if you took into account the spirit or conscious energy of the things that crossed your path.

The best way to shift your consciousness toward the spiritual aspect of the material is to experience it. As a teacher, there is almost nothing as exciting or fulfilling to me than to be with someone the first time their awareness shifts intentionally to the energetic. One of the great things about working with adolescents is that they are often so open to experience. I was leading a group of high school students in an arts-based mentoring program through the series of exercises described below. We were gradually opening up to the energetic quality of a simple stone through a series of drawing and writing exercises. What surprised me was how matter-of-fact they were about the wonderful revelations they were experiencing and sharing. Almost every student seemed to perceive, at some level, a whole new world opening up within the stone, and yet they shared their observations with a curious calmness. Not that I needed drama. It was just that in working with adults I was used to at least a few expressions like, "Oh my god! There are colored lights floating around you," or "Things seem to be shimmering," or "I hear music when I hold this stone close to my ear." With these students it was as if they took this vision-shifting for granted. What I failed to remember was just how important it is for adolescents to appear cool—to look as if nothing surprises or phases them.

It was only after class that they began to come to me individually. One amazed student shared: "I started to see pictures of a war being fought with cavalry and swords. I thought I was making it all up at first, then I tried to stop making it happen and I kept seeing it. I feel like I know so many details, I could write a report on it. I don't think I was just imagining it. Something changed. What do you think I was seeing?"

Another student shared that she had seen colors around things when she was younger but didn't know what it meant. She remembered that when she talked about it with her mother, she realized it was not something her mother saw. Eventually she stopped seeing these colors as well. Rediscovering her ability to see energetically was like reuniting with a long-lost friend.

The following set of exercises will begin to open you up to the energetic quality of objects. I've always been drawn to stone, so these first exercises use stone as a subject. Stone has particular qualities that are useful for developing energetic awareness. It holds energy patterns—one might say memories—for long periods of time and is particularly easy to work with.

THE STRONG EYE AND BORDER WORK: SEEING AS A DREAM ARTIST

With this exercise, you will learn to change the way you see things—opening yourself up to more information than the physical structure of the eye/brain complex normally admits to.

IN the 1970s, anthropologist Stanley Diamond reported that studies done on desert Bedouin tribes indicated an amazing capacity for distance vision. Long before anyone else in a group could distinguish a figure or feature in the landscape, the Bedouin Arabs could describe it. At first researchers thought it might be some physiological improvement of the eye's ability to see, but tests indicated no difference in the actual functioning of the eye. When researchers finally got around to asking the tribal informants why they thought they could see so far away, the answer was stunningly simple. "From the time we are very young," it was explained, "we *expect* to see things at a great distance."

The Aborigines speak of a way of seeing called "the strong eye." This refers to a kind of X-ray vision by which a shaman can see into a thing to diagnose disease or the source of dysfunction. It also covers a specific technique that allows one to see energetic landmarks. This technique is very similar to what I call vision-shifting.

To practice vision-shifting with "the strong eye" technique, begin outdoors. Take your dream artist's journal and stand or sit in a relaxed posture. Look off into the horizon and squint your eyes. Narrow your focus as if you were shifting a camera from normal to panoramic view. Think of your vision as being wide and diffuse. Don't squint hard. Try to relax the muscles around your eyes while still maintaining the narrowed field of view. Don't focus your attention on any one point of the horizon or foreground. Take it all in. If you find yourself focusing on a specific object, let it go and return to your softened general field of view. After you are able to hold this way of seeing for several minutes at a time, you will begin to notice movement or glowing light or flashes that draw your attention. But, when you focus on them there is nothing there. I find this similar to watching a pond for jumping fish. You see a fish jump in your peripheral vision but by the time you look the fish is gone. If you try to look for the one spot where the fish will next jump, you will always be off. But if you soften your gaze and widen your field of view, you will see the fish jump.

You can think of this softening as the kind of vision the Impressionist painter Monet must have used when seeing the light falling on haystacks or dappling across his water garden at Giverny. Use your dream journal to map the energetic traces you see. You needn't worry about whether you are sketching realistically. You can use simple lines and stick figures. In addition to giving you a whole new perspective from which to draw inspiration, this is a useful technique for finding lost items, or for opening yourself up to encounter the right object in a search.

The second technique for vision-shifting comes from the Celtic tradition of honoring the points betwixt and between two things. I call this "border work."

When I experience vision-shifting, I often find myself in the waking world one moment and in the dreaming world the next. It is a feeling of being betwixt and between. Vision-shifting through border work is an excellent way to take a compass reading on your direction in the middle of a busy day or to take a fresh look at a piece of art you are creating. It can help you by tapping the intuition of your dreaming mind at a moment's notice.

Vision-shifting usually comes over us with little intention on our part, but we can experience it more willfully. By practicing border work we not only shift our way of seeing, we also shift our way of being.

This technique works best by finding liminal points—points of energetic transition such as the boundary between water and land or earth and sky. Once you are practiced at it, you will find liminal points all around you. Find a comfortable place where you can sit for a while and focus your attention on the point in between two things. With a tree, this might mean the point between roots and earth or leaves and sky. At the seashore, this might be the point between wave and sand or ocean spray and sky. Try not to focus on either single element, but on the point between them.

There is something of the Zen koan to this exercise. It is the sound of one hand clapping or the tree that falls in the forest. Stay with it. Imagine yourself into this space. Spend as much time in this space as you can, before allowing yourself to be pulled out by distractions.

If you don't have the luxury of time in nature, it is also possible to find these liminal moments in your own breath. Sit quietly and attend to your breathing. Focus not on your inhalations and exhalations, but on the spaces in between. Don't hold your breath at either point, just place your attention into the pauses between your own breaths.

Whether you are utilizing "the strong eye" or the border work techniques, there will come a moment when you experience a shift in awareness. Things will become clearer, more alive, and more intense. In the beginning it may not last long; but with practice, you will learn to slip into these spaces of *no time* at will.

STONE WALK:
FINDING AS A DREAM ARTIST

This exercise will allow you to learn what it means to incorporate the intuitive guidance of momentary shifts into trance states as part of your waking life.

TAKE a break now and go find a stone. What you are looking for is a stone you can hold easily in your hand. It should not be much larger than a golf ball, but it may be as small as a marble. It might be rounded or flat. It might be smooth and polished or rough and angular. You might already have stones around you, but it would still be useful to take a walk to find a new stone. It doesn't matter if you live in the country or the city; as long as you can go outside, you will be able to find a stone.

Once you are outside, take a few deep breaths. Pay attention to your senses. Close your eyes. What do you hear—birds, wind, waves, traffic, music, conversation? What do you smell—pine, saltwater, exhaust fumes, cooking food, cigarettes, flowers, the perfume of people passing by? Is it cold, warm, humid, dry? From which direction is the sun shining or the wind blowing? Don't evaluate or judge any of these sensations, just experience them for a moment.

Now begin to walk. Don't walk too fast. There is no place in particular you are going. But you needn't walk absurdly slow either. Scan the ground ahead of you as you walk. Soften your eyes. It's hard to describe exactly how to do this, but try squinting your eyes and allowing your focus to go a little soft. Rather than looking at things, try to be aware of your whole field of vision at the same time. Use "the strong eye" technique described earlier. This may seem awkward at first, as if you might run into something, but you will find as you relax into it that you are actually more aware of what is going on around you than when you focus intensely on seeing something. It will also be difficult because things will distract you and pull you into a focused way of seeing. This is fine. It is actually what you are hoping will happen. Don't fight it. If what distracts you is not a stone or a sign of stone, simply soften your vision and continue.

When what pulls you out of the state of soft vision is a stone, stop for a moment. If you are walking down a city street, you might be hard pressed to find a single stone. When you see one, it might seem to call out to you—to pull you to it. On the other hand, if you are walking along a pebble-strewn beach or following a streambed through a forest, it won't be difficult to see *a* stone; what will call out to you is *the* stone.

Before you pick the stone up, notice where it's lying. Is it part of a pattern you can discern? Is it pointing in a particular direction? Is it partially buried or covered up? Is it lying flat or on its edge? Is it moist or dry, clean or caked with dirt?

Next, still without picking it up, try to identify what it was about the stone that attracted your attention. Was it a pattern or marking on the stone, or was it the placement of the stone in a larger pattern? Was it the glint of some quartz or metal vein running through the stone? Was it the shape of the stone itself? You may not know for certain, and that's okay. It's enough to ask yourself the question. This information will be useful in understanding your stone and telling its story.

Now you are ready to pick up the stone. If you live in a city, you may, by now, be feeling very self-conscious. You have, after all been staring intently at a rock on the sidewalk or gutter for the past minute or two. Make it easy on yourself and pick the stone up briskly. Hold it in your hand or put it in your pocket and walk on. If you are alone in a more natural landscape, you don't need to move on so quickly.

At some point, before returning home, you will want to examine the stone more carefully. If it is dirty, brush some of the dirt off. If you are near running water, you might choose to rinse it off. Hold it in your hand, feel its weight and shape. Does it nestle into your palm? Do you like the shape and feel of it? Does it feel the same or different if you hold it in a different hand?

Close your eyes for a moment and clasp the stone in your hand. Ask the following question (you can do this out loud, but if you are around other people you might want to do it silently): *Is this the stone, or should I keep looking?* Don't censor yourself, or agonize over this. Accept the first answer that pops into your head. Think of this as the voice of the stone, or your own intuition; either one is okay. Trust this first voice. Don't try to talk yourself into another answer.

If the answer was *yes, this is the stone*, kneel down as if you were picking something up, touch the ground briefly with your fingertips and thank the earth for bringing the stone to your attention. (It is always nice if you can touch real soil when you do this, but your intention of gratitude will pass through the concrete and asphalt if necessary.) We will discuss more formal offerings and exchanges for stone later, but for now it is enough that you honor the earth with a simple thank you.

If you have your stone and have expressed your gratitude, it is time to return home. If the answer was *no, keep looking*, repeat the process described above as you continue your walk. Carry the stone you picked up until you are drawn to another one. When you pick up the new stone, exchange the one you have been carrying for it. Never just throw a stone away casually. Place it back on the ground gently. Remember, it did call to you, and even if it wasn't the stone for you at that moment, it still might be magical for someone else. Continue this process until you find the stone that gives you the answer *yes, this is the stone*. Thank the earth as described above and return home.

You may find the right stone immediately or it may take you some time. This is not a reflection of your ability or affinity for stone. Finding a stone quickly is no indicator of highly developed skills of attention and intuition. Sometimes the right stone demands that you work to find it.

When you return home, carefully wash and dry your stone. Keep it with you for at least a couple of days. If you have your own work space, get your stone out and keep it near where you can see it. Set it on the night table near where you sleep. Refer to it as you read about ways of working with stone. You may choose to honor it through some artistic process or to make it part of a collection. You may work with it more deeply through dreamwork or shamanic journeying. It may become a charm you choose to carry with you, or it might be given as a gift. It might even be returned to the earth as an offering. The important thing is that you've opened yourself up to finding stone in a sacred and attentive manner.

TRUE SIGHT: CLEANING YOUR EYES

*This exercise will allow you to develop the ability to
look past your own preconceptions of a thing and see it
with wonder.*

N o w that you have a stone that you can hold in your hand, locate a clock or watch that you can use to time yourself for three minutes. You can do this exercise with any small object if a stone is too hard to find. Don't take too long to find something.

Now, force yourself to observe your stone for a full three minutes. Set it in front of you on a bare surface and against a background that offers few distractions. Turn off the television and radio. Study the surface of your stone. You can turn it over and around in your hand. Really look at it. If your mind wanders, gently bring it back to observing. This exercise often works best when you are a little tired. What you are attempting to do in this three minutes of intense observation is to bore your rational mind and trick it into shutting down for a moment. The rational mind doesn't really see. It considers real attention to detail a waste of time. Its function is to look long enough to identify and classify. Then it can move on to something else, leaving a kind of visual cliché in the place occupied by the object. This is a useful ability. It allows us to perform complex tasks quickly, but it also keeps us from really seeing what we look at.

The kind of true sight we are trying to develop here is similar to what Yogic and some Buddhist practitioners call "third eye sight." This involves opening the third eye (usually seen as located on the forehead, between the eyebrows). In these practices, it is the third eye that sees what is really there—that shatters the illusion created by the rational mind.

You'll know when you've accomplished this task of opening up to a different way of seeing because what you are observing will suddenly shift in your hand. It might actually feel like movement, or it might be a kind of intensification. This is hard to put into words because we don't have the language for this kind of experience. It's as if a thing becomes more itself than it was a moment before. If you are observing a stone, it will become more richly itself. You will notice patterns and textures you hadn't seen. Some people describe their objects as suddenly becoming more beautiful or more fascinating. Sometimes this shift comes over you suddenly, sometimes the change is more gradual, but stay with the exercise for at least three minutes. Even if the shift is not dramatic, you will notice new things about your object. The more you practice, the easier it will be to slip into this state of true seeing.

ENGAGEMENT:
LOOKING AS A DREAM ARTIST

With this exercise, you will learn to back up and
ask basic questions and then listen, really listen
for the answers.

FOR this exercise you will need a couple of sheets of drawing paper and a pencil. You might use your dream artist's journal. You'll also need a stone or small object. It might be the same one you've been working with, or it might be a new one. To begin with, sketch an outline of the stone in the center of your piece of paper, leaving enough room around the edges to add some writing. Don't worry about how good or how realistic the sketch is. You can trace the shape of the stone if you prefer. Just lightly draw an outline that captures some sense of the shape of the stone. Now, hold the stone in your hand. Ask yourself what your senses tell you about it.

1. How heavy is it?

Instead of answering this question with an actual weight, compare it to other things. For example, the stone I'm holding weighs a bit less than a hen's egg, a bit more than a votive candle. I've not run to the refrigerator or to the nearest altar to do this comparison. These are two items I'm familiar with. They're also evocative things. They extend the web of relationships I'm weaving. List the weight comparisons you come up with on your sheet of paper along the perimeter of the outline you sketched. Another way of doing this might be to sketch the comparison objects alongside the drawing of the stone. Again, don't worry about the quality of your drawing.

2. How dense is it?

This is a subjective question, of course. As with its weight, you needn't calculate its actual density. What you are looking for is a feeling about its density, about how tightly packed are its molecules. Some stones, like pumice from lava flows, are porous and lightly packed. Other stones will feel quite solid and dense. What would it be like to move through your stone? Would it be an exploration of a linked system of caves or would you need to follow one tiny crack through the stone? How small would you need to be to move through it? Is your stone so dense, so solid, that to pass through it you would need to shrink to the size of a single molecule? Add these impressions to your stone sketch.

3. What shape is it?

Look at both your stone and the sketch you made of it. Does its shape remind you of anything? In all of these questions we are engaging the stone for associations, not for measurements. Let your mind play with the shape of the stone. Turn it over in your hand and look at it from other angles. Do you see anything in its shape that reminds you of other things? List those things on your page or sketch them.

4. What does it feel like?

Close your eyes and lightly brush the surface of the stone with your fingertips. Bring it up to your cheek or lips. What does it feel like? Is it smooth or rough, glassy or pockmarked, cool or warm, rounded or edged? What are other things that have similar surfaces and textures? If you were describing the texture of this stone to someone who could not see or touch it, what words, what analogies would you use? Add these words to your growing list.

5. *What color is it?*

How many different colors can you find in your stone? Some stones are striated with different colors—veins of quartz or metal ores. Other stones are banded with distinct shades of gray or tan. Still others are speckled with flecks of color. Describe as many of the colors or shades as you can. You might see a wet slate gray beside an early morning mist gray in close proximity to a band of oatmeal tan with a threadlike vein of rust red. Allow your comparisons to be evocative and playful. They can also be personal comparisons in a language that only you can understand. If I said that a stone was the color of Natasha's paws, it would mean nothing to you, but would instantly evoke for me the color of dirty white blending to brown. Natasha is one of my cats, and this creates a strong association for me. What are your associations? List these colors on your drawing.

6. *What are the patterns of your stone?*

So far, we have looked at weight, density, shape, texture, and color. Now look at your stone for pattern. Are there any distinctive patterns or designs on the surface of the stone? This time, instead of using words to describe them, draw them onto your stone outline. If you are unsure of your ability to draw, work lightly first so that you can erase if you choose. Remember that you needn't do a realistic representation of your stone. Instead, think of yourself as a scientist making notes about the patterns that you observe. Turn the stone over and around if necessary. Overlap patterns or draw another outline to represent the stone seen from a different side. Shade in your patterns with the edge of the pencil lead. Some stones will have wavelike patterns from the compression of strata. Others will have striated bands formed from different material, such as quartz. You may find pieces of a different variety of stone within your stone, or you may see fossils. You might see a pattern formed by the shape or texture of your stone.

SCANNING: ENERGETIC SIGHT

*In this exercise, you will learn to experience your own
energy field as a tool of perception.*

So far we've been using traditional and commonly accepted senses to explore stone. We've used sight, touch, intuition, and active imagination. Now we will open up to a more energetic form of sensing. We will be bringing stone into our energetic fields with awareness and intention.

Begin by washing and drying your hands. While this step is not absolutely essential, it is a kind of ritual act that focuses your attention on what you are about to do. Next, you will need to sensitize your hands. There are several ways of doing this. Some people clap their hands together one or more times. Other people shake their hands loosely until their fingers begin to feel like limp appendages. My own method is to rub my palms together in a circular motion until I feel the heat of friction building up between my hands. The important thing is to find a method that works for you.

When your hands feel ready (trust your intuition), hold them five or six inches apart, palms facing in, as if you were holding a melon. Feel the energy between your hands. Some people feel a tingling in their palms; other people feel it in their fingertips. It may feel stronger in one hand than in the other. It might feel like an itch or it might seem like an elastic cord connecting palm to palm or fingertips to fingertips.

Bounce your hands gently back and forth. Try compressing and expanding the energy between your hands. How far can you go before you lose awareness of the energy? If you do get distracted or lose touch with the sensation, start again. Try to see the energy between your hands. If you can't see it with your eyes open, close them and imagine the ball of energy you are cradling.

Some people find it easy to sense this kind of energetic field, others have to practice a bit more, but everyone is capable of it. If you practice it often enough you may not need to prepare your hands in any way before beginning to perceive the energetic field.

After you are comfortable with what this feels like, practice it with a stone in front of you. Set the stone on a cloth within easy reach of where you are. Sensitize your hands and begin to feel the energy pulsing between them. Now open them slowly and turn your palms out toward the stone. Keep your hands moving over the stone lightly, several inches away, and feel for any sensations emanating from it. You might be more aware of sensation in your fingertips or it might be your palms that are the most sensitive, but give yourself a chance. Every so often you might want to reposition the palms to face each other—reconnecting with your own energetic field.

What should you expect to feel? Well, if this is new to you, you might feel a little silly. If you don't feel something immediate and dramatic, you might be tempted to dismiss the whole experience or to conclude that you have no ability. Stay with the experience a while longer. Pay attention to tingling sensations in palms or fingertips. Be aware of changes in temperature. Does one place feel cooler or warmer than others? Can you sense any difference in air density close to the stone? These can all be ways of perceiving energetic fields.

One more thing to be aware of is whether you seem to consistently sense the energy field more strongly with one hand or the other. Most people will find that they have a greater sensitivity for receiving in one hand and a greater capacity to send or direct with the other. Don't worry if you don't notice a difference.

While focusing on the feeling in your hands, also be aware of the thoughts, images, and impressions that come to you. Do sudden strong images come to your mind? Are the images ones you recognize from your life or are they new to you? Open yourself up to these images, but don't linger on them. In a later chapter we will explore this imagery further. For now it is enough to note the images the stone triggers.

When you energetically scan a stone, keep your dream artist's journal nearby. Begin by writing the date and time at the top of the page. Sketch the stone you are working with or trace its outline. Write a little of what you know about the stone such as:

- Where did you find it?
- What size is it?

- What color is it?
- What is its texture?
- What patterns are visible on the stone?

As you scan the stone, write down or sketch any strong ideas or images that come to you. Don't try to interpret them. Just record them. If words or sounds come to you, record these as well. Writing down your impressions reinforces your ability to receive them.

You may want to go on and do further work with the material you received from the stone—weaving it into a poem or story or painting or sketching it—but before going on, give the stone or object you worked with a name based on your impressions. Feel free to be romantic, poetic, and even mythic in the naming of it. Naming your things will help them come fully to life. When I look at the stones I have collected, I see Fat Rain Stone, Moon Thunder, and Polar Bear Surfacing Stone.

Listen to your objects and they will tell you their names.

DEEP READING: HEARING THE STORIES THAT OBJECTS TELL

This exercise will allow you to develop an openness to the consciousness of objects by interacting with their energetic fields.

WITH basic scanning, you were getting to know your own field of energy and that of the stone. With reading, you are focusing your intention even further. Begin by preparing your hands as you did for basic scanning, but this time place the stone on the palm of one hand and cup the other hand over it.

Pay attention to the feeling in your hands. Sometimes stones will feel warmer then you expect to. Sometimes they will be cooler. How do your palms feel? Do they itch or tingle? Now direct your attention to your abdomen, specifically the area from just below your solar plexus to several inches below your navel. Many people who are developing psychometric skills feel an energetic response in this area. This response might be a grumbling stomach, a tensing of muscles, a funny tingling, a sense of warmth or cold, or a peculiar sensitivity. In time you will come to understand what this means for you specifically. Gifted psychometrics associate different messages with the signals that they experience. You might notice nothing in this area of your body. Don't worry about it, just move on to the next step.

Ask yourself the following questions:

- What is my first impression of this stone?
- Where has this stone been?
- Who has held this stone before me?
- Why has this stone come to me?

Write down the answers to these questions in your dream artist's journal. Don't censor yourself. Trust your first impressions. If you hear a dialogue, write it down. If it happens too fast or is too long, try taping the dialogue and transcribing it later.

Deeper into the Dreaming

VISION-SHIFTING is the first of the journeys you will make into an altered state of consciousness. Reread what you've written and sketched in your journal. Some of it will seem fairly commonplace, but some of it will surprise you. You may feel as if you've imagined some of the images, feelings, or sensations you received. That's okay. If you've done nothing more than limber up your imaginative powers, you're already allowing the dream artist to emerge in your practice. If you've worked with the same stone or object through all four exercises, ask yourself how you feel about that stone or object now. Do you have a new appreciation for it? Do you have a new connection to it? These exercises can take even the most skeptical person into the world of the dreaming. The more you practice these exercises the more flexible you will become in your way of thinking. You will also begin to find that you are more open to the spirit in the material.

Now that you have begun to access the dreaming world through its material shadows, you must practice your new skill. Don't wait for special occasions. During your day, when you are forced to wait in some line or in some reception room, pick up an object and hold it in your hand. Go through the process of attending to the material form of the object, then use your intuition to open yourself to its energy or spirit. Carry a stone with you on which to practice. Take short, slow walks in which you allow yourself to see the energetic world around you. Record your experiences in words, colors, simple diagrams, or drawings in your dream artist's journal.

But it's important to remember that as interesting as these experiences are, a dream artist is not merely a tourist in this realm. All objects will speak if you develop the power to listen to them, but not all objects will have important things to say to you. Your intentions—the questions and requests you put out into the universe—will bring significant objects and images into your field of consciousness. Attending to these objects with your intention in mind will bring forth images, words, songs, and scenes. Remember these things. Write them down. These are the things you are looking for. These are the raw materials with which you will work.

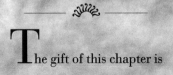

The gift of this chapter is

awakening.

We enter into the dreaming—the shamanic state of

consciousness—every night. Waking up to that world, the

imagery and meaning of it, can enrich our spiritual practice as

dream artists. The exercises in this chapter will help you

remember and understand your dreams as well as work with

them as source and resource.

chapter 4

Dreamwork: *Night Dreams* as Source and *Resource*

*If "everyone who dreams is a little bit shaman" as the Kagwahiv say, then
every approach to dreamwork that honors dreams as coming from a source
beyond ego might be considered "shamanic."*

—ROBERT MOSS

Conscious Dreaming: A Spiritual Path for Everyday Life

Do you dream? A lot of people say they don't dream, when what
they mean to say is that they don't *remember* their dreams. There are
many ideas of what dreams are—from the dismissive modern stance
that dreams are simply a neurological reordering process that occurs
during sleep to the indigenous belief that dreams are a gateway beyond
time and space to another reality. Some schools of thought place great
emphasis on understanding or interpreting the one true meaning of a
dream. For a dream artist, it is more important to fully experience
dreams to reflect upon them, to honor them, and to use them as a source

of divine inspiration. We don't attack them like a problem that must be solved. We play with them.

Every Tuesday afternoon my friend and fellow dream artist, Victoria Rabinowe, gathers a group together to play with their dreams. Selecting a different metaphor each session, Victoria leads her fellow dreamers through a series of playful exercises designed to provoke and stimulate new ways of seeing dream material. "What if your dream was a gateway?" she might ask. Before analyzing or seeking to interpret their dreams, she encourages the group to find objects that represent elements of their own dreams. The class proceeds to construct gateway shrines—physical manifestations of their dreams. The shrines are decorated and honored with candles, flowers, and found objects. Some found, altered, or created object represents each element of the dream. Victoria encourages her dreamers to write in the voice of different dream elements. Some imagine themselves as gatekeepers, others as those hoping to pass through the gate. There is no attempt to explain or interpret the dream in a rational, logical manner; rather the dream is played with like a child plays with a toy. Voices and personas are tried on. Points of view are shifted. When meaning comes, and it almost always does in this process, it is a meaning that is deeply felt—understood at some soul level. The process does not end here though. The gateway shrines are used to explore the issues of the dream more deeply through dream incubation and further ritual engagement.

Night dreams are an important part of a dream artist's life. If vision-shifting seems too fleeting and shamanic journeys require too much commitment, you still have your night dreams to explore. Night dreams offer a rich banquet of imagery from which to sample. Creating art from dreams and dream imagery is one of the most commonly accepted practices among artists. Whether they are identified as such by title or not, a good percentage of the paintings and works of art on display in any museum are influenced, if not inspired, by artists' dreams. The dream artist is different only in the depth to which he or she explores the imagery of the dreaming mind.

There are many good books on how to work with dreams (see bibliography), but what the dream artist needs to know is how to remember dreams, how to work with dreams through reentry and incubation, and how to translate the symbolic language of dreams in images and artifacts. As dream artists, we don't need neat explanations for our dreams. We need the raw material with which to play, to create, to cross-pollinate our waking life experiences, and upon which to expand. Our dreams, both the pleasant and the frightening, are a sea into which we joyously and fearlessly dive.

Outfitting: The Dream Journal

YOU ALREADY HAVE a dream artist's journal. You may simply wish to record and process your night dreams in this book. But if you get serious about logging your dreams, you may want a separate book for this purpose alone.

A dream journal may be lined or unlined. Some art supply stores sell books that are divided up to provide lined areas and open space on the same page. Ask yourself if you prefer to write out your dreams, to sketch images from or diagram your dreams, or to do some combination of both. There are commercial dream journals available that are very beautiful and evocative. Some of these dream journals prompt you with questions or offer specific spaces to fill in. If this inspires and motivates you to record your dreams, by all means invest in a dream journal of this sort. I know dream artists, however, who use inexpensive spiral notebooks, so don't let the expense or the search for the perfect dream journal keep you from getting started.

I recommend that your journal be small enough to keep on a bedside table without being so small that it's hard to write in. It should also be convenient to work with. If the spine is so stiff that you have trouble keeping it open while you write, you may hurry to finish and miss recording important details. Consider also that you may want to take your dream journal with you during the day. Is it portable?

Everyone develops a favorite style for recording their dreams in their dream journals, but consider some of these techniques to add variety and new insights to your dream recording:

1. Make a word and image map of your dream. Instead of starting at the top and writing down, start in the middle or in a corner of the page. Record the dream geographically.

2. Record your dream in your own hieroglyphics. Create a key for what each symbol means and tell the dream with only symbols.

3. Draw a single image to capture the spirit of the dream.

4. Write at odd angles to the page. Write in long meandering trails around the page.

5. Don't worry about writing in complete sentences or run-on sentences. Express yourself in words and phrases.

6. Write in different colors of ink to match the moods within a dream. Use different colors to signify shifts within the dream where things seem to have blurred into another dream.

7. Number the significant elements or events of your dream.

8. Use a highlighter or underlining to make note of recurring dream elements.

In chapter 1, you read about dedicating your dream artist's journal to a sacred purpose through a simple ceremony. You can do a similar kind of ceremony to consecrate (give over to a sacred purpose) your dream journal.

In addition to the journal itself, you will want to keep a pen next to your bed. Some pens have lighted ends that allow you to write in the dark. If you don't get one of these and you think turning the lights on in the middle of the night to record a dream would disturb someone, you might also get a small flashlight or one of those tiny lamps designed for reading in bed.

Some people have more success with initially recording their dreams by speaking into a tape recorder and transcribing them into their dream journals later. If this seems like an approach that might work better for you, get a microcassette recorder or a digital voice recorder. If you choose a microcassette recorder, you have the option of getting one with voice-activation. This certainly keeps you from fumbling with the tape recorder in the dark, but it might also document snoring and other embarrassing sounds. Setting the recorder up to record and pushing the pause button can make it easier to get the recorder running in the dark.

You may want to pick up a starter set of acrylic paints. You already have all of the other supplies you will need for this chapter.

T hough we may take it for granted, entering the world of night dreams is as much a journey as any waking world expedition. Dream artists explore their dreams in search of imagery. For some people it might simply be a matter of saying, "Ready? Set. Sleep!" But, most of us, at one point or another in our lives, have difficulty accessing our dreams. To utilize the raw material of our dream imagery we first need to learn to recall it.

DREAM RECALL:
THE ART OF REMEMBERING

This exercise will teach you to develop a creative and intuitive resource that is always available to you for problem-solving and clarification.

W E all dream. We don't all remember our dreams, but we do dream. Dream recall is something that can be learned, improved, and practiced. I've provided a set of practical tips—listed below—that can help you remember your dreams, but the first step is to decide that you *want* to remember them. If you already remember your dreams easily, you may not need the advice provided below, but it helps to familiarize yourself with it for two reasons. First of all, others may ask you how they can learn to better remember their dreams. If dream recall has always come naturally, you might not know what practical advice to recommend. Second, you may find yourself having occasional difficulty remembering your dreams. Even in a dream-sharing group—a gathering of people committed to sharing their dreams and helping each other understand their dreams—people sometimes go through long dry spells where they cannot recall their dreams. I think this is a natural defense mechanism. Once you've accepted or experienced that dreams reveal your soul's deepest fears and concerns, there can be a backlash in your psyche that says, "No! We're not going to go there." So for weeks some part of us will interfere with our ability to remember dreams. This can be very frustrating, but it's always temporary and can be overcome by returning to some of the basic steps listed below.

1. Set an intention to remember a dream.

This is the single most important thing you can do to improve your dream recall. As you fall asleep at night, repeat to yourself as many times as you can that you will remember a dream in the morning. It also helps if you make a ritual out of it. Light a candle. Ask your dream artist for help in remembering a dream. Write the following day's date in your dream journal. Place your dream journal and a pen (and maybe a flashlight) beside your bed and within easy reach. Blow out the candle before going to sleep.

2. Keep a dream journal or tape recorder by your bed.

As mentioned above, you can use your dream artist's journal or you can purchase a separate dream journal, but you need to log your dreams every morning. Even if you tape record your dreams (one of my friends calls her own voice mail system, which she has on speed dial, to record her dreams in the middle of the night), you need to take time to write out the dream in as much detail as possible. Make sure that you have the necessary recording tools close by your bed.

3. When you wake up—lie still for a while.

What causes us to be able to experience dreams as being so lifelike, without actually moving, is that our body is flooded with a chemical that inhibits major muscle response while we sleep. In this way we can have a dream experience that is real enough to cause our pulse, heart rate, and respiration to climb without actually running a fast mile. The memory of a dream is keyed to the body posture we were in when we dreamed it. As you wake in the morning, try not to make any dramatic movements. If you catch yourself having rolled over, simply roll back into the previous position and move to step 4.

4. Rehearse the dream several times before moving.

Before stretching, rolling over, getting out of bed, or engaging in any other physical activities, rehearse the dream. Replay it in your mind and try to recall as much detail as possible. Follow the chain of events as far back as you can go in the dream. Repeat this process several times as if recollecting the plot of a good movie, but be careful not to fall back asleep. Move to step 5 only after you think you have as much material as you can remember.

5. Record the dream in words and pictures.

Use whatever tool works best for you to log your dream. If it works better to record your dream into a tape recorder, that's fine, but later in the day you will want to transfer it to your dream journal. When you do use a journal, consider combining words and sketches. I've found it useful to record dreams in a first-person, present-tense, stream-of-consciousness narrative. This seems to reinforce the quality of being in the dream. I relive it as I recall it. I also find it useful to add little pictures, maps, and diagrams to my text.

Begin with the objective details of the dream. Write out as much as you remember, as far back as you remember. Story is important, but the imagery and details of the dream are even more important. Don't try to give meaning to anything as you write—just write. If you only recall a single image, record that in as much detail as you can.

And what if you can't remember anything? Write the first things that come into your head. Write down whatever spontaneous images or thoughts occur to you. Sometimes this can trigger dream recall. It also sets a pattern of recording. It puts your psyche on notice that even if you don't like the discipline of writing, failure to remember a dream won't exempt you from the process. I've also had the experience of discovering that what I wrote when I couldn't recall a dream was as interesting and important as some of my actual dreams.

After you have described the objective details of the dream, record your subjective responses. How did you feel about events within the dream? How did you feel upon waking? Did any emotions or experiences from the dream linger? Finally, give the dream a title—a short sentence that summarizes the dream.

6. *Vary your sleeping/waking schedule.*

If you still have difficulty remembering your dreams, look at your sleep schedule. Are you getting enough sleep? Does the sound of an alarm jolt you awake? Try setting your intention to recall a dream over a weekend or a holiday where you have the time to sleep late and wake slowly. Conversely, if you always sleep late and wake slowly, try setting an alarm for the early hours of the morning to see if you have better recall.

7. *Be persistent, but don't judge yourself.*

Don't give up. If you aren't used to recalling and recording dreams, it may seem awkward or unproductive at first. Stick with it. You are creating a new habit. Don't worry if you can't recall epic dreams right away. Some of the most useful dreams are fragments and single images. Don't be critical of either your ability to recall your dreams or of the dreams themselves. If you have nightmares or dreams where you violate social taboos or personal codes of behavior, it doesn't mean that you secretly want to do these very things. Morality in the world of dreams is subjective. The spirit or energetic realm sometimes uses our own fears and the strong emotional experiences of our past to communicate important information.

8. *Join or form a dream-sharing group.*

Dream-sharing groups gather to share and help in the unfolding of dreams. They really reinforce one's capacity to remember a dream. If you're skeptical about whether dreams really have meaning at all, sit in on an established dream-sharing group and listen. It's hard not to be amazed by the wealth and relevance of information that comes through group dreamwork. If you feel comfortable, ask if you can continue to come. If not, try another group. Not all dream-sharing groups are created equal.

So what happens when dreams stop coming?

Sometimes, even when we are practiced at the art of recalling our dreams, the flow of dreams seems to be interrupted for a period of time. If that happens to you, consider one of the following possibilities:

1. We don't really want the guidance we are receiving.

Sometimes spirit, through our dreams, calls for us to make life changes that seem too radical, too uncomfortable, or too difficult. This predetermination can make us deaf to the guidance of spirit through dreams. It can also result in dramatic and frightening nightmares as spirit uses our soul's worst fears to get through to us.

2. We fail to honor our dreams.

If we continually receive dream guidance from spirit upon which we fail to act, the well of guidance, in effect, runs dry. Spirit, soul, subconscious—whatever you choose to believe is acting through your dreams—likes to be fed through ritual. Try painting your dream or find an object to represent it on your personal altar. Make a nature offering in gratitude for the dream's guidance even if you are unable at the time to follow it.

3. We are under the sway of strong emotions.

When our days are filled with trauma, worry, grief, anger, fear, or even intense love and erotic passion, we can temporarily shut down from receiving dream guidance. It's almost as if we need the respite more than we need the guidance.

4. Our sleep cycle has been disturbed.

Illness, drug use, change of routine, the arrival of a new baby, the arrival or departure of a new energy within a household can all disturb our dreaming life.

Each of these cases, it's important to note, is just as likely to produce an excess of dreams, or a plethora of highly memorable dreams, as it is to cause dream recall to be interrupted. But whatever the cause of the disruption, the link to spirit guidance through dreams can be rebuilt by returning to the steps listed in the Dream Recall section.

Once you have reached a point where you are remembering and recording your dreams, there are two additional techniques that will help you to delve more deeply into the meaning of your dreams and utilize your own dreaming consciousness more effectively. These techniques are dream reentry and dream incubation, and as you'll see in the example given below, they can help with the dream artist's work in a number of ways.

> *Michael dreams he must pass through a series of rooms in an art gallery to reach a room that he understands will be displaying his own work. Michael, a man in his mid-forties, has only recently begun to act upon a life-long desire to paint, so he is excited about getting to the room that contains his paintings. At each connecting doorway between rooms of the gallery, a person stops and asks him for something in order to get into the next room. He gives away everything he has in his pockets before he reaches the doorway to his own display and is worried that he has nothing left to give away. The person bars his entry to the fi-*

nal room, and Michael is peering around the guardian, trying to see what his artwork looks like when he wakes up.

Michael was, needless to say, disturbed and anxious from the dream. He could instantly put several interpretations to the dream, but none of them felt complete. I suggested that Michael move into a relaxed, meditative state and reenter the dream. This time he was to consciously address each of the doorway guardians, asking them why they were there and what they expected of him. He was also to try to change the ending of the dream and enter his exhibit space. This technique, based on the exercise Carl Jung called "active imagination," often strikes observers as being wishful thinking and fantasy; but my experience is that, more often than not, it adds new insight and context to the original dream.

In Michael's case, the spontaneous conversations, in which he spoke in the voice of both himself and his dream guardians, suggested that he had been too willing to give up whatever he had to reach his goal. He reexamined the objects he had given away to each guardian and began to explore what they represented to him. He had given away the change in his pocket, his wallet, his watch, and finally his wedding ring, before realizing that he had nothing left to give up.

Rather than directly interpreting these symbols, Michael found objects to represent them and placed them on a small dream shrine. By playing with the arrangement of his found objects, he addressed some of the deep beliefs he had about what being an artist meant. He realized that he believed artists had to be poor, had to give up traditional ideas of status in the community, had to devote all their time to their art, and could never have stable relationships. By creating a shrine, he began to see the value in things he had assumed he would have to give up, and the ways in which they could actually *contribute* to his life as an artist. His vision of his own future as an artist evolved to allow for more balance and less of an all-or-nothing attitude.

—————————————— ·ᘓ·ᘓ· ——————————————

DREAM REENTRY:
FINDING YOUR WAY BACK

*With this exercise, you will learn to transform dream
scenarios through imagination and intention.
This technique can be used for both night dreams
and waking reality.*

T H E technique Michael used in the example above is what is commonly called "dream reentry." It means, quite simply, to use the power of imagination to return to the landscape of a particular dream. It can be used to resolve unfinished issues from the dream, to confront challenges that seem nightmarish, or to simply explore further pleasant and intriguing dream scenarios. It is, in essence, as simple as lying down in a quiet room where you will not be disturbed for twenty minutes, relaxing, remembering the dream setting in as much detail as possible, and interacting with the characters and elements of the dream through dialogue and action. To try dream reentry for yourself, follow these steps:

1. Set aside some time when you will not be disturbed (turn off the ringer of the phone, let family members know that you will be unavailable for a little while) and when you are not so tired that you are likely to fall asleep.

2. Put on some soft droning music. Lower the lights. Make contact with the four elements by lighting a candle, burning a bit of incense or sage, touching stone, and touching the water in your bowl. Relax and set your intention for sacred work. Have your dream journal handy for preparation and to log your dream reentry experience. Some people like to keep a tape recorder running while they document their dream dialogue out loud. Others do this silently and record their conversations afterward in writing.

3. Reread your dream journal to familiarize yourself with the dreamscape to which you are returning. Set an intention for the dream reentry. Why are you reentering the dream? What do you hope to learn, clarify, experience?

4. Lie down on the floor in a comfortable position and progressively relax your body by tensing and relaxing feet, legs, torso, pelvis, abdomen, chest, hands, arms, shoulders, neck, face, and head. Breathe slowly and deeply from your belly, but don't force your breath.

5. Visualize the scene in as much detail as possible. See yourself back in the dream. Instead of allowing yourself to be swept away by events, exert some control. Ask questions, confront aggressors, and try going in new directions, manipulating objects, reading books, signs, and messages. Shift your perspective. Allow yourself to become different elements or characters in the dream and give a voice to what you've become. Remain focused on your intention. When you become too distracted, or the scenario leads too far away from the initial dreamscape, or you realize you're drifting off into other dreams, return to the waking world.

6. Write your dream reentry experience in your journal. Treat it with no less respect than you would a night dream. Honor the reentry experience by incorporating elements of the dream reentry into your artwork.

While dream reentry as a personal practice is highly effective, it is also highly beneficial to experience it with a partner or group. When done in this manner, as in the process Robert Moss describes in his book, *Conscious Dreaming: A Spiritual Path for Everyday Life*, as "dream tracking," one person or a group agrees to go through the same relaxation and reentry process on behalf of another. This can be a powerful way to get new perspective on aspects of a dream. It's important to state, however, that even if one agrees to allow someone to reenter his or her dream, the purpose is not to provide the one answer or interpretation for the dream, but rather to unfold the dream's multiple layers. The other thing I invariably find when I participate in dream tracking is that no matter how specific or profound the message is to the person for whom I am dreaming, there is also some piece of dream reentry wisdom meant for me.

Taking dream tracking a step further, purposefully dreaming for others can also be a powerful experience. I dreamed for a woman who is a friend and an artist. She had been having difficulty creating and was being especially hard on herself and the work she had done in the past, though my perception of her work has always been that it is exceptionally powerful. This was my dream:

I'm lying on a small rug in a room. The woman artist is also there, as is a third person. We all sit up and face each other in a triangle formation. The woman begins to talk about her art, and I notice a figure unfolding behind her. At first this figure matches her silhouette perfectly. But as it opens up, I see a shamanic figure of a woman in a floor-length cape of deep blue and green feathers. Her hair is a wild tangle of feathers, bones, and red glass beads, and she wears beautiful jewelry at her neck and from around her wrists, ankles, and ears.

As the woman artist talks about her work, she gestures overhead with her hands. Each time she extends an open hand up into the air, the shaman woman lays a beautiful beaded pouch, or sacred necklace, or other artifact into her hand. My friend lays these objects in front of us, unaware of their source and dismissive of their value. I watch, wide-eyed and amazed at this display. I'm struck by the power of the artifacts and their source and surprised that the woman does not realize from where her gifts originate.

As is the case with most of the dreaming we do for others, there is truth here for the dreamer as well as for the woman for whom I was dreaming. This is her story, but it is also mine. One of the things blocking her creativity was the personal investment she had in being an artist. The work was hers, so the responsibility for the lack of work was also hers. The more she didn't create, the more she doubted her ability to create. The best thing I could offer my friend was not a prescription, but a combination of attentiveness and the willingness to share my life experience. My journey as an artist and a person had helped me understand that *I* am not the creative force behind my artwork. I am creative because I access a kind of sacred creative energy—the potential of the dreaming world. As I have journeyed inward to understand the source of my creativity, I realize that to truly acknowledge what I am experiencing in the process and product of creation—an expression of spirit in the material—I need to confront a different, more sacred, more magical world. This is how I came to the world of the shaman—the world of the dream artist. I have no doubt that my friend will create again when she is ready to reopen the channel to that divine source that had always inspired her work anyway. What she will come to realize is that understanding the source of her creativity and giving herself the space and the conditions that her creative source demands will open up in her a whole new world of creative endeavor.

DREAM INCUBATION: SEEKING DREAM GUIDANCE

*Through this exercise, you will learn to get intuitive
guidance for specific issues in your life or ask for
specific artistic advice through your dreams.*

THE second useful technique for dream artists is called "dream incubation." This is to the dreaming mind what setting an intention is to the conscious mind. Dream incubation allows you to ask questions of your dreaming mind, to request guidance on life events, and to clarify or amplify previous dreams. In the ancient Greek world, people sought healing dreams in the temples of Aesculapius. They would prepare themselves to dream through special dietary practices, ritual bathing and cleansing, prayer, and ceremony. In the proper frame of mind, and with a clear request for assistance or guidance, the dreamer would sleep in a specially prepared chamber, ready to receive the wisdom of the dreaming world. Though the more you prepare, the more likely you are to receive a dream specifically related to the question you asked, you can experience a simple form of dream incubation by following these guidelines:

1. Before going to sleep at night, allow yourself a few minutes to sit with your dream journal. I find it helps to spend some time writing about the issue you want assistance with. If it's a personal issue, describe it and describe how you feel about it. If it's a question of artistic guidance, be clear about where you are stuck or in what areas you would like inspiration.

2. Start a new page to record the dream you intend to recall the following morning. Write the next day's date at the top of the page and state as clearly as possible your question or what it is you would like to receive from the spirit world through your dreams.

3. While it is possible to ask big questions like, "What should I do with my life?" and "Why am I here?" It sometimes is more productive to take smaller bites. Ask for guidance rather than answers. Instead of asking, "Which job offer should I choose? Try asking "What do I need to know or do in order to make the best choice between these two jobs?"

4. If your intention is to dream something helpful for others, as I did with my artist friend who had been doubting her talents, you may, with their permission, set an intention to dream for them. But when the issue is one about which you are or may be in conflict with another, it is most productive to ask for guidance or clarity on your own role in the situation rather than asking how to "fix" another person.

5. Before falling asleep, repeat your question or request over and over again as a mantra.

6. Record whatever you remember of your dreams upon waking, even if it does not seem instantly relevant. It may take several tries to get clear guidance, but stick with it. Once you've devel-

oped the ability to program your dreaming consciousness, you have a constant connection to specific spiritual guidance.

Dream reentry and dream incubation form a continuum between the waking and dreaming worlds. In his book, *Secrets of the Talking Jaguar*, Martin Prechtel describes the creation of "Dream Thrones" or physical manifestations of dream experiences in an altarlike arrangement. "Once a shaman has his or her spirit throne, then he or she could talk to the spirit, asking questions after feeding the spirit on its Dream Throne. The replies would occur in a dream. This back-and-forth dialogue between shamans and their power, from dreams, is a prerequisite and signifies the spirit's endorsement of a shaman's desirability."

Understanding the Language of Dreams

So WHAT IS DREAMING consciousness? What are dreams? What do dreams mean? How are we to understand our dreams? As you travel more and more in this inner space, as you make your waking life more dreamlike and your dreams more real, you will form your own conclusions. What I can provide at this point are simply some of my own observations about dreams that I think will help you as you work with yours.

To begin with, I think it's important to point out that you don't need to understand all of your dreams. Some dreams will speak to you in clear and precise detail, giving you instructions, revealing guidance, initiating you through songs and stories of power. Other dreams will seem to be less important. They might be worked with or just as easily let alone. But some dreams will call you to engage in a game of understanding.

One of the reasons that I think dreams baffle us is that we, as a culture, have lost the ability to read poetry. When faced with a poem, we immediately want to know what it means even though it is seldom the intention of the poet to mean just one thing. A poem suggests, implies, creates for us new connections, and takes us to new vantage points;

when we read it as a textbook, we come away more confused. The same is true of dreams. It is not in the nature of a dream to mean just one thing. A dream carries truth on many levels at once. There may be literal truth in a dream—a foretelling of events to come or practical guidance for the near future. There may also be psycho-personal truth in a dream—information we need to better heed the call of our souls. Often there is a kind of communal or cultural level of wisdom imparted in the dream. And, it is also possible to see cosmic or universal truths unfolding in dream messages. The trick to understanding a dream is to not hold any one interpretation too tightly. Gather interpretations as you would pretty shells on a beach. Draw what truth or beauty you can from each interpretation without investing in its correctness. Pay attention to your body's reaction to each interpretation. When you find one or more that "sit well" with you, know that this is what will be most useful for you in the moment. It does not mean that other interpretations are less true or less correct. It means that, in the moment, this answer best fits your question.

For this same reason I think that it is good to avoid consulting authority figures when it comes to dreams. Dream dictionaries tend to cut short our speculative play with a dream in the same way that reading a detailed commentary about a poem disconnects us from truly experiencing it as a poem. Consulting someone skilled in the language of dreams can be helpful if their process includes far more time questioning than postulating, and if, in the end, the result is several possible interpretations. This may seem frustrating, but if someone reduces a dream to one possible meaning, all you've really learned is what one meaning out of many possible meaning resonates with that person. Conscientious dreamworkers always offer their interpretations with the observation that, "If this were my dream . . ."

The best authority on your dreams is you. You will never read a better book about dreams than your own dream journal. Read more poetry. Write some poetry. Read your dreams like poems. Write your dreams as if they were poems. Look for similarities within your dreams. What elements recur in your dreams? Make your own recurring elements your personal dream categories. Come to understand the nature of your categories. One way I've found to access the meaning of my dreams in this way is through dream mapping. In the following exercise, I'll show you how to put this technique into practice.

DREAM MAPPING: MANIFESTING A DREAM

This exercise will teach you to see the images of your dreams come alive in the waking world. You will learn to develop your ability to combine and play with found imagery.

FOR this exercise, you will need a piece of illustration or matte board (about 11 by 17 inches), scissors, magazines you can cut up, some white glue, a couple of small and medium-sized paint brushes, and some acrylic paint (a couple of colors will be fine). This exercise combines all four of the dream artist's ways of working: finding, arranging, altering, and making.

Use your dream journal to select a particularly vivid and detailed dream, or select several dreams that occurred over a short period of time. If you haven't been recording your dreams, try to recall and record one tonight before doing this exercise. If you're still having difficulty remembering your dreams, try putting on a relaxing piece of music and allowing yourself to just select images intuitively.

Select a magazine with a lot of pictures that you will not feel bad about cutting up. Travel magazines are usually good for this exercise. If you need to use several magazines instead of just one, that's fine, but don't use more than four (trust that what you need is in those four publications). Have handy a pair of scissors. Take a moment to recall the dream or dreams in as much detail as you can.

When you have the dreamscape in mind, begin flipping quickly through the magazine. Cut out any image that in any way reminds you of the dream. You might see exact matches—object for object or animal for animal. You might not find a leopard, but you might find a woman wearing a leopard print skirt. You might find pictures where only a small piece of the image reminds you of your dream. Cut them out anyway. You might choose an image because it reminds you of the mood of the dream or your emotions as you dreamed the dream. You might also cut out words that remind you of your dream, but for the most part, look for images.

Work fast, trust your intuition, and let the images speak to you. Cut out whole pages or roughly cut out images so that you can work quickly.

In about twenty minutes you should have a nice selection of images. You have, in effect, found a physical manifestation of your dream imagery in the waking world.

The next step is to carefully trim the images you've saved. Cut away the background with detail scissors or an X-Acto knife. Try arranging them on your board. Shift them around several different ways before committing to glue down. You can fill a lot of the board, but you needn't cover the entire space. Consider overlapping pieces and creating relationships between the parts you've cut out. You can arrange them in the order of the dream or move them about until the overall image is more visually satisfying. Play with them. If they want to tell you a new story, let them.

When you are ready, glue them down with white glue and a brush or a glue stick. If you use the glue stick, make sure to cover the whole back side of your images for good adhesion. If you use white glue squeeze out the air bubbles so that the images will lay flat when you're done. Allow the glue to dry.

Next, take the paint and fill in all the empty space between the images. Paint over anything that you don't want to show. Paint right up to the edge of what you do want to show. Paint neat or paint fast and messy. Use several colors. Mix the colors and swirl them right on the board. Spatter the piece with color if you want. Sprinkle the painted places with glitter. Try painting over some images and wiping away the paint to reveal them again. Use cotton swabs to wipe away paint or clean up edges if you need to.

Let your dream map dry.

Look carefully at what you've created. What story does it tell you on its own? How does it amplify the images of the dream? Look for new relationships between images. Look especially for the effects and bits of images you hadn't intended to show. Use the piece as a backdrop for an altar.

This exercise shows that you can find, alter, arrange, and even make images. You may wish you had done it differently, but you now know that you have the ability to do it. If you take on no other media, you can still be a wonderful dream artist with collage techniques alone.

Sometimes your dreams will speak to you with a clarity that is astounding. If you need to make a choice between two things, you may dream of choosing the right thing. But more often your dreams will speak to you playfully, with puns and metaphors and meaning that must be teased from the dream. I began this chapter with a quote from a fellow dream traveler: Robert Moss. Before I met Robert, I knew of him from his books and tapes. He has done a lot to bridge the gap between shamanic work and contemporary dreamwork, inventing and adapting many useful techniques.

One night I had the following dream.

I'm dancing in a place that is both a circular room and a moss-covered forest grove. I'm doing a dance I understand to be a Boundary Dance—a ritual testing of the boundary between worlds. I'm dancing it with a partner that I cannot always see through the trees. My partner always stays opposite me on the circle. We are dancing to a deep drumbeat, stamping our feet on the forest floor and regularly striking the walls with our fists. I understand that what we are looking for is a soft place in the wall—almost a physically transparent place—a passage into the other world.

As I dance, I realize that my partner is a polar bear. Polar bear often comes to me as a power animal and guide, but this polar bear is different. He is roughly my height, with a shaman's medicine bundle about his neck, an Australian cavalry hat with cocked brim and white feathers in the headband, and an oar as a staff.

When we have danced to near exhaustion, we take a break and move to the center of the circle we've been defining by our dance. The drumming continues, but we lie down on the soft ground and look up at a night sky through the canopy of trees.

The bear says, "So, where are you from?"

"Norfolk, Virginia," I answer. "And you?"

"Down under," he says as if it should be obvious to me.

"Australia?" I ask, though I know "down under" and Australia are usually synonymous.

"No, France," he says. He is not being sarcastic. I wonder if there are polar bears in either Australia or France.

We watch the night sky as stars begin streaking together to form an oval galaxy with a dark center. We realize this galaxy is somehow the way into the other world we've been looking for. The galaxy transforms itself into an oval opening in the ceiling of the forest/room we are in. It is too high up for either of us alone, but we figure out that one of us might lift the other up through the opening, then climb up that person. We discuss who should lift whom. It is decided that while the bear could lift me easily, I might not be able to support his weight as he climbs up my body. Though it is something of a strain, I lift the bear to the opening and then climb up myself.

We are both hanging from the edge now, laughing at our predicament. We pull ourselves through and find that what seemed to be an oval galaxy when we looked up at it is now an oval pool—smooth and inky black. We look to see if we can see back through it but all we see are our reflections. Then the earth seems to shift and we find that the pond has become a framed oval mirror set in a stone wall.

The bear says, "Now that's a dream gate!"

I could have consulted a dream dictionary to find out the "meaning" of the symbols within the dream, but instead I played with it a bit. I liked the imagery of the dream and sketched it in my journal. I began to wonder about the bear and his oar. Was he an oar-bear? Was he a paddle-bear? I thought of rowing. Is he a row-bear? I realized that row-bear sounds like the French pronunciation of Robert. The bear said he was French. Perhaps this is a Robert as well as a row-bear. The next day I got an announcement for a lecture and workshop with Robert Moss. I remembered from his tape series that Robert spoke with a healthy Australian accent. All at once I realized this was the Australian bear I'd dreamed about. I'd been with Row-Bear of the Moss.

I decided to take the workshop, but my schedule didn't seem to allow for it. A couple of weeks prior to the workshop date, my schedule changed and I was even asked to present a workshop prior to the Friday night lecture. To honor the dream, I painted a stone with a mirror image in a field of colorful stars. I gave this to Robert when we met. As I related my dream to him, he shared that his family was in fact from France, though he grew up in Australia. He'd also just returned from a visit to Australia and made a gift to me of a shell, hand-painted by an Aboriginal artist, depicting the constellation from which this artist believed his people originated.

Dreams are considered by many cultures to be a direct expression of the vast and mysterious nature of life. They come to us free of the corruption and machinations of our all-too-human need to control our own destinies. Look to your dreams for a truer picture of your life and your situation. If you are living out of balance, your dreams will tell you. Consider that your dreams are the fairy tales of another culture. Bring them back as stories of power. Bring back the memory of images of power, whether they are sublime, ecstatic, or horrific. If you handled or observed objects in your dreams, bring them back as images sketched in your journal. Capture snippets of conversation. Sing or play the tunes you hear in your dreams.

One Monday afternoon, several hours before attending my regular dream-sharing group, I took a short nap and dreamed this dream.

I've arrived for dream-sharing group early and am discussing the nature of dreams with a fellow dreamer. I'm excited to share that I've discovered that dreams are either doors or windows to the spirit world. Most of the time they are windows. We are allowed to see through them and take back useful information about our daily lives. But sometimes they are doors. We pass through them, and the energetic pattern of our lives is forever changed. This happens more often than we think. The problem is that if we don't make a place for that change in our waking world, the change in our energetic patterns sets up a longing, an unfulfilled desire, an annoying ache, or a sense of frustration. I'm explaining how we must first understand when we've passed through a door, as opposed to approaching a window, and second make a place for change in our lives when I wake up.

Well, it seemed easy enough in the dream . . .

Now that you've added vision shifting and active dreamwork to your set of creative resources, it's time for one more method of accessing the realm of spirit: the shamanic journey.

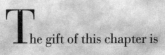

The gift of this chapter is

freedom.

Developing the capacity to enter into a shamanic trance—to

cross the border into nonordinary reality at will and while

maintaining control of your experience—gives you the ability

to travel to any place that ever has been or will be imagined.

The exercises in this chapter will help you access the

unseen world directly.

chapter 5

Journeying: *Shamanic* Trance
for *Creative* Inspiration

*Shamanism is the intentional effort to develop intimate and lasting
relationships with personal helping spirits by consciously leaving ordinary
reality and journeying into the nonordinary realms of the spirit world.*

—TOM COWAN

Shananism as a Spiritual Practice for Daily Life

Where would you go if you could go anywhere?

The shamanic journey technique is one of the most useful tools of
the dream artist. Shamanic journeying will help you understand your
night dreams and more fully live your waking life. It can lead you to a
wonderful new source of artistic inspiration and creativity. It will help
you develop your own unique imagery and artifacts. It will answer any
question you have about your art. It can be done in a group or as a solo
practice. It is simple to learn and works the first time you try it.

A shamanic journey is a self-induced trance state through which an
individual can enter dreamscapes of spirit. It does not require drugs, is

safe to do, and allows the practitioner to have the perception of control over the experience. The shamanic journey is used for personal and communal healing work, empowerment, exploration, and to seek guidance and inspiration. It is one of the primary techniques for establishing direct dialogue with spirit. It is deeper than the experience of vision-shifting and offers more control than dreamwork. It is the place from which one begins to more fully practice excavating the symbols and artistic inspiration of your dreams.

As a dream artist, you will want to call to yourself certain kinds of energy. This energy can and often does appear in animal form in non-ordinary reality. Most shamans have a primary relationship with one or more power animals; as a dream artist, you will want to have a power animal connection of your own. But there are also mentors and guides in the dreaming that embody the spirit and energies of art, craft, and creativity. You will want to develop a relationship with one or more artist guides. The combination of power animals to guide and protect you and artist mentors to advise you will open up a series of special places that you can go to for artistic inspiration, technical information, and assistance with the alchemical process of transforming your shamanic dreams into art.

M̲y friend Doug Zaruba puts a prerecorded drumming tape into his tape player, adjusts his headphones, and pulls a bandanna down over his eyes. He is a jeweler, a dream artist, and an experienced shamanic dream traveler. He is in the middle of a project to design a set of rings carved with sacred symbols and has come on this journey for guidance and inspiration. He works not just with surface appearances but as a true dream artist, with the underlying energetic patterns of things. Within minutes his body relaxes into the insistent rhythm of the drums.

He finds his passageway to the upper world—a series of steps carved into an ancient pyramid extending up to the sky. He calls his power animal to his side, and a sleek black panther is in-

stantly with him. He climbs the steps and makes his way through a layer of clouds that shroud him in mist. It is disconcerting at first, but his power animal leads the way. He has shared his intention for this journey with his power animal and trusts it to take him where he needs to go. If this was a place he had visited before, he could will himself there in an instant, but he is looking for a new source of information.

He passes quickly through a number of different landscapes before coming to a cavelike library inhabited by an old man dressed in Victorian clothing. Doug sits in conversation with the man for what seems like several hours, though in waking world time, the whole journey only lasts thirty minutes. He is shown books and copies patterns and symbols onto parchment sheets provided by the keeper of this library. He is not quite finished when he hears the callback signal of rapid drumbeats. He reviews quickly what he has copied and what the signs mean with the old man and asks if he may return at a later date. He thanks the man and asks his power animal to return him to the stone steps. In an instant, he is there, then descending the steps, then waking back to his physical body.

Quickly he copies the symbols in his journal just as he had done on the parchment. He struggles a bit with the meaning of the symbols, but manages to outline the significance of each. Later he will work these symbols into a set of rings, aligning them with the energy of the specific individuals who purchase them.

Making a shamanic journey—entering a controlled trance state—is a technique anyone can learn. The more you practice it, the deeper and more real the experience will become for you. Shamanic journeys are induced meditative or trancelike states that allow us to enter into the dreaming while retaining conscious control of our actions.

Shamanic journeys can be induced by a variety of techniques, such as meditation, visualization, body work, breath work, and rhythmic entrainment (a strong rhythmic beat that alters our brain waves). Any or all of these techniques may work for you, but you will want to find your own most significant trance trigger. This will be an auditory, a visual, or a kinesthetic experience, usually supported by a secondary and sometimes a tertiary trigger. For me, conscious dreaming is most often triggered by the pulsing rhythm of drums, rattles, or click sticks, supported by internal visualization, breath work, and muscular relaxation. Sound or auditory stimuli are most likely to induce my brain into a safe trance state. For others, the trigger is ecstatic dance or body postures. Still others are shifted into the dreaming by visualization or intense concentration while staring at mandalas, labyrinths, or geometrical patterns.

The core technique of the shamanic journey practiced by a great number of contemporary shamanic practitioners was developed by anthropologist Michael Harner. It involves listening to live or taped drumming while lying in a darkened room. Shamanic practitioners then visualize a place of transition into nonordinary reality. They see themselves passing through a hole into a long dark tunnel through which they follow a light and emerge in the lower world. Or they might see themselves climbing a kind of *world-tree* into middle or upper worlds.

I came late to a formal understanding of the techniques of shamanic journeying. I had been making journeys into nonordinary reality since childhood and had discovered that auditory stimulation was my own best path into the dreaming. I rely on the drum or rattle for my journeys only about half the time. Other forms of music such as drone sounds (chanting, didgeridoo, sitar) also work to take me into the trance state. I can now enter this state by simply closing my eyes and rolling my consciousness inward. But for introducing shamanic journeying to those new to it, the drum and rattle are highly effective. This technique is extremely useful because it is safe and easy to do. It requires no drugs. It can be practiced alone with minimal equipment, and success improves dramatically with practice.

Since rhythmic sound works well for most people, it is the method of trance induction I will introduce here. But, I suggest that you remain open to the great variety of techniques available and, more importantly, that you find the one that best matches your style and personality.

Those new to journeying might wonder if this isn't all just a case of very active imagination. After all, a shamanic journey begins with the dreamer actively imagining a portal between worlds. I can only answer this by suggesting that you try the technique for yourself. It is true that sometimes you can feel like you are forcing images to come to you, but other times you will be amazed by what occurs spontaneously. I'm always most impressed by dialogue. When I ask a question, I often get a lengthy and detailed answer faster than I could think up an answer in ordinary reality. Frequently the language and the phrasing are different from what I would choose if I were saying the same thing.

To help you experience the shamanic journey technique as it relates to the needs of a dream artist, I will review the equipment and supplies you will need, describe the basic steps involved, encourage you to make an exploratory journey to both the lower and upper worlds, and suggest three journeys of particular importance to dream artists—the power-animal journey, the artist-mentor journey, and the great museum journey.

Outfitting: An Urban Shaman's Tools

THE BASIC SHAMANIC journey begins, as any archaeological expedition might, with an outfitting of basic equipment. At a minimum, you will need a sound system, a recording of drumming, notebook and pen, and a cushion and blanket.

Sound System.

Even if you are lucky enough to belong to a drumming circle or have friends who will drum for you, you will find that you can journey much more frequently and flexibly if you have your drumming recorded. Live drumming is a powerful experience, and I urge you to journey to live drumming or rattling as often as you can. If you are going to make dream archaeology a regular practice, however, you will want to be able to journey any time you choose.

Any sound system will suffice, but I suggest a personal stereo system. This will allow you to make your journeying a private process.

Shamanic journey recordings are available on CD and on tape. Recordings on CD have the advantage of flexible programming and better sound, while a tape system has some advantages if you are going to move or dance while listening to the music.

A Drumming Tape or CD.

Prerecorded drumming is available on tape or CD from the sources listed on pages 237 to 239. Purchasing a prerecorded tape or CD is the easiest method of proceeding, but you may choose to record your own. If you are going to make your own recording, you will need a drum, rattle, or click sticks. The rhythm should be between 228 and 240 beats per minute. Time yourself for short bursts of ten seconds to figure out the right rhythm. You should hit about 38 to 40 beats in ten seconds. This is a strong driving rhythm. Don't accent beats or vary the tempo or rhythm. You are working to entrain the brain's rhythms to this sound.

You will probably want to begin with a recording of at least fifteen minutes. At fifteen minutes, pause the drumming, and then strike the drum deliberately for seven beats. Repeat this three more times, then begin drumming as rapidly as you can for about a minute to a minute and a half. Pause again and do another set of seven deliberate beats repeated four times. This process is called the callback, and it signals you that the journey is over and allows you about two minutes to return.

Notebook and pen.

You will want to record your journey immediately after you return. It helps to have a book in which you record all your journeys. You may use the dream artist's journal you began in chapter 1, your night dream journal, or a separate book altogether. You will be logging the details of your explorations and excavations. Your notebook will become an important document, so get something that pleases your senses. It should reflect the nature of what you will be writing in it.

Some people do keep separate books for night dreams and shamanic journeys, but my own preference is to keep them together. It's easier to see patterns, relationships, and synchronicities when all the journeys into the dreaming are recorded together. Structured dream journals might work well for you, but I generally recommend a blank book for logging your journeys.

Any pen or pencil will do, but my favorite tools are a set of colored markers with a fine tip at one end and a brush-like tip at the other. Colored pens or colored pencils are fun to play with and may inspire you to sketch or record more playfully.

A glue stick is also a useful tool to have around for when you want to attach found two-dimensional materials to your journal pages.

Bandanna or cloth.

If you will be journeying in daylight and the room or space you're in can't be made dark, a bandanna across your eyes may be used to eliminate distractions.

Blanket or mat and cushion.

You will be journeying while lying on your back on the floor. You should be comfortable enough to not be distracted from your journey, but not so comfortable that you fall asleep. You may want a cushion under your head and a mat or blanket beneath you. Regular shamanic practitioners develop relationships with the blankets on which they make their journeys. The more you use the same blanket, the more of a magic carpet it becomes. A good blanket can become empowered with the spirit of journeying, Again, if you are selecting a blanket to use regularly, pick one that pleases you aesthetically. If you are drawn to natural fibers, select a cotton or wool blanket. If those things aren't as important to you, the new plush fabrics and fleeces made from recycled plastics are soft and comfortable.

If it's cold enough to be distracting, you might also want a blanket to pull over you while you journey.

For shamanic journeying itself, you will need nothing more than the materials listed above. As you evolve in your practice as a dream artist, however, you will begin to assemble additional supplies in two categories: personal power objects and art supplies and tools. We've already discussed art supplies and will deal with them more specifically as they are needed for specific exercises, but you may wish to begin making or looking for personal power objects sooner.

Personal power objects might be bought, found, or given to you as gifts. I believe an object you make yourself will have the most power, but found objects or gifts from others can also be strong carriers of spirit.

Your own set of ritual and ceremonial objects might include rattles, drums, or other rhythm instruments. You may want to have personal artifacts of power for the corners of your journeying blanket. This defines your sacred traveling space and helps you throw a protective field around yourself. You may also want a personal altar of cloth or some portable construction. The altar might honor your guides, teachers, and power animals. It can also honor the four directions. The altar-making suggestions in chapter 7 can be adapted to create portable altars.

You will also eventually develop your own variation of the native American medicine pouch or the Celtic crane bag. Don't underestimate the power of the objects you begin to gather. Since you are drawn to the visual and the aesthetic qualities of things (otherwise, why would you be reading about art as a sacred practice), it's enough in the beginning to understand these objects as visual and tactical triggers for your imaginative processes. The deeper you allow yourself to move into the realm of spirit, however, the more you will understand the true power these objects contain.

You needn't gather all these power objects, tools, and supplies at once. Remember: This is a journey, and it's almost a rule in mythic journeys that the tools or weapons with which the hero begins a journey will be lost, stolen, or turn out to be useless without a certain level of mastery. The tools of real value are usually won or found along the way. You will better understand what you need as you progress on your journey. If you do purchase items at the outset, I suggest that you shop for the best-quality materials you can afford. Cheap, shoddily made tools and supplies will have cheap and shoddy spirit. Money doesn't equal spirit, but when money is spent on materials and craftsmanship and you can feel the difference, there is a correlation.

The Shamanic Journey: Basics

YOU HAVE ACQUIRED the material objects—the tickets—in preparation for your shamanic journey. The next step is to engage in a ceremony, or ritual, to mark the beginning of the journey.

Ceremony

IT'S my own belief that ceremony is important to shamanic journeying, but it's also difficult to talk about it without being prescriptive. Most shamans engage in some ceremony prior to journeying. Usually, this will have deep roots in the culture from which the shaman comes. It may also have been handed down through several generations. Undoubtedly, if your mother's grandmother passed a ritual down to you, it will have great power for you. It is not always true, however, that the rituals you learned from a specific shaman will have any more potential power than those you learned from your guides in the spirit world.

My rituals reflect both my studies of various cultural traditions and my experiences in nonordinary reality. As such, I feel that the specifics of the rituals are not meant to be passed on as though the power resides within the ritual itself, but what I will offer are some guidelines.

Before beginning a journey, cleanse and consecrate your space. This can be done by lighting a candle with clear intention, smudging with sacred herbs (sage or cedar for cleansing; sweet grass, cinnamon stick, lavender, or copal smoke for attracting positive energies), shaking a rattle, or ringing a clear bell. I usually honor the directions of north, south, east, west, above, below, and within.

Define your space. If you are working on a blanket, place personal objects of power on each of the four corners of the blanket. I place a wolf fetish in honor of my primary power animal—a guardian spirit in animal form—at my right shoulder and a crystal seer stone for clear vision at my left shoulder. I have a grounding stone at my left foot and a feather for flight at my right. In addition, I will place a rattle near my right or left hand. These objects help me define the sacred space within which I will work. I also envision a protective egg of turquoise light around me and the space I've defined.

I begin each journey with a prayer and a statement of my intention. Just as in dream incubation, it helps to have questions stated clearly in advance.

As I begin the journey, I call in my protective spirits, guides, and mentors. When the journey is completed—after I have emerged from the trance state and record my journey—I thank these same entities. I try to carefully close each session with an offering of gratitude and humility. I gently return the power objects I use to their pouches and places. It's my understanding that ritual focuses both attention and intention. It matters less what the actual ceremony is. What counts is that there is some structured activity that focuses our minds on the task ahead. The value of repeated use of the same ritual is that it more quickly entrains our minds and focuses us.

Embarkation

A shamanic journey uses your visual imagination combined with the rhythmic power of the drum and the physical posture of the dreaming shaman to transport you into nonordinary states of reality—what I call the dreaming. You begin by relaxing into the sound of the drum. You lie on your back with arms and legs uncrossed. With your eyes closed, you imagine one of a series of personal openings, passageways, or starting points for journeys into another world. The starting point you choose will be based on whether you intend to journey into the lower world, the middle world, or the upper world.

Most shamanic cosmologies describe three worlds, though within each world there are often a great variety of levels. The lower world should not be confused with the Western or Christian concept of hell. It is, instead, a primal—almost mythical—landscape. The middle world is very much like the world we live in, only energetically more transparent. The upper world is often described as an airy place of crystalline structures, mystery schools, and great teachers.

We will begin with a lower-world journey by imagining a hole or opening into the earth. Once you've fixed this opening or starting point in your mind, you will move through it, and, with the help of a guardian spirit or power animal which you will acquire, you will explore and fulfill the intention of your journey. When you hear the drum's callback signal, you will retrace your steps and return to your passageway, exit, and return to your physical body. You will then log your journey in your journal.

Finding Your Opening

A journey to the lower world begins with a descent through a hole or passageway that leads down into the earth. This might be a cave, a hole in a hollow tree, a crack in the earth, or any opening that calls to you. It can be of any size because your dreaming body will simply adjust itself to fit the opening. It should be an opening you've seen before so that you can visualize it clearly and imagine it in full detail. If a place comes to mind easily, use it. If not, you can find your opening by consulting your dreams or asking for guidance in the waking world.

1. Your opening might be a place about which you've had recurrent dreams. If you can't recall any places clearly, and if you've kept dream journals in the past, reread them and see if something you've recorded calls to you.

2. Incubate an opening. Before falling asleep at night, repeat to yourself several times that you want to dream about a passage into the lower world.

3. Go for a walk in the woods or a park. Walk more slowly than you normally would, as if you are stalking something. Look for hollow trees or holes that lead into the ground.

4. Flip through a magazine like *National Geographic* or a travel magazine that has lots of beautiful photographs of places. Let something call to you.

Ideally you should make a drawing of your opening into the lower world in the front of your journal. Include as much detail as you can. If your opening came from a photograph in a magazine, cut it out and glue it into your book. If you can visit your site, sketch it from life and/or photograph it from various angles. Add these photographs to your book. It doesn't matter whether you draw or photograph well. Before the invention of the camera, drawing was considered a basic part of a scientific education. Drawing helped you to see what you were observing in more detail. Photography also can help you to see better. The important part of this exercise is to pay sacred attention to this opening.

Find a comfortable position and close your eyes. Without the drumming, take a few moments to imagine the opening you've chosen. See it in detail. Imagine yourself going through the opening. On the other side of the opening is a dark tunnel. It may be very dark at first, or it may be dimly lit. Picture the details of the tunnel. If you can see nothing, feel the walls. Sense what the tunnel is like. Is it cool or warm, moist or dry? Experience the tunnel, but don't proceed any further. After a few moments, see yourself turning around and exiting through your opening.

It's important that you clearly imagine as much of this as you can. You will find that when you do this with the drumming, the experience will take over, and you will find yourself not so much imagining as experiencing.

THE LOWER WORLD:
YOUR FIRST SHAMANIC JOURNEY

*With this exercise, you will learn to use journeys
to the lower world to tap your uncensored, primal,
creative energy.*

WHEN you are ready, you should try an exploratory journey into the lower world with drumming. You will return to the opening of the tunnel you imagined. You will proceed down this tunnel. What you see at the other end of the tunnel will be your shamanic lower world. I could describe what *I* see, but it will not be the same for you. The dreaming is your world to explore.

It's also possible that you won't *see* anything. Not all shamanic practitioners experience the dreaming visually. Some people hear their journeys, as if they were being described simultaneously with their occurrence. Other people just know what happens. Their experience of the dreaming is misty and vague in the visual sense, but they are certain of what occurs and whom they meet. Be alert to the fact that your journey may be a visual experience, an aural experience, a kinesthetic or somatic experience, or some combination of these. You can have rich and successful journeys regardless of which shamanic sense you favor.

Now it's time to try an exploratory journey. Your intention for this journey is to visit and explore the lower world. Arrange for a time when you won't be interrupted. Turn the ringer off on the phones, draw the curtains to darken the room, make sure that dogs and cats won't disturb you. Make yourself comfortable by lying on the floor. Uncross your arms and legs. Put a bandanna or cloth over your eyes if the room is not fairly dark. Put your headphones on if you're using a personal sound system and have the controls within easy reach.

Take several long, slow, deep breaths from your belly. If you're tense, try tensing and relaxing your body one area at a time. As you breathe and relax, repeat your intention for this journey: *I enter the dreaming to explore the lower world.* When you're ready, begin the drumming tape or CD.

As the drumming begins, visualize your opening. See it in all the detail you can. Pass through your opening into the tunnel. Find the light and follow it. Even if it isn't clear or distinct, it will be there. Follow the light until you reach the other side of the tunnel. If you don't see it right away, walk forward awhile and it will appear. If for some reason the tunnel becomes blocked, find an alternate route. There *will* be another way,—this tunnel is not designed to defeat you. Follow the light to the end of the tunnel. It's important to remember that when you go down into the tunnel, you are not literally going into the earth. You are passing through an opening into another world. When you reach the source of the light, you will be through the portal into the lower world.

You will find yourself in a landscape. Explore this landscape. Get to know it well. It will be country you will pass through again and again on future journeys. Look around and pay attention to details. Think about how you might map this location. If you see animals or people, make note of them. If an animal or person addresses you, you may choose to engage in conversation. Ask questions about this world. Ask to be shown around, but try not to stray too far from the opening to your tunnel.

When you hear the drumming callback, return to your tunnel and follow your route back to your personal passageway.

Take a few moments to reorient yourself. Remember what you saw as clearly and as completely as you can before you open your eyes. When you're ready, open your eyes and log your journey in your journal. Sketch what you remember. Diagram or map your route. These activities make the experience more real and more familiar. If you accept what you've seen or experienced as manifestations of spirit or divine guidance, that's fine, but at this point it isn't necessary that you accept anything. For now, it's enough to record them.

It is important to remember that the dreaming world of the shamanic journey is the same reality as the world of our night dreams. It's filtered differently because we have maintained only a small degree of conscious control over the experience. This awareness allows us to ask questions directly and to be shown, told, or even to read the answers to our questions. The return from a shamanic journey requires less unfolding of metaphors and deciphering of meaning.

—————————— ·ᴥᴥᴥ· ——————————

THE UPPER WORLD JOURNEY: BROADENING YOUR EXPERIENCE

With this exercise, you will learn to use shamanic
journeys to the upper world to access information
about specific creative techniques and applications.

AFTER you have experienced a lower world journey, you might want to try an upper world journey. As you might imagine, an ascent into the upper world requires a different route. There are fundamental differences between upper and lower world journeys. The experiences, the characters, and the nature of the places are different. Again, it's important to remember that upper and lower worlds in the shamanic tradition do not correlate to the Christian tradition of heaven and hell—they are merely different. My own experience is that lower world journeys are very earthy and physical. They tend toward sensual and primal imagery. My journeys into the upper world move toward light and pattern and abstraction. If I wanted to know about making a clay bowl, I'd journey to the lower world. If I wanted to mark that bowl with the patterns of sacred geometry, I'd travel to the upper world. The best way to understand the difference is to experience it yourself.

Your intention for this journey is to visit and explore the upper world. In much the same way that you discovered your door to the lower world, you will need to imagine your method of ascent to the upper world. Use the dreaming mind and waking request for guidance techniques suggested for finding the lower world entrance, but this time look for a way up. It could be an opening into an attic. Many tribal shamans lived in huts with vents in the center of the ceiling for smoke from a central fire to escape. This was often their route of ascent. Another popular method of ascent is a "world-tree." This mythic tree straddles the lower, middle, and upper worlds. By descending down through its roots, one accesses the lower world. By climbing high into its branches, one enters the upper world. Find your route. Imagine a tree or passage up that will take you to the upper world.

When the drumming starts, visualize your tree or opening and imagine yourself climbing up. Look up and find the place where it feels like you will pass through into a different world. This may feel like climbing up out of a hole in the ground. Remember what Jack must have felt like when he climbed the beanstalk and stepped off in the world of the giant. Keep climbing, soaring, or levitating, until you pass into the other world. Climb up and through.

Investigate this new world. Notice in what ways it seems different from the lower world. Do you think you could tell which world you were in if you forgot which way you had gone on a journey? If you see people or animals, ask questions. Ask to be shown around. If not, just wander some. When you hear the callback drum, return the way you came to reenter your body.

Lie still for a moment. Collect your thoughts. Remember as much detail as you can about your journey. Log your journey in your journal. Again, it is important to sketch, map, or diagram what you saw, heard, or felt. This activity deepens your connection to your experience.

Your first journeys may seem forced and awkward. This will pass. You'll soon be comfortable and adept at the transitions you'll be making in the dreaming world. Your first journeys may seem to rely heavily on your own power of imagination. Again, don't worry about that. As you come to trust the process, the accuracy and relevancy of information you bring back from your journeys will amaze you. You'll find it goes far beyond what you think you can imagine.

Exploration and Excavation

THE SHAMANIC JOURNEY is interesting and useful in its own right, but our task is to learn how to use it for and apply it to the process of making art or engaging in a creative practice. For this purpose, we look at three journeys that can be extremely helpful to the dream artist.

They are the power-animal journey, the artist-mentor journey, and the great museum journey. These journeys help us build relationships with dream guides and seek out places that can provide inspiration and instruction.

The first of these journeys is to locate an ally and guide called a power animal. A power animal is guardian spirit, which takes the form of an animal to protect, guide, and empower. You may already feel a strong connection to a certain animal totem. You may have a power animal already and not know it. The Aborigines believe that whenever a person is born, an animal twin spirit is born in the wild. You may also have several power animals at any one time. Wolf, Owl, and Polar Bear are my primary power animals. I have kinship connection to Hawk and medicine connections to Stag and Turtle. They've guided and accompanied me on many journeys into the dreaming. Wolf helps me balance my need to be social and my need to spend time alone. Polar Bear brings me strength and courage and a certain amount of playfulness. Owl serves my need to know and understand things and is also my guide in the upper world.

As a dream artist you will seek a power animal that helps you with the work of manifesting your dreams as art. The power animal you attract for this purpose might become a primary power animal for your life or it might become a secondary helping spirit for when you are journeying for artistic and spiritual inspiration.

THE POWER-ANIMAL JOURNEY

In this journey, you will give form to the spirit that
serves as your guide and guardian.

Y OUR intention for this journey is to meet your power animal. Follow the directions for a lower world or upper world journey. When you reach the other end of the tunnel or climb through the hole in the sky that leads to the upper world, call a power animal. Ask that a power animal come to you. If nothing comes to you immediately, explore a little bit. If one animal comes and stays with you, this is probably your power animal. If many animals reveal themselves, look for an animal that you see three different times. This will be your power animal. Some teachers recommend that you not become attached to insects, reptiles, or domestic animals, but I believe the spirits of these creatures can be powerful helpers to dream artists. Could a weaver want a more useful power animal than a spider? As a painter, I wish that my strokes were as sinuous as a snake's tracks in the sand. As a photographer, I've learned much from the stillness of my cats.

When your power animal makes itself known to you, ask it how you may call upon it. Ask it to show you around. It knows the dreaming world much better than you do. If you feel like running, swimming, climbing, flying, or playing with your power animal, do it. Study your power animal for unusual markings. What makes this owl distinct from other owls?

When you hear the callback drum, thank your power animal, retrace your steps, and return to your body. Record everything you can remember from your journey. If you can draw your power animal, do so in your journal.

❧ Honoring Your Power Animal

To keep this connection with your power animal alive and vital and to draw on it in waking life, consider the following:

1. Draw or paint your power animal.

2. Visit a zoo, a wildlife park, or a wilderness area and photograph your power animal.

3. Carve your power animal from wood, soapstone, or plaster or model it with clay or plastic modeling compounds.

4. Cut out images of your power animal from magazines or purchase prints of your animal to hang on your wall and glue in your notebook.

5. Collect shed and found materials from your power animal (antlers, feathers, paw prints).

6. Dance your power animal. Put on music and move the way your animal would. Dance as your power animal would dance. Become your power animal. Experience the world as it might.

7. Be attentive to when your power animal or the image of your power animal shows up in waking life. Listen for its message.

8. Feed your power animal with offerings left out in nature. I feed Wolf spirit by carrying dog snacks on my neighborhood walks. Every time I feed a dog, I do it with the intention of honoring my power animal.

9. If your power animal is a member of a threatened or endangered species, take some action on behalf of that species. Donate money or time to preserve wildlife and habitat.

Your power animal will help you in the next two journeys you make. The first of these is a journey to find an artist-mentor. Your artist-mentor may come to you in the appearance of a famous artist. In his book *Dreamgates*, Robert Moss reports meeting with a guide who took the form of the artist Albrecht Dürer. Moss is quite clear on the fact that this guide was not *the* Dürer, but a guide in the form of Dürer. Your mentor might look like Picasso, Matisse, or Monet. Then again, he or she might not take the form of a recognizable artist. Your artist-mentor in the dreaming world will guide you in the manifestation and realization of your dream images. You may have several artist-mentors eventually, but for now we will focus on one.

THE ARTIST-MENTOR JOURNEY

*In this journey, you will give form to the spirit that
teaches and inspires you as a dream artist.*

YOUR intention for this journey is to meet your artist-mentor in the dreaming. You want a mentor who is kind and compassionate, but also one who will expect only the best from you. Your mentor might be playful and humorous or solemn and serious, but you want someone to whom you can go for guidance. Imagine the ideal teacher who would teach you exactly what you needed to learn in exactly the way you would want to learn it. This guide will answer questions of technique for you, but his or her real purpose is to nurture your creative spirit. Keep these characteristics in mind as you begin your journey.

Again, you can journey to the upper or lower world. Once you are in the dreaming, call your power animal to you. You should see it right away. Ask your power animal to take you to your artist-mentor. How you travel with your power animal will vary. Sometimes your power animal will fly you to a place, and you will see the terrain over which you are flying. Sometimes you will be led on foot or across water. Sometimes your power animal will lead you into a mist and just on the other side of the mist will be your destination. Sometimes you will just appear where you need to be.

When your power animal leads you to your artist-mentor, note your surroundings and observe his or her appearance. Speak to your artist-mentor. Ask questions. Ask what name you should use when calling him or her. Ask to see what your artist-mentor is working on. You are, in effect, interviewing this person for the role of artist-mentor. You need to be comfortable with this spirit. If you are not, if you feel that you are being bargained with, or compelled to do something, walk away. Your power animal will protect you and can remove you from this place in an instant. This happens very rarely, but it's important to know that even in the dreaming you have the power to choose the relationships into which you enter.

If you like your artist-mentor, ask how you will meet again and what kinds of questions you may ask. Spend time with your artist-mentor. When you hear the callback, thank your artist-mentor, excuse yourself, and ask your power animal to return you to your opening back to the waking world. Return to your body and spend a few moments recalling the experience. Log your experience in your notebook.

Honoring Your Artist-Mentor

To deepen your connection to your artist-mentor, consider the following ideas:

1. Sketch your artist-mentor in your journal. If you can't sketch to your satisfaction, consider photocopying a picture from a book or clipping a picture from a magazine. This will be easy if, for instance your artist-mentor came in the form of Pablo Picasso or Isadora Duncan. Finding photographs of these people will not be difficult. You might have to find a picture of someone who looks similar to your artist-mentor or someone who makes you feel the same as your artist-mentor did.

2. Map or draw your artist-mentor's studio or workspace.

3. Recreate something your artist-mentor was working on.

4. If you noticed any signs or symbols around your artist-mentor or woven into his or her clothing, you might reproduce these.

5. Put your artist-mentor's name around a candle and light it in honor of his or her creative guidance.

6. Take an art class in a specific medium or technique. Shop around for a teacher who has qualities similar to those of your artist-mentor.

I met my first artist-mentor in a wonderful studio in a forest of giant sequoia and redwoods. I climbed spiral steps that wrapped around a tree trunk and led up at least ten stories. High in the trees, just below the canopy of foliage, I found a triangular tree house attached to three trees. A porch wrapped all the way around it and there were three stories to the structure. My artist-mentor was an old man with white hair and a great toothy smile. He said that I should call him Wally, which was the name of my first art teacher in college, a good friend who died several years ago. He described himself as principally a mapmaker, and he showed me the maps he drew and painted. They were breathtakingly beautiful. Some were jeweled, some sewn with golden thread. I've never been able to replicate what I've seen him do, but I've brought back pieces and ideas that have ended up in my work. I've spent many hours at Wally's studio and traveling to the places he has shown me.

One of those places is what I call the Great Museum. This is the museum for all the works that artists have ever dreamed of doing. If you can imagine the Louvre in Paris, The Smithsonian Museums of Washington D.C., and the Metropolitan Museum of New York City combined with Russia's Hermitage Museum, and perhaps the Vatican's collection of art, you still wouldn't have a collection nearly as large as the Great Museum I've visited in the dreaming. You can find your own Great Museum in the dreaming world; your artist-mentor can help you get there.

THE GREAT MUSEUM JOURNEY

*In this journey, you will give form to the source of your
creative legacy. Find the place that invites you to
observe, learn, and discover.*

T H E intention for this journey is to visit the Great Museum. This collection of art and artifact from prehistory into the far future will always reveal something new and wonderful. Just as you turn to your artist-mentor for advice and guidance in your own creative practice, you can also visit the Great Museum for inspiration. Within the Great Museum not only can you see the art of prehistory, you can descend into the caves themselves to see the work in context. You can even choose to meet the artists and see them at work. The Great Museum is your limitless resource for ideas and images.

Once you are in the dreaming world, call your power animal to you and visit your artist-mentor. Ask to be shown the Great Museum. Your artist-mentor may accompany you or he or she may give directions to your power animal. Again, you may travel by one of several different methods, but you will end up at the Great Museum.

Take your time on this first visit. You will not be able to see it all. Pay attention to acclimating yourself and learning your way around. Look for maps, floor plans, and guides. Ask for directions if you are traveling alone. If you are with your artist-mentor, let him or her lead you on this first visit. Ask to see a famous work of art with which you are familiar. Does it look the same as you remembered? If it looks different, remember how it differed. Remember that you are looking at the essential spirit of a painting that was manifested in your waking reality.

Also ask or look for information about a piece of art's spiritual purpose. What was it intended to do? Sometimes I find this information on the identifying cards beside works of art, sometimes I have to ask.

When you hear the callback, ask your power animal to return you to your passageway back to the waking world. Remember to thank your artist-mentor and your power animal. Return to your body and take the time to relive the adventure. Write down as much of your journey as you can recall.

❧ Honoring Your Visit to the Great Museum

To make the Great Museum a real place in the waking world, consider the following suggestions:

1. Visit actual museums. Make a date with yourself to visit a museum or art gallery once a month. Note what you like about the museums themselves.

2. Collect postcards and images of works of art that you are drawn to or moved by. Paste these into your Dream Artist's Journal.

3. Sketch a map or plan of the Great Museum as you recall it. Add to your map with each trip you make. After you've made enough trips, consider creating a large map of the museum. Make an art project out of it.

4. Sketch, draw, paint, or describe the works of art you see in the Great Museum.

5. Visit the Great Museum in a night dream through dream incubation (see chapter 4).

I have a friend who makes a contribution in the waking world every time she visits the Great Museum. Just as some museums have entry fees, my friend puts a dollar into a jar when she visits the Great Museum in her dreams. She uses this money to fund art supplies and trips to museums in the waking world that do ask for donations. This helps her connect her journey into the dreaming with her waking life in a tangible way.

A Note About
Middle World Journeys

So FAR WE have not talked much about middle world journeys. I mentioned them in the context of doing vision-shifting, but you can also access the middle world through shamanic journeying techniques. Journeys to the middle world are a way to travel in spirit to familiar places from your waking world. Shamans use middle world journeys to check out hunting grounds for game, or visit distant kin, or travel backward or forward in time, or to find lost people or objects. Middle world journeys can be extremely useful.

Journeys to the middle world are similar to journeys to the upper and lower worlds. As the drumming starts, go to your usual point of departure for an upper world journey. Have an intention in mind ("I want to check on the health of my Aunt Sue" or "I want to visit my childhood home"). Before ascending, call your power animal to you and ask to be taken to a specific place you know in waking life. Your power animal will fly you or transport you to the dreaming version of this place. Please note that what you see here may not be what is actually occurring in the waking world. What you see here is in answer to your question or request.

For dream artists, a middle world journey can be a good way to find out what kind of image or artifact individuals need to heal, to learn, to be empowered by, or to find magic in their lives.

Y ou now have the tools, techniques, and resources you will need to begin the dynamic translation work of the dream artist. Though you have been experimenting with the techniques all along, it's now time to more deeply explore the processes of finding, arranging, altering, and making—the techniques you will use to slow your dreams down into physical form.

T he gift of this chapter is

sanctuary.

Making yourself a place to work provides sanctuary for your

creative soul. Sanctuary offers more than protection. It gives

us a place in which to rejuvenate and reenergize. The

suggestions and exercises in this chapter will help you to

manifest your own sacred space.

chapter 6

Sacred Space:
Inside a Dream Artist's *Studio*

For the magician's intelligence is not encompassed within the society; its place
is at the edge of the community, mediating between the human community
and the larger community of beings upon which the village depends for its
nourishment and sustenance.

—DAVID ABRAM
The Spell of the Sensuous:
Perception and Language in a More-Than-Human World

I n his book, *The Spell of the Sensuous*, author David Abram points
out that the tribal shamans of Southeast Asia tend to occupy a specific
and meaningful geographic space in relation to their villages. While
they do not live in the middle of the village as priests or religious func-
tionaries, they also do not live the secluded lives of mystics and as-
cetics. If a village is located in a clearing near a thick forest, the shaman
will live on the edge of the forest—a part of the community and yet distinct at the same time.

Abram suggests that this is because the shaman must literally and symbolically walk in two worlds—the dreamlike and often enchanted world of the forest and the rational ordered world of society. This is a useful idea to hold onto as we begin to look at how we will work as dream artists. For walking the path of the dream artist is nothing if not the art of living fully and simultaneously in both the waking and the dreaming worlds. Where we work, what we choose to have around us, and how we relate to our tools is often as important as what we do.

To a dream artist, place and space are important. Where you choose to do your work can affect you deeply. The quality of a building, a room, a corner, a desktop is significant. The imagery you surround yourself with can support or stifle your creativity. Your relationship to your tools empowers you. As a dream artist, you sensitize your self to the spirit or living essence of material things and places in a way that has impact, not only on what you do, but how you do it, where you do it, and with what tools. It's tempting to dismiss this and move right into the work itself, but this is an important part *of* the work. Defining a studio, creating an altar or shrine to your own creative energies, and entering into a sacred relationship with your tools is all part of becoming a dream artist. Remember that living as a dream artist is a way of being as much as it is a way of doing.

Outfitting:
Defining Sacred Space with Music

I CAN'T IMAGINE creating a studio without music. I can't imagine working without music. Some music lifts me up and amplifies my energy. I want this music playing when I have physical tasks to accomplish. Other music helps me vision-shift by returning me to a light trance state while I do repetitive work like painting pattern or design. Music helps me define the space and time in which I'm working as being sacred.

There has never been a better time to find recorded music designed for trance work. On pages 237 to 239, I've made some specific recommendations of recordings I use personally and in my workshops, but here are some general principles that you might wish to consider when selecting music.

1. Think of the music you use as your own personal soundtrack. In movies, soundtracks prepare us for what is going to happen. They signal the arrival of certain characters by weaving in that character's specific theme. If you use the same music regularly when you work in a certain way (awake and energized, light trance, deep trance, etc.), you'll find that simply hearing your theme puts you into that state again, ready to work.

2. Most new age bookstores have music sections with tapes and CDs that are perfect for this work. The store clerks usually let you sample the music.

3. Look at the number of tracks on the recording. If it has fewer but longer tracks, it will probably be better for uninterrupted trance states. If it has many tracks, make sure that they are similar in feel so that every time a track changes, it doesn't pull you out of your trance state.

4. The more recognizable the melody, the more the recording will tend to pull you into its own world. This is not always a bad thing if you want to explore the musical world an artist has created.

5. Recordings with lyrics that you understand will always command some part of your attention. Again, this is not necessarily a bad thing. When I'm doing something physically challenging, I like to play music to which I can sing and dance along.

6. Vary your music to see how different styles affect your work. If you like classical, try world beat music. If you prefer soft, rhythmless, new age meditation music, try something more primal and rhythmic. Try movie soundtracks. If you liked the place to which you were taken in a movie, chances are that the soundtrack will take you right back. Try listening to soundtracks from movies like *Dr. Zhivago, Lawrence of Arabia, Star Wars, Out of Africa, Dances*

with Wolves, or *Titanic* without being whisked away to those places all over again, and you'll understand what I mean.

7. Consider nature recordings as background music. Several companies sell the recorded sounds of the rainforest, the ocean, a mountain stream, an African savanna, or the sounds of whales. Sometimes these recordings feature subtle synthesizer tracks. Other times they are straight recordings of natural sounds. These environmental recordings can shift your consciousness and your attitude in significant ways—locating your studio in a virtual jungle or beach house.

In the last chapter I suggested that you get a portable CD or tape player to use while doing shamanic journeys. If you already have one, it either has built-in speakers or is designed to be used with headphones. Headphones are great for doing work that is static, but speakers are better when you need to move around. If you already have a portable CD player and don't want to invest a lot of money in a sound system, consider getting a small set of multimedia speakers from a computer store. They are portable and usually inexpensive, but deliver nice sound that can easily fill a small room.

As your collection of music grows, consider cataloguing it according to its effect upon you. That way you can use the music purposefully to reinforce the sacred nature of the space and the work you are doing.

The Dream Artist's Studio

I LOVE WALKING INTO an artist's studio. There is usually so much life and energy concentrated in such a small space. I've been in many artists' studios, and I can always tell whether a studio is an active place or a memorial to a once-vital creative urge. I can also tell a lot about the artist from how he or she keeps a space. A messy and chaotic space sometimes suggests what the artist's product will look like, but more often it reflects the artist's attitude to his or her creative energy. This is not meant as a judgment. Great art can come from chaos or from order, but some artists have a painful, anxiety-ridden relationship to their own creative process that reveals itself in how they choose to work. Actually, I think this is one of the myths of modern art—that artists must be dysfunctional, angry, tormented, and prone to excess and abuse. Because this myth is so pervasive, it tends to attract the dysfunctional, and even more absurdly, it compels talented artists to manufacture angst as a kind of credential.

As with all myths, however, there is often an underlying truth. Artists sometimes do plumb depths the rest of us avoid. They often explore excess on our behalf. They face the shadow in themselves and uncover the shadows of culture and society. These are shamanic tasks as well. The shaman experiences symbolic death and rebirth on behalf of the community. Sometimes shamans like many artists, spend their whole lives in conflict over the work they are called to do. Shamans live eccentrically, sometimes excessively, to restore sacred balance. The studio of the artist or the sacred space of the shaman reflects the work done there and the relationship of the artist/shaman to that work.

When I first entered college, one of my teachers was artist Wally Dreyer. Wally has since passed on, but in my student days, he would invite me to his studio, an old carriage house on the beautiful wooded grounds of an historic house and museum. He taught me to cut window mats for my photographs, and to care for and present my work in the best possible manner. He taught me printmaking and invited me to help create a plaster cast for a life-size bronze statue made by his wife, Gay. He was a mentor to me, drawing me into the world of the artist. His studio was like his life, richly layered, piled, and cluttered with experiences realized or represented in physical form. Wally was a photographer and printmaker, but what he seemed to do best was collect things. Old signs, license plates, machine parts, found objects, memorabilia, and what many would consider trash found homes in Wally's studio. Ancient printing presses, photographic equipment, weathered frames, and stacks of art made navigating the space difficult, but for me there was always the promise of treasures waiting to be discovered. The building he worked in seemed to resonate with meaning for me. It was always a sacred space.

The universe has a cyclical way of working, and now, nearly twenty years later, I find myself occupying the same carriage house. For the past several years, I've used it as a studio for high school students learning to become dream artists. Painting, storytelling, sculpting, and ceremony still keep the spirit of the place vital. I'm certain that Wally would like knowing that his studio was part of a continuing tradition of creativity.

A studio is a place to do the "work" of art. It can be a raw warehouse space, a renovated loft, a basement or garage, a room, a closet, or even a desktop. The big comfortable chair in which I sit when writing is a kind of studio for me. It faces a wall decorated with objects and imagery of particular significance to me. I have an altar near me with candles that I light before I begin writing. Cut glass prisms dangle in the windows, throwing rainbows around the room in the late morning light. Flowers and plants fill the room with color and the scent of living green things.

A studio always serves two purposes: the practical and the spiritual. As much as we've concerned ourselves to this point with accessing the world of spirit—finding inspiration, illumination, and guidance, something that can happen in any setting, the making of art is a profoundly physical process. Working with materials and tools requires space— space to work, space to store materials, space to organize tools, space to let work cure, dry, harden, or merely rest. That space should honor the nature of the tools and materials with which you will be working, the size and form your creative expression will take, and the logistics of your own personal ways of working.

If you choose to carve massive blocks of stone with pneumatic power tools, you will need a space that allows easy access, a lot of open space, and a location that doesn't drain your energy through conflicts with irritated neighbors. Painting large canvases with acrylic paint may simply require an open wall of a garage. Sometimes the space we have available is a constraint that helps us choose a medium with which to work. History is full of artists whose greatest work came in answer to the challenges of where they worked. Michelangelo was challenged by the size, the shape, and the difficulty of painting the ceiling of the Sistine Chapel. The early impressionists painted small canvases because they were drawn to work outdoors under natural light. Jackson Pollock painted huge canvases that covered nearly the entire floor of his tiny studio. He worked without the ability to step back and view his work from a distance.

Perhaps the most important reason for finding or creating some kind of studio space is to facilitate work in progress. If every time you want to paint, or model with clay, or carve wood, you need to concern yourself with the task of clearing off, setting up, and cleaning up, you will be spending most of your creative energy just getting ready. As an artist, as a dream artist, you need to be able to work intensely with a piece, set it aside, and return to it easily.

You may have the luxury of devoting a room to your work as a dream artist, but a corner of a room, even a surface that is yours alone can serve as a studio space. The practical side of your studio space will be defined by the resources available to you and the needs of the medium in which you choose to work. Don't fixate on what you don't have. Not having the perfect space can be a great excuse not to engage in creative work. Not being able to work in the medium you've decided that you were meant to work in can also serve as a good excuse for postponing your creative journey. Find some space, somewhere.

The second function of an artist's studio, in some ways the more important function, is spiritual. Depending on an artist's belief system, he or she may have more secular terms for the quality a studio holds. A space might have an emotional feel that reinforces the processes an artist engages in. It might psychologically bolster and support an artist through a difficult period. It might energize an artist to work. A dream artist sees this as the guiding or helping spirit of a place. It is this spirit that makes a studio a sacred space.

For a dream artist, there are three elements that define a sacred studio space: intention, serendipity, and discipline. While you may be lucky enough to inherit a studio space that is already blessed with spirit, as I was with the carriage house of my mentor, you must still assume the responsibility for maintaining that space as sacred. And, if you begin with the only space you can find and need to make it sacred, to commit it to a purpose, you need to understand what makes a space, especially a studio, sacred.

Think of your studio, no matter how large or how small, as sacred ground dedicated to the spirit of creativity. All sacred ground is sacred in a reciprocal relationship. This means that the work you do in your studio is sacred because it is done on sacred ground, and the ground is sacred because you are doing sacred work upon it.

You will actually have two sacred studios: one in the dreaming and one in the waking world. Your studio in the dreaming world can inspire you and give you ideas for designing, arranging, and decorating your studio in the waking world. Let's begin by using a shamanic journey to explore the sacred studio in nonordinary reality.

YOUR SACRED STUDIO JOURNEY

This journey will allow you to understand that your
sacred creative space exists in both the waking and the
dreaming worlds.

Y OUR intention for this journey is to visit a special art studio in the dreaming world. This is a sacred studio, which means that the work you do here will have spirit and power. It doesn't mean that you can't have fun and be playful in this space. Sacred means that what you do has meaning in spirit. Your sacred studio has all the tools and materials you could want to create anything you can imagine. It is your version of the space in which you found your artist-mentor. Imagine the perfect space for creating and keep this in your mind as you journey.

Using one of the shamanic drum recordings listed in Sources of Music (pages 237 to 239), prepare yourself for a shamanic journey. If you need a refresher, review the steps described in chapter 5. Once you've emerged in either the upper or lower world, call your power animal to you. Either your power animal or your artist-mentor can take you to your sacred studio. If they ask you what you would like in the way of a studio, be as specific as you can. If they do not ask, trust where they take you.

When you arrive at your sacred studio, ask your power animal how to gain entrance to it. Your space will be marked by a particular sign or symbol. There will also be some secret by which only you and those accompanying you can enter the space. Remember this secret.

Once inside, explore your sacred studio. How big is your space? Is it small and intimate or large and cavernous? How many rooms does it have? How many floors are there? What media can you work with here? Are there empty spaces for future media you might try? How is it lit? What can you see through the windows?

Also look to see if any work is in process. You might find a guide in residence who looks after the space when you are gone. If so, ask him or her about the place. Ask to be shown around. You may be asked whether you wish to find the studio exactly as you left it each time or whether you would prefer it tidied up. Spend some time in the studio. Let it recharge you.

When you hear the callback signal on the CD—a pause followed by four sets of seven distinct beats, rapid drumming, and a repeat of the four sets of seven beats—leave your sacred studio, closing the door behind you. Thank those who have helped you and ask your power animal to take you to your passage back to the waking world. Return to your body. Recall as much detail as you can and log it in your journal.

⁂ Honoring Your Visit to Your Sacred Studio

IN some ways, your sacred studio is the most important of the places you've visited in the dreaming so far. It is your sanctuary and creative retreat. To honor your sacred studio, consider the following suggestions:

1. Draw or paint an image of your sacred studio from the outside. This can be in your journal or on a separate sheet of paper.

2. Draw a floor plan of your sacred studio. If you would like something different than what you remembered or you would like to add space, drawing it will change it in the dreaming. The next time you return, it will be as you drew it (usually).

3. Ask yourself how you can create a studio for yourself in the waking world that is sacred. These might be little steps at first, but take them.

4. Was there a project in progress in your sacred studio? Can you manifest that project in the waking world?

5. If you have a space for a studio, mark it the way the entrance to your sacred studio is marked.

When I return from a visit to my sacred studio, I feel relaxed and creatively energized. My sacred studio is a stone tower with many floors. Each room feels intimate and ordered, which is how I like to work. I have rooms for woodwork, for painting, for fine projects, and for drawing. I also have a special room for meditating and doing rituals for and with the things I make. My favorite room is on the top floor. It's a lighthouse structure with windows all around. Beneath the windows are bookshelves that rotate to hold far more books than it would first appear they could. In the center of the room is a large old leather chair that rotates to allow me to see any view I choose. This is where I write, and think, and plan.

YOUR SACRED STUDIO IN THE WAKING WORLD

This exercise will demonstrate that the ability to return from an exploration of nonordinary reality and give form to your vision is at the heart of the dream artist's practice.

BEGIN with intention. Intention is the energy with which we fuel our work as dream artists. Intention can be as simple as defining the space in which you work as being safe, nurturing, and energizing to you. Stand in the center of your room or stand in front of the table that will be your studio. Begin to see it as sacred space. What might reinforce that perception? What signs or symbols do you associate with sites that are consecrated? The list below consists of materials that can be used to enhance the sacred quality of any studio space. Consider adding some of the following elements to your studio space:

- Candles—for the element of fire and the quality of light
- Incense—for the scent and the image of smoke rising
- Aromatherapy burners or candles—for the scent
- Fresh flowers—for the color and the scent
- Plants—for the living energy they bring
- Water—for cleansing and fluidity in bowls, fountains, or aquariums
- Stones—for the element of earth
- Crystals—for the energy they transmit
- Feathers—for air, wind, and spirit
- Mirrors or reflective surfaces—for the way they bounce light
- Mobiles or things that hang and dangle—for movement
- Cut glass prisms or pendulums—for the rainbows
- Chimes—for the sound and movement
- Branches or pieces of wood—for their color, form, and shape
- Pieces of fabric—for the color, pattern, and texture
- Sound system—for music

Remember that what will make this space special is not the objects you add, but the intention you have to make it so. You needn't spend a lot of money to do this. Found objects or pieces you already own will work fine. Your space should attract you sensually. It should look, smell, sound, and feel calming and energizing.

The second set of enhancements to consider adding is those things that support your intention to do the "work" of art. Do you have reproductions of works of art you admire? Consider pinning them up on a wall or bulletin board. How about photographs or images of artists? The people you admire need not be artists. They might be teachers, spiritual leaders, athletes, scientists, politicians, or celebrities. They must simply have some quality that you would like to emulate as you do the work of a dream artist. Do you have pictures of yourself from particularly creative or energetic periods of your life? Do you have pieces of art you've done? What about displaying your certificates, diplomas, or awards? Posting these things is not a tribute to your own ego. It reinforces your intention to live a creative life.

Some people have inspirational quotations, sayings, or personal creeds posted in their studios. For myself, if I were to define my beliefs as a dream artist in the form of a creed it might look like this.

As a dream artist:

1. *I return to my creative source through the dreaming.*

2. *I honor my encounters with spirit with the best of my gifts.*

3. *I faithfully manifest the essence of my dreams in the material world by finding, altering, arranging, or making.*

4. *My art has a purpose, a power, and a spirit of its own.*

5. *To live in balance, I must give back to the dreaming.*

The third set of material enhancements one might add to a sacred studio space bridge intention and serendipity. Serendipitous things are spontaneous and playful. For this reason, they are hard to prescribe, but they might include toys, masks, costumes, strange found objects, odd collections, gifts that have meaning simply because of the people who gave them, musical instruments (especially if you don't know how to play them), picture books, travel memorabilia, postcards and greeting cards, and almost anything that feels right for the space. I have a sign on my door—brought back from the San Diego Zoo—warning visitors not to "annoy, torment, pester, plague, molest, worry, badger, harry, harass, heckle, persecute, irk, bullyrag, vex, disquiet, grate, beset, bother, tease, nettle, tantalize, or ruffle the animals," which pretty much sums up my attitude to being disturbed while I'm working. Don't neglect humorous or playful items out of some sense of what a proper artist's studio should look like. They are an element of every working artist's studio I've ever been in. The only place from which they are absent is in non-working display spaces designed to look like studios. The element of play, the ability to find new connections and links between disparate objects is an energy that must be nurtured and honored.

Also, don't forget the sacred studio to which you journeyed. If you've not made that journey yet, try it now. What does your sacred studio in the dreaming look like? Did you remember the mark or sign on the outside door? Can you incorporate that into your waking studio? Are there other design elements you might incorporate into your studio? If you sketched or drew a floor plan for your studio in the dreaming, perhaps you might display it in the studio you're designing.

You needn't add all of these things at once. Your space will grow organically over time if you are open to the possibilities described above.

By now you have set the intention that the space in which you work will be sacred space, and you've reinforced this with objects and images. You've also introduced the elements of serendipity, playfulness, and chance to build energy and avoid taking yourself too seriously. Your studio should be a place where you enjoy spending time. Is there a comfortable place to sit? Can you meditate or do shamanic journeys there? If you find that you don't want to be in your studio any longer than you absolutely have to, try taking a second look at how you've decorated or embellished your space. If you find no fault or need for improvement there, consider your relationship to doing the "work" of art.

***

FACING THE GUARDIANS—DEALING WITH ARTIST'S BLOCK

*Every dream artist faces creative blocks. Learning to
address those creative blocks energetically in this
exercise will allow you to honor what is blocking you
and to overcome it.*

ONE way of thinking about creative blockage is to consider those blocks as mythical creatures. This is how they were personified in the myths, legends, and magical tales our ancestors told. To enter your own sacred studio space—to begin doing the "work of art"—you need to pass the guardians. If you've created some space for yourself and filled it with reminders of your intention and your playfulness, but still find it hard to settle into working in that space, it may be that the gateway to your studio is too well-guarded. The bad news is that, though you may not have been aware of them, these guardians have all the power they need to keep you from fully entering your own creative space. The good news is that your past experiences set those guardians in place and, though they may be stubborn, they are subject to your control.

Make a list of the guardians at the door to your studio. Put yourself into a relaxed meditative state and begin to write. Another way of getting to know your guardians is to incubate a dream (following the instructions in chapter 4) in which you ask to meet and understand your guardians. Identify what they are and how they got there. For instance, did someone once tell you that you had no talent? That's now a guardian. Is your inner judge or critic too powerful? Are you afraid of failure? You're not alone. Are you afraid of success? Surprisingly, this is even more common than fear of failure. Success brings change. The guardians of stasis don't like change. Do you feel guilty about taking time to create? Do you feel unworthy of the time you would grant yourself? Is your guilt only an internal message, or are there people around you giving voice to your feelings of guilt? Are you afraid of what would happen if you surrendered control? Do you busy yourself with little tasks that always seem more important than practicing your art? Are you too busy?

List each guardian at the top of its own sheet of paper. Draw, doodle, or color an image for each of your guardians. Add words or explanations if you feel so moved. Alternatively, you may model or sculpt your guardians out of clay. You may also choose to find a figure or object to represent each of your guardians. Whichever approach you choose, don't judge your work. Be specific about your guardians. Be honest. After you have given form to your guardians, you have two options for dealing with them.

❋ *Option #1:* Honoring Your Guardians

GATHER your guardians around you. One by one, ask what they are protecting you from. You may find that one guardian is protecting your relationships from the pain and disruption success might bring. Another guardian might be protecting a fragile self-image from the possibility of failure. Ask what must be done to appease them. Guardians don't always need to be fought. Sometimes it is enough that they are honored and acknowledged. This may be done through vision-shifting, through dream incubation, or through shamanic journeys. If you have drawings of your guardians, try hanging them on the door to your studio or near the space where you work. If you have models of your guardians, try setting them in a place of honor. Whenever you enter your studio, before you begin to work, take a moment to acknowledge your guardian or guardians. Leave them a little symbolic food or flower offering.

❋ *Option #2:* Vanquishing Your Guardians

PARTICULARLY nasty guardians often need to be vanquished. In many myths and fairy tales, the guardians are battled and destroyed. While I don't think this is necessary all the time, you may find this approach useful.

Set aside time for a ceremony. Build a small fire outdoors, in a grill or brazier, or in a fireplace. Sit in quiet contemplation of each of your drawings. Call the spirit of each guardian into the piece of paper. Thank the guardian for what it has protected you from, but be firm in your intention not to need that protection any longer. Then, without anger, set the intention to eliminate this guardian. Pass the image into the flame and allow it to be completely consumed. Toss a handful of incense, sage, or cedar chips onto the flames between each burning. If you have clay models, you might consider consigning them one by one to a pond, stream, lake, river, or ocean. If you have more resilient found objects, consider reverent burial.

It is useful to remember that once you've made it clear that this is your space and that you do have the right to be here, your guardians can be made to work for you. They can keep the negative energy of others from entering your space. They can protect you and watch over you while you work. They can even remind you when you are bringing heavy or negative energy into your sacred studio space. Use images or objects that represent your guardians as a marker of transition. Thank them for the work they do and set your intention to be protected by speaking to your guardians as you pass into your sacred studio space.

Having faced your guardians and appeased, honored, acknowledged, or defeated them, the third step to consecrating your sacred studio comes with discipline. It takes discipline to find time to work in your studio. If you can't work, can you at least spend time in the space? Your very presence charges and enlivens the environment. After I have been away from the carriage house studio I use for my high school art program, I can feel a difference in the space itself. I often arrive early to turn on heat or air conditioning, sort supplies, or prepare for ceremony. I feel a potential in the place, but it takes movement, music, some candles and incense, and finally the students themselves to generate the kind of magic I associate with the space. Your own studio, even if it's only a desktop, becomes sacred space cumulatively, over time, as you apply discipline to your life to engage in creative practice.

Part of what makes a space sacred is our relationship to the tools we use in that space. Selecting and using tools in a sacred manner is as important as how we decorate our space.

Outfitting: The Dream Artist's Tools

Do you remember how it felt to get a new box of crayons when you were a child? Do you remember how they smelled as you opened the box? Do you remember the feeling of potential in a box of sixty-four crayons? Do you remember the built-in crayon sharpener in the big box?

I enjoy tools. I enjoy them almost as much for what they are as for what they can do. I haven't taught school in any formal sense for ten years, but every August I get the uncontrollable urge to buy school supplies. I like well-made tools and that difficult-to-describe feeling of quality that some materials and supplies have and others lack. I know artists who are dismissive of their tools and think little of the supplies they use. For these artists, any tool will do and there is little need to attend to or care for the tools they use. They often craft things that are very beautiful or impressive to look at. But, as I watch them work, I often notice how artists of this temperament seem to be at war with the very process of making art. They have trouble finding the tools they need. They get angry at tools not well-suited to the tasks to which they are applied.

For me, process is very important, and my relationship to the tools with which I make art is little different than my relationship to the sacred objects on my altars and shrines. Even before I had an explanation for my actions, I knew that cleaning my cameras and lenses before a photo session was about something more than ensuring their smooth and trouble-free operation. The slow, almost meditative process of cleaning my equipment prepared me, allowed me to merge with my tools, allowed for their "toolness" to fade away. They became extensions of me. I know—without being able to prove it—that my car runs better and is happier when it's clean. My computer equipment also appreciates being clean. My carpentry tools work better when they are kept clean and well-organized. It isn't just that I work better when my tools are clean and organized; there is something more to this relationship. I'm not a mechanic or an engineer. Sometimes I can figure out and solve problems when they occur in cars and computers, but little that I do seems to have as much impact as simple cleaning and maintenance. This is why I feel that I'm in a reciprocal relationship with my tools. It's also, I've come to believe, the way of the dream artist.

This is not a cookbook or project guide, so I won't be recommending which tools you will need. Each dream artist will have different needs— this is a personal journey. But I can provide some thoughts and observations about entering into sacred relationship with the tools and supplies you choose to use.

1. Get the best-quality materials you can afford, but don't let the quality of your tools and supplies become an excuse for not working ("If I can't have Berol Prismacolor pencils, I just can't draw.").

2. Just because you have expensive materials and tools does not mean that your work will be better. You may feel better about the work you do, but that's different. Wonderful discoveries and compelling pieces of art can come from the simplest of tools and materials. Try to avoid buying into hierarchies of media. Oil paints are not better than acrylics, and acrylics are not better than tempera paints. They're just different.

3. Add tools slowly, as you need them. You will appreciate a tool designed to do a specific task even more after you've made do with a less appropriate tool.

4. Treat your tools as a collection. Acquire tools purposefully and mindfully, know the tools in your collection, and know where they belong. Become a connoisseur of tools. Get to know what makes a top-quality tool or material.

5. Find, make, or invest in containers for organizing your tools and materials. This helps you make much better use of the creative time you've carved out for yourself. You can see what supplies you need to replenish, you know where to return tools after you've finished using them, and you can more easily move tools and supplies to where you will be working. Find ways to organize small things that are easily lost or mixed up with other small things.

6. Clean your tools and keep them organized. You needn't be compulsive about this. I'm not a cleanliness freak—I don't alphabetize my canned goods. There are times when my messes pile up, and I don't always clean and maintain my tools at the end of a project. I do find, however, that I need to clean and prepare my tools before starting a new project. Sometimes every possi-

ble work surface in my basement studio gets covered with stuff. At those times, I come to hate being down there. I'm terribly unproductive and find excuses for not engaging in projects. Finally, though, I will tackle the mess, cleaning and reorganizing. My productivity and my whole attitude about work then shifts so dramatically that I'm always amazed.

7. Use the sharpening of pencils and the laying out of supplies as an opening ritual before you begin working. Allow time to clean brushes and put things in order, even if you aren't going to put them away, as a closing ritual.

8. Feel free to develop special relationships with certain tools. It's okay to have a favorite hammer, paintbrush, camera, modeling tool, or brand of supplies. Honor these relationships with special containers or places for these tools and supplies. It's also okay to not want others to use the tools you take such good care of. Keep other tools on hand to lend if asked.

9. In addition to cleaning and maintaining your tools, consider cleansing them with ritual smudging. Smudging means to pass a tool or object through the smoke of burning sage leaves, sweet grass, cedar, or copal (which can be found at almost any new age shop) with the intention of clearing the tool of any unwanted energy and dedicating it to the task before you. Sprinkling it with rainwater or leaving it out overnight in the light of a full moon can also be effective for cleansing and energizing tools.

10. Finally, before beginning to paint, draw, sculpt, or work with any tool or media, give yourself a few minutes to practice the following meditation:

Gather the tools or materials you will be using around you so that they are within easy reach. Select one tool (pencil, brush, crayon, pastel, etc.) as the primary piece through which you will establish a bond with the other tools and supplies you'll be using.

Hold that tool in your drawing hand. Sit in a relaxed position on the floor with legs crossed or in a chair with both feet flat on the floor. Keep your spine straight and breathe deeply. Fill your belly first, then expand your lower ribcage, and then fill your lungs. Visualize your crown area (top of the head) opening up to a beam or column of white light. At the same time visualize another beam of light being drawn up through the soles of your feet or your perineum. Bring both of these currents of energy together at the base of your spine and raise them up your spine circulating through your torso and radiating out to your hands. Understand that this light is a creative life force that you are tapping into and that is now flowing through you. Let it connect you to the tools and materials you will be using. Visualize it expanding out as a bubble of energy that encompasses the tools and materials you've drawn around you. Allow it to fill the room. Ask to work in harmony with your tools and materials. Invite any spirit guides you may be aware of to work alongside you. Express your gratitude for having the opportunity to act as a channel for this creative energy. When you feel full and complete, begin your work.

Having the tools of a dream artist is one thing—using those tools is another. We can use tools in a way that is both a meditation to and an honoring of our creative souls, but this requires that we wake up to the nature and history of our ways of doing.

Have you ever thought about how you learned to do all the things you know how to do? When you drive a car, do you ever think about who taught you to do it? How about when you are riding a bike, folding clothes, scrambling an egg? Was it a parent, an uncle, a grandmother, a brother or sister who taught you? Who taught them?

One way to think of a life is as a collection of ways of doing things. My distant ancestors learned to survive in a harsh and threatening environment. Their bodies learned to survive the onslaught of destructive diseases. I carry that learning with me today. My great-grandparents did things in a certain way that their children and their children's children emulated. I learned little ways of doing from my grandparents and parents. I learned other ways of doing from friends, from teachers, and from people I admired. I learned to do things I saw in movies and on television. Everything I do connects me to a great chain of others. They live on through my ways of doing, the ways of doing I pass on to my students and nephews and nieces.

WAYS OF DOING

Becoming conscious of our ways of doing allows us to work as if we were the products of generations of artists and artisans. In this exercise, you will learn to use this awareness to increase your confidence and energy.

W E are collections of ways of doing. This is true whether we are aware of it or not, but sometimes I think it's important to remind ourselves of this interconnectedness through ceremony. While it's possible to ritually honor a way of doing that you're already aware of (this is a powerful way to honor a parent or grandparent and see yourself as a connected being), for this exercise I suggest using the shamanic journey technique to learn a new way of doing—one that relates specifically to your work as a dream artist.

To do this exercise as a shamanic journey, follow the directions for an upper world journey in chapter 5. Set your intention to meet an ancestor spirit and to learn a way of handling an art material or working with a tool. Don't be surprised by the appearance of the spirit that presents itself to you. Ancestor spirits may be within your bloodline or outside of it. At a workshop I gave once, a middle-aged white woman received guidance from an ancestor who appeared as a young African warrior. He taught her to carve in a specific manner, and she was open enough to listen and learn. Ask politely to be taught a way of working with a specific tool or material, or leave that up to this mentor spirit. Practice what you're shown until you think you can bring that way of doing back from the dreaming. Ask questions if you feel the need. When the time comes to leave, thank the ancestor spirit. Let your mentor know that when you practice this in the waking world it will be done in gratitude for the gift he or she has given you. Return to your body in the waking world.

Immediately record your journey in your journal, writing down as much detail as you can recall. Diagram what you learned if it helps you to commit it to memory. Next practice it. Transform the memory of this way of doing into a physical thing. Incorporate this way of doing into a ceremony or an actual piece of art you are working on.

When Elizabeth, a student of mine, began practicing this exercise, it had special meaning for her. She was adopted and always felt cut off from her past. Most of us take for granted the stories we hear about our ancestors in our childhood, but these stories give us a sense of who we are and what we might do with our lives. Think about a child displaying an unusual talent. One of the first ways of addressing this phenomenon for parents and family members is to figure out who the child "gets this from." Remembering that great-aunt Ellen was quite a painter in her day, or that your great-grandfather had once been a published poet somehow means that this gift or talent is accepted. To not have access to these stories in childhood can leave an empty place.

We had been experimenting with some basic painting techniques, and Elizabeth felt drawn to the act of painting but never felt her colors were right. When we took a break in our work to do this exercise as a shamanic journey, this is what she experienced.

Once in the upper world, I called my power animal to me and was guided by my large black rabbit to a thatched cottage in an open meadow. I wandered through the cottage noticing small paintings of flowers everywhere. Eventually I passed through the cottage and out the back door. From the back of the cottage I could see a beautiful garden and a meadow filled with wildflow-

*ers, butterflies, birds, and a middle-aged woman in an old-fash-
ioned dress. She had bushy red hair and was a little fat, but as
she turned to greet me I noticed that she had a really friendly
smile and a warm face. She was standing at an easel painting
and invited me over to see what she was working on. It was a
painting of flowers, like the ones I'd seen inside.*

*I was immediately excited and asked her if she could teach
me to paint flowers. She dabbed her brush on her easel with a
kind of circular motion then quickly painted a little flower on my
forehead. I couldn't see it, but I knew that's what it was. "You
don't want to paint flowers," she said. "You want the secret of the
flowers' color."*

*She showed me how she mixed colors on her palette and on
the canvas itself. She did it by drawing a tiny amount of one
color into another color with a circular movement. Sometimes
she would mix several colors with a little white. Then she would
go back and add more dabs of the same color, but this time she
didn't mix them in completely. When she painted on the canvas it
first looked solid, but it had a kind of shimmer to it. When you
got close, you could see the shimmer was from the little streaks of
other color.*

*She even let me practice this technique. She told me that she
was an aunt to my mother's great-grandmother and that she had
lived in a place called Cape Inverness. When I heard the callback
drum, I didn't want to return, but I remembered to thank her. She
invited me to come back anytime.*

Elizabeth tried mixing paints the way she had been shown in her
journey. This was a technique that I had not taught, she had not previously tried, and that no one in the class had previously demonstrated. It
worked well for her, and though she did not paint flowers, the colors in
her paintings from that point on were very special. She taught other students to mix colors this way, always remembering to thank and credit
the ancestor she had encountered. She was also affected by the possibility of having an ancestor who was a painter. From that experience on she
was more confident in her abilities and her identity.

• • •

I'd like for you to consider two more aspects of your sacred studio space—that you might have more than one studio space, and that your studio will evolve over time.

I have several studios. I have the old building I use when I work with students. I also share a loft space with a friend that we both use for workshops. These spaces are used by others, so my efforts to define them as sacred must be nonintrusive or portable. I light candles and incense, I use music and portable altars, and I arrange the room in a way that is conducive to creative work—all in an effort to define the space as sacred. What things could you carry with you to make a space sacred? In addition to candles, sacred herbs and incense, and music, I bring special stones, feathers, shells, a bowl for water, noisemakers, figurines, and brightly colored cloth.

I've already described the room in which I do my writing, but I also have a basement workshop for heavier and messier work. And I've created a virtual sacred space on my computer in my office. Special objects and guardian spirits sit on my computer monitor and tower. Candles burn beside me and things of special significance are within easy reach.

You should also realize that your sense of your studio will evolve. It will change as your exploration of new media continues. It will grow along with your need to work on larger pieces or store more of your work. It will reflect new influences as you discover the patterns of Navaho weaving, or the colors of Van Gogh's sunflowers, or the erotic temple sculpture of Hindu India, or the sacred architecture of Bali, or the mandalas of Tibet. Let your studio display what you are passionate about. It will also change to reflect the dream artist's mode of creative expression you choose to explore—finding, arranging, altering, or making.

The gift of this chapter is

discrimination.

Every artist will tell you that the single most significant (and

often most frightening) thing they do is make choices. The

suggestions and exercises in this chapter will help you utilize

discrimination based on energetic criteria and sensitivity.

chapter 7

The Sacred Hunter:
Practicing the Arts of
Finding and Arranging

*The urge to collect is the natural response of the human psyche to an
aesthetic object that speaks directly to it, stirring memories that lie
deeply within. Collecting confirms the indigenous belief that the
human psyche reads and understands symbols and that attraction to
beauty is a function of psychic awareness.*

MALIDOMA PATRICE SOMÉ
The Healing Wisdom of Africa:
Finding Life Purpose Through Nature, Ritual, and Community

No object crosses your path by accident. If an object attracts
your attention—catches your eye—you can be sure there is meaning
behind it. You may debate what that meaning is, but the more you experience life as a dream artist does, the less doubt you will have that there
is meaning.

It's appropriate to begin discussing the manifestation of spirit in material form with a quote about collecting and finding because, in many ways, this is the root of art making. While *making, altering,* and *arranging* may have more prestige in our contemporary way of thinking about art, *finding* is the artist's and the dream artist's core skill. We find the right lighting for a photograph, the best point of view for a painting, the finest piece of marble for a sculpture, the most exciting form to emulate or transform in clay, the correct stones to arrange, the most intriguing objects to combine. Our ability to find demonstrates that we are alive and able to interact with the spirit in things. Finding is both a starting point and an expression of the dream artist's practice that is complete in itself.

Outfitting:
A Ritual in Preparation for Finding

FINDING IS THE foundation upon which all our work as dream artists is done. It is the confluence of intention and attention. Intention is the asking of a question; attention is listening for the answer. Whether we know it or not, we are always setting intentions. Some of our intentions are negative, some are positive. The shaman or dream artist learns to take control of the power of intention—to apply will to intention. Intention is like the flashlight you use when finding. The more general the intention, the broader the beam of light, the more likely you will be to find something. The more specific your intention is—the tighter the focus of the beam—the more likely you will be to find a particular thing. A general intention might be to find a stone to empower with the gift of containing grief. A specific intention might be to find an object to represent a character or event in a recent dream.

Many of the ceremonial dances of native peoples are preparatory. They prepare the hunter to hunt, the gatherer to find, the warrior to fight, and the loving couple to conceive a child. You can practice your own ritual of preparation by following the instructions below or adapting them to your own needs.

This is best done in the morning as both an active and a passive form of preparation. Give yourself ten minutes of time in which you will not be disturbed. Use your dream artist's journal to record your intention. Distill down to a single sentence what it is you are looking for. Be as specific as you need to be, but realize that what you find may be totally different than what you believe you are looking for. Sit in a comfortable position, close your eyes and take ten long, slow, deep breaths. With each inhalation, ask for guidance and assistance from whatever power you choose to invoke. This may be your image of a god or goddess, an ancestor spirit, a guide or mentor, a power animal, the spirit of a place or element, or simply the universe itself as an animate energy. In effect, you are asking to be blessed or guided in your search, much the same as a hunter/gatherer might ask that an expedition to find food or medicine be successful. With each exhalation put your intention to find a specific thing out into the world. Repeat the sentence you wrote in your journal out loud or to yourself. If you've been unable to decide what it is you are looking for, you can ask that you find the thing you need.

Remain in this relaxed state for about five minutes after you've completed your sequence of ten breaths. To complete the ceremony, make a small offering in gratitude for the help you will now receive. Lighting some incense or a candle, placing a cut flower in water, burning some sweet grass, or sprinkling some beer, tobacco, or cornmeal on the earth are all ways of expressing gratitude.

Practicing Finding:
Becoming a Sacred Hunter

THE EARLIEST SHAMANS WERE, like other members of their tribe, hunters and gatherers. They were part of the cultures in which they lived. The art of finding, like the practice of hunting and gathering can be described as a collection of ways of doing things. To find sacred things, we must prepare ourselves for the finding as we did in the "Ritual in Preparation for Finding" described above. We must both see what we are seeking in our mind's eye and be open to the dialogue of what we actually find. For finders—sacred hunters and gatherers—there are four steps. We must know where to look. We must know what to ex-change for what we take. We must honor what we find through cleansing and clearing. And, finally, we must be able to listen to and learn from the voices of the objects we find.

Finding—Step 1: Where to look?

WHAT you find is affected by where you look. Being sensitive to place will make you a better finder. The easiest way to describe this sensitiv-ity, this energetic mapping, is by example. Let's take stone as the object of our search. I love stones and have a particular affinity for the energy of stone, but you can apply this method of energetic mapping to any ma-terial that you are called to work with.

When I describe finding stone as a sacred act, I don't mean that the search must be solemn and pretentious. Watch a child look for the per-fect pebble in a pile or while walking along a shoreline and you will see a perfect example of sacred searching. A child can become totally ab-sorbed by the task of attending to the subtle differences between stones. A stone can come to your attention as easily when you are laughing as when you are concentrating intensely.

There are a number of ways stones can come to you, but let's begin with finding them. If you want to acquire stones without purchasing them, you will need to look for stones in places where you are relatively free to pick them up and take them with you. Fortunately, this includes most of the planet. Some exceptions might include private property or national parks, but in most places no one will begrudge you the stone you pick up and take with you. Please note that we are talking about a single stone, not a backpack, or a wheelbarrow, or a truckload of stones.

Searching for stone in a sacred manner should take into account three factors: where you look, when you look, and what you look for.

The kind of stone you will find is often determined by where you go looking. The coast of Maine has beautiful stones that have been rounded and smoothed by the waves. The streambeds of the Appalachian Moun-tains are filled with flattened river stones of gray slate. The Rocky Mountains in Colorado have sparkling chunks of quartz-flecked granite. The canyons and peaks of Sedona, Arizona, have pastel stones streaked with red, gold, and brown. The shores of Hawaii are speckled with round pebbles of black volcanic pumice.

If you are looking for stone of a certain physical quality, you will want to hunt for it in its own territory. Keep in mind, however, that stones do migrate. I have found stones, that, geologically speaking, had to have been born hundreds or thousands of miles away. These are often very special stones; they have sought me out.

On a deeper level, you might search for stone according to intuitive properties. I have listed some possibilities below, but your imagination will be a better guide than any recipe. If you have access to wilderness areas or natural settings, make an expedition out of your search. Try some of the following:

- *Sandy beaches*—for that rare, little smooth pebble, a princess stone, for magical promise
- *Rocky beaches*—for stones that understand cycles, rhythm stones
- *High mountain streambeds*—for river stones in their childhoods, stones of expectation, a good birthing stone
- *Streams and rivers*—journey stones, stones for travelers
- *Waterfalls and rapids*—change stones for manifesting the energy to make changes, good healing stones
- *Rivers at the confluence of many mountain streams*—grandfather and grandmother stones, stones for wisdom
- *Rocky mountains and cliffs*—rough-edged stones of spirit, ascendant stones, especially those that are long and narrow
- *Rockslides and avalanche sites*—portable stones of spirit
- *Volcanoes*—for alchemical stones; for fire, air, and, earth; if they are rounded stones, they bring the fourth element, water
- *Caves*—for stones of introspection, especially good for dreamwork
- *Deserts*—for passionate stones
- *Forests*—for stones of seduction and enchantment
- *Fields*—for marking and building stones, good for cairns and constructions
- *Swamps, bogs, moors*—lost stones

My preference is always to seek stone in the most natural of environments, but it is not the only option. There is magic all around us. If you are hunting stone in built landscapes, consider the following:

- *Path stone*—pebbles and stones that line paths, driveways, and walks are often journey stones—good for travelers as temporary companions. Crushed gravel has spirit, but it often hides itself. Treat crushed gravel pebbles gently, as you might an injured or frightened animal.
- *Street stones*—loose stones found on streets are like stray dogs, happy to have a home. They always repay a kindness.
- *Construction stones*—stones from demolished houses and buildings can have a lot of spirit. Sometimes that spirit is positive, as in the case of homes, churches, places that have seen a lot of life. Sometimes that spirit is negative, as in the case of prisons and sites of great violence. Most of the time, the spirit is neutral. Try to learn something about the building the stone came from.
- *Excavation stones*—sometimes stones are uncovered in the process of building or gardening. These are sleeping stones— good for dreamwork.

There are, of course, other places you might find stone in a city or neighborhood. There are usually parks and little open places where stone can be found and adopted with little ethical consequence. Try to avoid taking stone from private property. Getting caught in the middle of the night prying up your neighbor's paving stones or dismantling his stone wall may have legal ramifications, will probably be embarrassing, and is certainly an energetically indefensible act.

While we are on the subject of things to avoid, watch out for bits of concrete, eroded fragments of brick, little balls of asphalt, and aggregate scraps (aggregate is stone chips and dust mixed with a bonding resin to form artificial marble for floors and walls). Sometimes these things can masquerade as stone, but they don't have the same kind of energy.

As you might have guessed by now, there are some places that can be very powerful sources for stones, and these are energy vortices and sacred sites. Energy vortices are points around the earth that vibrate at noticeably higher frequencies. You actually feel different when you are within one, though this varies with the sensitivity of the individual and the strength of the site. Sedona, Arizona, is well known for vortices and they are well documented in a number of books. The prophet and healer, Edgar Cayce, identified Virginia Beach, Virginia, as an energy center. Energy vortices are often connected along lines of geopathic or geomagnetic force, called "dragon lines" in the Chinese art of Feng Shui and "ley lines" by researchers in the countries of strong Celtic heritage.

There are books that discuss the theory of energy vortices and even guides to major identified sites, but with practice you can find smaller vortices yourself. Become aware of sudden shifts in your mental state or changes in physical sensation that are not easily explained. These changes can be signaled by visual, aural, olfactory, or kinesthetic phenomena. Of course not all such moments can be ascribed to an energetic vortex, but if the phenomenon occurs repeatedly in the same vicinity, you might have discovered an energetic site. Stone from an energetic vortex and those that fall on the paths that link these sites together can be powerful tools.

Which brings us to the second category mentioned above—sacred sites. Most sacred sites such as Stonehenge, Chartres cathedral, Machu Picchu, Jerusalem's Wailing Wall, Mecca, Lhasa, are located on points of high energy. They are usually situated on the most powerful vortices. In addition, they have been energetically reinforced by thousands of years of continuous sacred attention and intention. As you might imagine, there is powerful stone here.

I cannot, in good conscience, however, advocate taking stones from these places. Sacred sites are usually protected sites. Many of them are on private property or are managed by governments or religious groups. There are usually laws that prohibit the removal of material from these sites. Even if the site you are visiting has no such restrictions on this kind of activity, it would still need to be done with great care and sacred attention. Could you take a stone away from a sacred site without getting caught or without affecting the site in any noticeable way? Undoubtedly. But as hard as it may be for one to imagine, if even a small percentage of the people visiting such sites were to take stones away with them, there would be a significant impact. Some of the more managed and heavily trafficked sacred sites have gift stores that sell stones from the site. This might be one way to acquire a stone from the site; but, in general, be wary of people who sell stone they claim to have taken from sacred sites. You have only their integrity to ensure that the stone was taken with permission. Use your intuition and your other critical faculties. It is something you should care about.

There is another kind of energetic site I should mention at this point, and that is scenes of great or repeated violence. I am tempted to call them anti-sacred sites, but I think I would reserve this term for some of the cold and energetically barren places we have erected in our attempt to overpower the earth and dismiss such subtle things as energy lines, fields, and vortices. Actually, many of our battlefields have become sacred sites through the incredible amount of energy that was released upon them and the mourning and attention paid to those sites by generations that followed. Battlefields, memorials to great pain and suffering, sites of national, regional, and local tragedy, both manmade and natural, can be energetically consecrated. Stones from these sites can have powerful personal meaning, sometimes reflecting past lives, other times encapsulating ethnic or racial heritage. Stones have long memories and aren't usually as affected by our living and dying as we might like to think. If your collection is heavily weighted with stones from these kinds of sites, they may affect you in ways that are unpredictable. You might also want to explore what it is that is drawing you to these kinds of stones. Is it atonement, contrition, guilt? Is there a lesson you need to learn through these stones?

If where to look for stones is important, when to look can be equally influential. Sometimes stones come to you when they are ready and your sense of time will mean little; but when you are setting out to find a stone, time can be a factor in your search. I like the liminal times of a day for hunting stone. Dawn and dusk have always seemed more magical to me, and I find I have better luck finding the right stone during these times.

While as a species we are not well-equipped for finding stone in the dark, a midnight stroll along a pebble strewn beach by the light of a full moon can yield surprising results. I once camped near a stream in the

Blue Ridge Mountains of Virginia. I slept fitfully in my tent, always aware of the sound of splashing water. When I finally surrendered to the call and rose to sit by the stream in the moonlight, I was rewarded with a beautiful rounded black stone, veined with quartz. It flashed at me from just below the surface of the sparkling water, and I knew I was to take it with me. I still have that stone.

Generally, the best time to find stone is during daylight hours. I think, however, that there is something to be said for the quality of light by which one searches. Just as I prefer dusk and dawn for stone searching, I also prefer gray days, cloudy and overcast. This is not to say that beautiful blue skies and intense sun will not reveal stone treasures, but I find myself looking up and out on such sunny days rather than down and in. Down and in is the way to look for stone.

Noon is my least favorite time of day for looking for stone. This may be a personal idiosyncrasy, or it may be the way the sun directly overhead flattens out all the shadows and surface texture that help me find stones. Whatever the reason, it is not a time that I actively seek stone.

Other time-related factors might influence your search. Lunar cycles can have a powerful influence upon us. In general, the waxing moon, from dark to full, is a time for new ventures, positive and aggressive action. The waning moon, from full to dark, is a time for incubation, planning, and introspection. If you were looking for a stone to commemorate a birth, you might choose to look for it in the cycle of the waxing moon. Memorial stones, on the other hand, reveal themselves best in the time of the waning moon.

Seasons of the year also can inspire our search for stone. Most people have a particular affinity for one season. Gardeners and people who long for the warmth of summer find spring an energizing time. Stones found in the spring are often the most active. They tell us stories of movement and growth. They are good for building and constructing and the initiation of new ventures. Summer stones are magical. They are especially powerful for spells and charms. They affect relationships profoundly and, of all the seasonal stones, they work their magic the quickest. Autumn stones are stones of transition. They are good stones for marking or facilitating passage. They are good stones for travelers and explorers. Autumn stones can be good meditation stones, especially if it is an active form of meditation, such as guided visualization, but the best stones for stillness are winter stones. Winter stones are storytellers. Listen to them, go inside them, and learn from them.

The solstices and equinoxes are energetically charged times to search for stone. They are the great pendulum swings of light and dark. The vernal and autumnal equinoxes, when the daylight and darkness are equal in length, are moments of balance. The summer solstice, the longest day and the shortest night of the year, is a time of passionate and often erotic energy. Its twin, the winter solstice, the longest night of the year is a time of memory, history, and wanderings in the realm of the spirit.

You might be drawn to other ways of reckoning time and these can inform your search for stone as well. The great cycles of Chinese, Vedic, Mayan, Native American, and European astrology can influence you. The important thing to remember is that the where and the when of finding stone should not constrain you. There are no set rules. There are tendencies, inclinations, and possibilities. Become attentive to the places and times when you are looking for stone. As you sensitize yourself to the potential—the language—of place and time, you will align yourself with those specific energies and open yourself to their messages.

Finding—Step 2: What to give in exchange for what we take

IN Peruvian shamanism, there is a concept called *ayni* (eye-knee), which means sacred reciprocity. Ayni demands that we give in proportion to what we take, that we express gratitude for what we have and what we receive by making symbolic and sometimes more material gestures to the world of spirit. For Native Americans along the northwest coast, the idea of potlatch meant that the most powerful person or family was the one who could give away the most. I think it's useful to remember these ideas when we are practicing the art of finding.

When taking objects from the natural environment, develop the habit of asking permission first. If there is an actual person to ask (for example, before taking a flower or herb sprig from a garden), begin asking permission here. But whether there is a person of whom to ask permission or not, I would encourage you to ask permission of the spirit world. Simply close your eyes or vision-shift inward for a moment. Ask if this is the object you were meant to find and if it is okay to take it.

Once when I was searching for a stone to give to a friend to commemorate a weekend workshop we had taught together, I went for a short walk down to a stream that ran through the property. The light through the trees made almost every other stone glint and catch my eye. I picked up a number of stones, asking for guidance and permission each time, but I received no strong impressions. Finally, I found a small, reddish stone embedded with quartz veins. When I picked it up, a large blackbird began cawing wildly a few feet over my head. I wondered for a moment if this was a sign to take the stone or a warning not to. I looked up and asked out loud, "Am I meant to take this?" Immediately the bird fell silent. It watched me for a moment as I backed away but made no more noise. I took a pinch of tobacco and sprinkled it on the ground in gratitude. Seeing this done seemed to satisfy the bird, for it quickly flew off.

Which brings me to my next point. In addition to asking permission to take something, it's always a good idea to leave something behind. I carry a little leather pouch filled with tobacco. Cornmeal, sage leaves, flower petals, seeds, beans, pebbles, or shells will also work. In a pinch, spit or hair will serve as an exchange as well. Another form of exchange might be the act of cleaning up some litter or debris in the area where you found your object. What matters most is that your exchange be done with reverence and gratitude. If you cannot make an offering at that moment, or if you forget to, make an offering of gratitude later. This may seem silly and superstitious. You may not really believe in spirits, but in making offerings of gratitude you develop your own ability to see connection and relationship. Practice it until it becomes second nature.

While a scavenger hunt in the natural world is a truly rewarding way of finding, there are other methods. One can *find* in stores—"shopping as sacred activity." While money can't buy spirit, the use of money in exchange for objects and images does not necessarily negate the spirit or sacred quality in things. For an urban dream artist, roaming thrift stores and yard sales, art and craft supply stores, and the galleries and shops of other artists can be every bit as sacred an activity as trekking through the woods. What matters again is intention. Did you set an intention? Are you searching in a deliberate and mindful way? Are you open to surprises and aware of the symbolic language of the universe? When you find that special object, consider barter as a form of exchange. Barter creates a different energy and a stronger form of relationship. If money is to change hands, do it with an open heart. Feeling you've been cheated or feeling as if you've cheated someone will cause spirit to flee from an object faster than anything else I know. And just because money has been exchanged, don't neglect to give thanks with an offering or a silent prayer. Honor the fact that spirit led you to this place at this time to find this thing.

Another way objects may come into your life is as gifts. Sometimes people will give you things they have found, or made, or that have been important to them. Learn to accept these little gifts graciously. The giving and receiving of gifts, which we will discuss in more detail in chapter 9, is a way of building relationships. If you've put an intention out to the universe, the universe may act through someone close to you to bring you the object you need. My students and clients often bring me shells, stones, sacred plants, and offering materials. Some of these remain with me; others are meant to be passed along. When people know that you are a finder, a collector, it will sometimes trigger their desire to participate in your practice by finding things for you. For years, I've collected bird feathers from my walks through my neighborhood. My sister-in-law now also collects feathers for me. Every so often she leaves me an envelope full of the feathers she has found, always calling attention to the oddly colored and unusual ones.

Finding—Step 3: Cleaning, cleansing, and clearing

CARING for the objects that come into our lives is important. Often the first thing we will want to do is physically clean an object. This cleaning process helps shift our attitude about what we've found. Investing some physical effort in cleaning and drying our treasures creates a bond between them and us.

Cleansing is to spirit as cleaning is to the material. The way an object should be cleansed depends on what it's made of. These are some possibilities:

- *Water bath:* Soaking an object in rainwater, spring water, mineral salts, or ocean water is an effective method of cleansing an object of dense energy.
- *Moon soaking:* Let objects sit out in the light of a full moon to balance a piece with an excess of masculine energy. This can be done in conjunction with water baths or salt and earth burials.
- *Solar charging:* Let objects sit out in sunlight on a clear day to balance a piece with an excess of feminine energy.
- *Salt or earth burial:* Burying objects in a bowl of mineral or sea salt or directly in the earth drains off dense energy.
- *Smudging:* Passing an object through the smoke of a sacred spirit plant like sage, sweet grass, cedar, copal, lavender, or pine is a powerful cleansing process that is safe for most objects. Incense can also be used for smudging, though, in my experience, it is a bit less effective.
- *Candle passing:* Light a white candle (for purity) and pass your object over the flame three times. The distance from the flame should be close enough to feel some of the warmth, but not close enough to risk burning.

Clearing is which, for most objects found in nature, will not be necessary (the one exception being natural objects found at sites where violence or heavy energy has been concentrated). Clearing is most important for objects that others have handled. Clearing is done through intention and is meant to remove the programming an object may have picked up from a previous owner. Objects can hold residual tension from the people who have been in close contact with them. If, for example, a little bronze goddess statue was owned by a woman whose belief in her own power had been weak, the statue may have picked up this intention and, even after having been cleansed of heavy energy, may still be maintaining a weak energy field.

After cleaning and cleansing your object, sit quietly with it in your right hand. The right side is traditionally most appropriate for giving or passing energy to another person, animal, plant, object, or the universe itself. The left hand is better for receiving. We honor this ceremonially by giving with our right and receiving with our left; but if you find that your right hand receives better and your left hand transmits more effectively, feel free to adapt the techniques to what is most appropriate for you. Form the intention to clear the object of any past programming it may be carrying. Fix this intention through three deep breaths. Hold each breath after the inhalation for a slightly longer count to build the clearing power within you. On the third breath, bring the object to your lips and blow your intention to clear it into the object.

Finding—Step 4: Listening to and learning from objects

USE the vision-shifting techniques described in Chapter 3 to hear and see the stories your objects will tell. You may also choose to sleep with the object on the left side of your bed, held in your left hand, or tucked under your pillow on the left side (remember that the left will be the most receptive side for most people, but you may be different). Set an intention to dream the story of your object, then pay attention to the dreams you have. Alternatively, or perhaps in addition to the techniques mentioned above, you might do a shamanic journey to better understand the nature or true heart of this object. Ask your power animal or spirit guides for assistance. Try to discover a name for the object you found. Learn about it with resources from the waking world.

———————————— ·~~~· ————————————

IMAGE HUNTING:
TWO-DIMENSIONAL FINDING

Learning to find in a sacred manner can also extend to
finding images, as this exercise will teach you.

FINDING is not restricted to three-dimensional objects. Photographers and those who sketch and draw are also finders. Photographers are, in fact, the consummate finders and arrangers. They find points of view, subjects, textures, patterns, forms, shapes, shadows, and light. When what they find does not match their internal vision, they arrange elements to manifest that vision. Polaroid instant cameras are wonderful tools for exploring and finding imagery. They are fairly inexpensive, usually simple to operate, and provide almost immediate feedback, which means you learn what makes successful images much more quickly. If you are drawn to photography as a medium and would like to pursue it as a dream artist, consider assigning yourself the following projects:

1. Make ten photographs that in some way reflect or represent elements of a recent dream.

2. Try creating ten self-portraits in which you do not actually appear.

3. List the five most important values in your life. Make one or more visual metaphor images to represent them.

After you've made the images, study them as much for what you actually captured on film as for what you intended to capture. Don't judge your images according to some notion of aesthetic value, rather ask how these images illuminate your understanding of the dream. Challenge yourself to make ten photographs of interesting things within fifty yards of your home. You can, of course, do these projects with digital cameras or 35mm cameras, but the feedback is not as immediate.

Finding can also occur with a pencil and a sketchbook or your dream artist's journal. Find and sit in a spot and draw an imaginary circular border around yourself. Make yourself sketch whatever you find within your border as if those things were the most interesting things in the world. Take your journal with you for a day and record the messages or images on the signs that seem to call out to you most. Record snippets of conversation overheard on buses and trains and in other public places. Imagine that these are messages specifically meant for you. Explore what they might be telling you about your life.

THE ELEMENTAL COLLECTION

Begin finding with a purpose and deepening your
connection to elemental energies with this exercise.

YOU may discover that finding comes naturally to you. Perhaps you already enjoy the hunt, the search, and the adventure of finding. To practice some of the techniques described above, set yourself the task of finding the following items.

1. Find five objects or images that represent the element of earth.
2. Find five objects or images that represent the element of air.
3. Find five objects or images that represent the element of fire.
4. Find five objects or images that represent the element of water.

Before you begin, set this as an intention. Take some time to do a little writing about these elements in your journal. Avoiding the temptation to consult other sources, make a list of some of your own associations to these elements. What colors do you associate with these elements? What physical sensations does considering these elements evoke? Are there archetypal images, symbols, or myths that come to mind when you think about these elements? Do you associate different cardinal points to these elements? Do you think of different emotional states or different ages?

After recording your thoughts, you may want to look at what other traditions have to say about the elements (just remember that they are not necessarily more relevant than your own impressions). Over the next couple of days, begin your morning with the "Ritual in Preparation for Finding" (page 142). Set your intention to find objects or elements to represent the elements. Some of these objects may already be in your possession; but, even if you have enough objects to put together the collection right now, limit yourself to no more than half of your collection being made up of things you already possess. Experiment with finding in both natural and urban settings. Allow yourself to be open to receiving gifts that fill your collection. Remember to ask permission for what you take and leave an offering of gratitude behind. You will use the items you collect in the next section.

Practicing Arranging:
The Art of Altars and Shrines

SOME PEOPLE WILL be especially drawn to finding and collecting as a way of expressing their creative energies. For some, collecting will be their spiritual practice. But those who collect passionately usually become arrangers as well. They find creative ways of organizing and displaying their collections. Arrangement, organization, and display are all arts of relationship. Objects can be arranged attractively in ways that merely take advantage of surface or material similarities or relationships; but when they are arranged according to intuition, sacred traditional patterns, spiritual guidance, or dream revelation, they become arrangements of power—altars and shrines.

Throughout history, power and spirit have been attributed to objects and images, but of almost equal importance is the arrangement of those objects and the placement of images within a composition. This is how the power and spirit of objects is worked with, balanced, aligned, and amplified. The location and arrangement of church, mosque, temple, and synagogue altars are as important as the objects that make up the altars. The Chinese have the discipline and art form of Feng Shui built around the sacred arrangement and alignment of things. Native Americans build medicine wheels of stone. Peruvian *curanderos* lay out elaborate mesas filled with sacred objects. The Yoruba and the Dagara tribes of Africa erect carefully arranged shrines to the elements. For the shaman, the construction of altars, medicine wheels, shrines, and sacred maps is a significant practice.

As a dream artist, you can benefit from learning the traditions of Feng Shui and other cultural cosmologies of organizing space, but developing your intuitive ability to arrange is equally important. As with finding, the art of arranging appears deceptively easy to the outsider. It is a process that is open to a great number of people, but doing it well can be as transformative as any art form. It takes found objects into a new realm by organizing and arranging them energetically.

When Peruvian shaman and teacher Oscar Miro-Quesada conducts ceremony, it is around a mesa. The mesa is a portable altar. It is a square cloth upon which he organizes a large number of stones, shells, feathers, candles, and plant and animal spirit medicine bundles. There are items to represent the elements, the directions, various energy bodies, and elements of the ancient Incan cosmology. There are also objects that represent his personal connection to various sacred sites and guardian spirits.

When shamanic practitioner and author Tom Cowan conducts his "Celtic Shamanism—Spirit of the Ancestors" workshops, he does so around an altar that includes candles, a sacred chalice, power animal representations, and the symbolic representation of workshop participants' ancestor spirits.

Malidoma Patrice Somé, a shaman and teacher from Western Africa, guides students through ceremonies intended to rebalance their relationship to the planet. He does this work around focal point shrines to the elements of nature: earth, stone, fire, and water. Each shrine is different, dictated by the element being invoked or honored, by the needs of the group, and by the surroundings in which the ceremony takes place.

Native American medicine man, ceremonialist, and teacher Sun Bear taught thousands through his workshops and books how to build ritual medicine wheels. These arrangements of stone with spokes to represent the months, the seasons, and the directions give form to earth-honoring practices and spirit alignment.

While they may appear very different in physical form and construction, these structures share at least one commonality. They are all based on cosmologies that map the unseen world and give form to the powers that animate the waking world. A collection of objects, even the most personally sacred or meaningful objects, arranged in a way that does not honor intuitive guidance or ancient wisdom traditions may look aesthetically pleasing, but it is not an altar or shrine. It does not create sacred space. This is the challenge for those of us who would be dream artists. The creation of living and dynamic altars and shrines is one of our primary responsibilities. The way we arrange things has healing power. By our arrangements we open portals to other realities. We establish lines of communication with the spirit world.

The construction of altars and shrines could be the subject of a whole book in itself. For our purposes, however, I would like to more precisely define the difference between altars and shrines and to suggest two broad strategies for studying and practicing the art of arrangement: the traditional and the intuitive.

The distinctions I draw between altars and shrines are by no means universally accepted, but they do seem to serve as a good foundation for identifying what circumstances suggest the need for a shrine versus those that call for an altar arrangement. To begin with, both altars and shrines define sacred ground. Both altars and shrines can also serve as liminal points between worlds. Altars and shrines contain objects corresponding to some kind of sacred mythos or cosmology. What differentiates the two is the purpose or intention behind their creation.

A shrine, even a temporary one, is consecrated to a specific spirit, element, deity, ancestor, or purpose. It has one purpose and one purpose only, to establish a link between a specific energy and the material world. The pond I tend in my backyard is a kind of shrine to the element of water. My wife has a shrine to her ancestors and family in her office at home. The high school students I mentor create shrines to their own creative spirits. These little three-sided structures contain objects and images that represent their values and their personal gifts and talents. Shrines are designed for leaving offerings of gratitude and appeasement. They can be used for making requests and seeking guidance. It is through shrines that the gods are fed. You've probably seen shrines in Chinese restaurants. If they are well-cared for, they contain cups of tea, oranges, bananas, or other fruit, perhaps a burning stick of incense. You can consecrate a shrine to personal healing or to the healing of a friend or loved one. You can create shrines to encourage prosperity and abundance, to enhance relationships, and to ensure safe travel.

An altar is a place of sacrifice and transformation. It's a working space, not dedicated to one deity, spirit, or purpose, but a channel to each in turn. Whereas one might create a shrine to the element of fire and have no obligation to earth, air, and water, an altar with only the element of fire represented would be out of balance. An altar is a map of the unseen world. The *curandero*'s mesa that I've learned to use as an energetic map is a kind of altar. It has stone in the south to give form to the element of earth. It has a shell in the west to give form to the element of water. In the north sit three hawk feathers to give form to air or wind, and in the east is a white candle for the element of fire. The center holds a collection of my most sacred stones, which represent the rainbow bridge between the worlds. This is also the place of transformation that the Inca called *pachakuti* or world reversal.

While I think there is real healing power in creating shrines for oneself and for others, an altar is a more personal tool. I might encourage others to create altars, but I don't feel I could create one for them. In my life I have one main altar, one portable altar, and many shrines.

There are two paths one might take to develop one's facility with arranging objects to create an altar or shrine, and they are not, by the way, mutually exclusive. The first is to study a wisdom tradition, such as Feng Shui, the Chinese art of placement, or the medicine wheel from the spiritual practice of Native Americans. Studying cultural traditions from Africa, the Americas, Australia, the South Pacific, Tibet, India, the Middle East, and even the European mystery schools will give you a cosmology to work with in your arrangement of objects. I recommend, however, that you find a tradition that resonates for you and stick with it.

While it can be useful to understand a wide range of traditions, in practice, it can be confusing. For a time I was overwhelmed by the differences in the world's wisdom traditions. Some cultures honor four elements, others five, six, or seven. The qualities assigned to different elements and directions are often different. Protocol and etiquette are decidedly different. The spirits and their areas of influence and the assignment of "masculine" and "feminine" qualities are inconsistent. Eventually, however, I began to focus on one question: Are the elements and qualities I know and value being honored in the altar or shrine arrangement and ceremony? I understand that some traditions map the sacred universe with water represented in the East. When I am participating in those ceremonies, I can shift my frame of reference easily enough. When I arrange objects in a ceremonial manner, I place water in the West and don't concern myself with foolish questions like which tradition is better or more authentic. The only thing to remember is that what gives shrines and altars their power is your knowledge and understanding of the cosmological map or spirit world-view upon which they are based. An arrangement without a map might look like a shrine or altar, but it will simply be a display.

The second way of developing your ability to arrange objects in a sacred or magical manner is to trust the intuitive guidance that comes from dreams, shamanic journeys, or vision-shifting. This is the path based on the idea that if you don't know the map (if one wasn't passed on to you from a family member, a master, or a teacher) you must uncover it on your own. Incubate a dream to tell you how to lay out a collection of objects. Make a journey to the upper or lower worlds to learn ways of creating shrines or altars. We create these arrangements to please and honor the spirit world anyway; we might as well find out what they like firsthand. Or, you might move into the relaxed, meditative state I've described as vision-shifting and just begin playing with the arrangement of your objects until you feel your way to a correct alignment and orientation.

With a shrine, it's not so important to have an underlying map or orientation. For an altar, the fundamental pattern upon which you mark points with objects is more important. In either case it's important to have established some relationship with an object or image before adding it to a shrine or altar. It's easy to throw a large number of beautiful objects together and create something that looks shrinelike; but for a shrine or altar to have real power, you should understand the meaning each object has for you before incorporating it into an arrangement. This is not to say that we don't come to know the objects in our arrangements better over time, but rather that we are better off beginning with simple shrines and altars and allowing their complexity to evolve in tandem with our understanding.

ELEMENTAL SHRINES AND ALTARS

Developing an energetic sensitivity to the way objects
wish to be arranged helps ensure that you are not
simply exerting your will or your ego in your work as a
builder of sacred altars.

IT'S beyond the scope of this book to cover the many different wisdom traditions, but there are some basic models with which to begin to experiment. In the last exercise, you gathered a series of objects representing the elements of earth, air, fire, and water. For this next exercise, you will use these objects and supplement them with others as you practice sacred arrangement.

Gather your elemental objects and any other sacred or special objects that you would like to work with in creating an arrangement. In your dream artist's journal, sketch or draw a symbol for each object or image. Give each object or image a name (moonlight candle, wind-rider feather, stone of sorrow). Be romantic and playful. Be mysterious. If a name doesn't come to you immediately, set the object aside and return to it later. Use the vision-shifting techniques described in Chapter 3 to listen for a name or more deeply understand an object. Record your observations about each object. What is it for? What does it represent for you? Where does it come from? Listen for its story. Try to distinguish how one elemental object for fire is subtly different from another. Reflect that difference in the title or in your observations. When you've completed this task, you should understand what each of the objects you are going to arrange means to you.

When creating a shrine or altar pattern, you can mark that pattern with pebbles, sticks, paint, shells, sand, or anything else that defines the area. Your objects—the things you've collected—can then be placed within this pattern. To create a shrine or altar arrangement, you can immerse yourself in the arranging first or you can visualize the map and pattern first. If you arrange first, you will still need to address the pattern that you've discovered and process it in your journal. If you choose to visualize a pattern first, you might work from the following possibilities.

• *The dragon line*—is a collection of like or related objects displayed in a linear pattern through which energy is directed or channeled. Line up your like elements and play with what order feels right. Consider visual characteristics like ascending or descending height to create a sense of rising up or sinking down. A shrine to abundance might begin small at one end and increase in size at the other. A shrine to aid someone's fight against cancer might begin with large objects at one end and progressively smaller ones at the other end. The objects themselves might range from decayed to healthy. A collection of seven objects representing the classical chakras and their energies might be organized by color and convey an intention to raise energy within the body.

• *The web of life*—a collection of objects that radiate out from a central point, good for dispersing energy into the world. One of the most interesting variations on this arrangement that I've seen is the community altar. Imagine placing an object that holds your particular energy in the center of a cloth. Radiating outward from the center would be objects holding the energy for your closest circle—those to whom you feel most connected. In some cases, this might be family, but you might also have friends in this circle as well. The proximity of objects to the central object would reflect the closeness of the relationship. Moving out in concentric rings might be objects representing friends, colleagues, acquaintances, or old friends with whom your contact has lessened. Look for connections between objects/individuals in the different rings and arrange them accordingly to create radiating arms. This is a powerful altar for maintaining contact and balance with relationships.

• *The honeycomb*—collections in clearly defined spaces such as printers' boxes or other divided containers. This keeps the objects in relationship with each other without fully activating their energetic potential. When I want to arrange and display objects without weaving them into relationship to each other, I use divided containers. In fact, I'm particularly drawn to divided containers. I like the sense of order they bring and how they help me manage the collections I find or create. I have a small antique cabinet with eight drawers. I've lined these with felt and use each one for a collection of a certain type. I have glass-covered tables with compartments for a series of hand-painted ceramic fish and arrowheads.

• *The sacred wheel*—a pattern similar to the web of life, but more formal. It incorporates personal symbols and values into a circular or spiral pattern that can be marked with stones, shells, or almost any combination of found objects or images. This is a good pattern for focusing energy and attention. The native American medicine wheel has twelve spokes representing the months of the year. Creating an altar in this fashion allows you to reflect on what has occurred in your recent past and to plan energetically for your future.

• *The world tree*—a design that owes its arrangement to the fractal geometry of natural branching forms. It's a kind of sacred Christmas tree, decorated with objects of power and intention according to the pattern of lower, middle, and upper worlds. Hang objects that symbolize your core gifts and talents and perhaps your primal concerns low on the tree. Use the middle branches to support objects representing your material and relationship concerns. Use the upper branches for objects reflecting your spiritual goals and the wisdom of teachers you admire.

• *The spirit mountain*—an outdoor mound shrine that reflects the universal belief in the spirituality of high places. Make a mound of earth or stones and arrange natural objects at different levels symbolizing your spiritual journey.

- *The sacred square*—a square piece of cloth with each of your elemental objects arranged on a different side. All your fire objects would live on one side, all your water objects on another. End up with a side for each element. It doesn't matter so much which side you assign to the elements as long as they are all represented. Think about what the center might represent for you in such a model. What other values would you assign to each side? What is the significance of the corners as intersections of two energies? Drop a pebble directly into the center of the square and see where it bounces. What does this tell you about your current state?

This exercise is really only intended to get you to begin thinking about the possibility of meaningful arrangement. There are an infinite number of patterns upon which to build shrines and altars. Don't limit yourself to indoor shrines. Shrines to the elements or to nature itself are world balancing. Imagine what it would be like to take a walk and discover little half-hidden shrines on your journey. Imagine giving this gift to others.

As with finding and collecting, arranging can be an art form and a path of creative expression complete in itself. I harbor a secret fantasy of someday being old and secure enough in my material needs to indulge my passion for arranging. Like Johnny Appleseed, I would travel from place to place in my community and farther afield building shrines, teaching children and adults to build shrines, and then moving on.

Finding and arranging are core skills for dream artists, but there is more we can do, if we are called to it. The next chapter explores the creation of spirit vessels, temporary homes for spirit and energy, through the techniques of altering and making.

T he gift of this chapter is

manifestation.

Whether you choose to exercise that capacity or not, you have

the ability to give form to spirit. The suggestions and exercises

in this chapter will help you discover that power.

chapter 8

Spirit Vessels: *Practicing* the Arts of *Altering* and Making

In ancient cultures art was the mediator between the human and the world of divine mystery into which consciousness was born. Before the role of priest was relegated to certain individuals, the prayerful power of creativity, whether expressed through dance, chanting, mask making, or painting, was recognized as a personal responsibility. In primal cultures the arts are still essential means of interaction with the divine, and the artifacts created in the service of worship retain an especially powerful presence regardless of their age or condition.

—ADRIANA DIAZ
Freeing the Creative Spirit:
Drawing on the Power of Art to Tap the Magic and Wisdom Within

As dream artists, we reassume personal responsibility for our relationship with the divine. We do this by fully engaging in the sacred creative cycle. This is a breathlike process. Inhale and we are inspired—literally and figuratively filled with the breath of spirit—by attending to our dreams and to the dreamlike states that allow us access to other realities. Exhale and we release spirit into the world—breathing life into the creations we craft and the work we do. In some sense, this is as close as we may come to knowing God as the supreme creator.

As I've worked with both adults and children over the years, it has seemed useful to introduce creative expression through the skills of finding and arranging. These are practices that do not carry with them the burdens and baggage that society has attached to being an Artist. And, while I don't now intend to suggest a hierarchy or a relative scale of value, it does seem that moving into sacred creative consciousness occurs along a continuum. Not everyone, of course, will follow this path, but I have found that finding, arranging, altering, and making flow together in an order that leads one ever deeper into an experience of the sacred creative cycle. When we find objects that reflect the imagery of our dreams, we are doing so by being open and receptive. We allow the energy of an object to speak to us. When we arrange objects, we are using patterns to work with those energies. When we reach a point where we begin subtly adding our own energies to objects, or altering, we have entered into the realm of the talismanic. And, when our energies fully interweave and interpenetrate those of the materials with which we are working, we become the makers of spirit vessels—fragile but beautiful containers for spirit to fill.

As we explore altering and making we are beginning to practice the art of energy exchange. The inner tools we've been refining—intention, attention, and intuition—still serve us well. The intention we set prior to altering or making, the intention we hold during the process, and the intention we breathe into a piece after it's completed, define the power of that piece. Our attention to the surfaces and materials with which we are working ensures that the vessels we craft will attract spirit. The intuitive sense with which we listen for guidance and reconnect with our original inspiration make our pieces sacred tools.

Outfitting: Sacred Symbols

SACRED SYMBOLS ARE markings or patterns of special significance. They are important because they are shorthand for our intentions. They hold energy in a thing or an image. They help spirit recognize the vessels you have prepared. There are a great number of ways we can find sacred symbols. Use the suggestions below to build your own library of sacred symbols.

1. Photocopy and cut and paste symbols from ancient cultures into your dream artist's journal. There are encyclopedias of symbols that are wonderful resources. These can be found in libraries and bookstores.

2. Use trips to museums to copy patterns from ancient civilizations into your journal.

3. Search the internet for glyphs and stone paintings.

4. Use vision-shifting by sitting with a pad of paper and a pen. Get into your relaxed and receptive state. With your eyes half-closed, allow your hand to draw. Be aware of what you are drawing without judging it. When you feel as if you are complete in your expression, review your drawing. Select little elements that seem interesting and recopy them in your journal.

5. Incubate your dreams for a week or longer. Ask to see the sacred symbols that you need to include in your work. When you wake up, record your dream. If you don't recall seeing any symbols, experiment with drawing elements of the dream as simple symbols.

6. Do a shamanic journey to visit the great museum or your own dream artist's studio. Look for your sacred symbols.

7. Be aware of the possibility of seeing sacred symbols or patterns all around you. Act as if the universe was conspiring to give you secret information through your everyday experiences.

Practicing Altering:
The Art of Amulets and Talismans

I dream I'm following a path that runs parallel to the sea along a cliff. I come to a man standing next to a pile of shiny black stones. He's not wearing a shirt, and I can see old scars down his back as if he's been whipped. He is broad shouldered and muscular. Every so often he picks up a stone and with a grunt of exertion hurls it far out into the ocean. After awhile a woman comes up and watches the man in silence. We do not speak, but she seems very sad. The stone-throwing man says nothing but looks at her and gestures to the pile. She takes a black stone from her pocket and tosses it into the pile. It's black and shiny like the rest of the stones. She turns to leave, but somehow she seems lighter and younger than she did a few moments before.

I dreamed this dream when a friend lost her only child in an automobile accident. The next day I set an intention to find a black stone for her, and sure enough a piece of smooth obsidian came to me. For me, water is sometimes associated with grieving and stones are containers for memory. These were both strong elements from my dream. I knew that I was to make a gift of the stone to her, but I was still missing one piece. I used a shamanic journey to ask for guidance on how to use the stones and was told the following:

We can only mourn for a finite period of time. Mourning fills us with dense energy and weighs us down. If we are strong we can carry our mourning a long time, longer than we are meant to. Spirits of the departed want to be honored, celebrated, sometimes forgiven, then released. Honoring our dead, remembering them, creates connection and continuity between past, present and future; mourning them overlong merely creates a life-draining bond. Stones can carry the weight of our grief. Releasing that grief into water cleanses us.

I offered the stone to my friend and asked her to carry it with her in the difficult hours, days, weeks, and even months ahead. At some point, I suggested to her, it would feel right to find moving water into which she could throw the stone. This is a ritual release, I explained. It's not forgetting or abandoning your son's memory; it's surrendering the weight of the mourning and grieving process so that you can continue to live your life. She reacted with quiet gratitude to the gift. In the midst of her overwhelming grief, I expected little else. I was not sure if she would be able to follow the instructions I had been guided to give her, but I gave the stone with the best intention for helping her heal.

I later learned from her that she had kept the stone for about six months, stroking and rubbing it when she felt the darkness of her despair most acutely. One day, however, she knew it was time to let the stone go. She drove out on a bridge and threw the stone into water. She found herself crying again, as she relived all the pain, but something shifted in that moment, and she realized that she was going to go on with her life.

The black obsidian stone I gave my friend was a mourning stone, a kind of talisman. Talismans and amulets are similar but different. Both are usually worn or carried. They are, at the very minimum, portable. Both are intended to affect the waking world by influencing the unseen world of spirit. The more traditional definition of amulets is that they are simple found objects—usually unadorned and unaltered—but they may also be crafted and intricately detailed pieces. Talismans are almost always crafted, sometimes by bringing together a carefully selected set of materials, other times by marking and engraving. The distinguishing element between the two that I find more useful is that amulets are designed to affect the wearer more generally and more broadly, bringing healing, good luck, prosperity, protection, or fertility. Talismans, on the other hand, are designed for more specific and narrow purposes, such as success in a particular endeavor. For this reason, I call an object like the little black mourning stone I gave my friend a talisman. It was selected and intended for a specific and focused purpose.

Talismans and amulets were the earliest art forms to explore the energetic or spiritually sensitive combining of materials. When magic was the technology by which the world was understood, the principle of sympathetic connection was a guiding principle. In an animated world, if a tree has a particular spirit, a piece of that tree—the leaf, bark, root, or wood—also contains the spirit. Marking a piece of that tree's wood with a stain made of crushed berries or a white hot stone applied a pattern that further refined the purpose of the piece and gave the wearer some control over the power. Binding the piece of wood to a stone taken reverently from a sacred site brought the spirit of the tree and the spirit of the stone into proximity. Adding the feathers of a specific bird mixed in yet another spirit power. Found objects, when modified and combined with other found objects, are the province of the dream artist as one who alters.

The easiest way to think about adding altering to your creative practice is to consider four ways of altering: marking, wrapping, carving, or combining objects in significant ways. Marking is the addition of symbols of personal or cultural significance to an object or image. Marking can be done with pen, pencil, charcoal, paint, adhesive bonded images, metallic leaf, etching acids, or carving tools. Wrapping is the binding of energy. It can be done with raffia, vines, leaves, flower petals, sinew, leather, twine, thread, or wire. Carving is the release of energetic form from a material. When the sculptor Michelangelo spoke of releasing the figure from the stone, this was the energetic act he was describing. Carving can be done on soft materials, such as clay, wax, or wood, or it can be applied to stone or metal. The fourth process for altering is combining. When we join two objects together, whether through wrapping, tying, binding, or fusing through heat, we are augmenting and boosting the energy of each of the pieces. This is a variation of the chemical wedding described by alchemists.

A dream artist might create a spirit vessel by using one or any combination of these processes. Some pieces might take advantage of all four approaches. Intention and attention are critical when practicing finding. The art of arranging builds on these skills and introduces more reliance on intuition. Altering requires that we dance back and forth between knowledge and intuition. To make art in a sacred manner, you must bring materials and the elements of an image together with purpose and at some level of understanding. This may be an intuitive process at the outset, in which you play with combinations of materials, patterns, and designs, but initial intuition does not eliminate your responsibility for the piece you create. You must understand what you're creating before you create it, as you create it, and after you create it.

If you are going to mark objects with paint or chisel, you should understand what your marks mean. If you wrap and bind materials, you should understand the energetic nature of the materials you're wrapping, as well as the wrapping itself. How does wrapping a stone in silk modify its qualities? If you carve something, what are you releasing? And if you combine two or more materials, what is the new sound they make?

I taught a workshop once in which a woman wanted to make a piece of art reflecting her intention for her relationship to her husband. Following a guided meditation and a vision-shifting exercise, she found two unique stones, one to represent her energy and one for her husband's, and begin wrapping them and binding them together with copper wire. She used copper wire for conductivity and crafted a nest out of twigs and feathers in which the stones would rest. She had reasons for everything she did, but her intuition told her that the piece felt forced. It represented what she thought she wanted rather than what was necessarily right for either herself or her husband. She unbound her stones and started over. Finding a piece of driftwood, she cleaned it and enlarged two indentations to hold the stones. She wrapped the center of the piece of wood with many coils of carefully aligned copper wire, until it looked almost batterylike. She pressed the copper wire into a crease in the wood so that one end ran to one indentation and the opposite ran to the other. The piece at rest, with two polished white stones sitting in their places at either end of the piece of driftwood, linked by copper wire, was not only more aesthetically pleasing, it was also a healthier intention for her relationship. It suggested balance and union of choice rather than union of desperation.

As with all the techniques and approaches we've discussed so far, the best way to learn these techniques for altering is to try them.

---— ⠿⠿ ——---

GIFT STONES

Learning to mark an object with pattern and design
gives you the capacity to empower an object, as you
will see in this exercise.

O NE simple form of altering is marking. Marking can increase or focus the energy of an object. In chapters 3 and 7 you practiced finding
and reading simple stones. You can build upon this work by creating
something I call gift stones. To do this, select a small pebble. Sometimes
I use a found stone, sometimes I intuitively select a stone from a collection of polished river stones I have. Try to select a small stone that can
be easily carried in a pocket. Vision-shift or use dreaming to match the
right stone to the energy you wish it to carry. The next step is to actually
mark the stone. Marking focuses your intention around the energy of the
stone and increases the stone's capacity to hold that energy.

To select the appropriate symbols, begin with your journal. Fill a
page with symbols that are important to you. Write down what each of
them means to you. After you've exhausted your supply of familiar symbols, begin to doodle. Draw symbols you like. Assign a meaning to each
of these symbols. Don't worry about whether they would be understood
by anyone else. Over a period of two weeks, incubate the request to see
important symbols in your dreams. Add these symbols to your collection. If there are any that baffle you, use a shamanic journey to better
understand the meaning of certain symbols.

Have you identified symbols that would serve to mark positive intentions, such as safety, prosperity, luck, or love? Select one of these
symbols and apply it to the pebble. If you have the tools and the skill, it
is sometimes possible to carve simple designs into pebbles. The easiest
path would be to paint it on with acrylic or enamel paint. Another option
would be to use a gold or silver metallic paint pen to draw your symbol. I
sometimes use gold leafing to apply symbols. It's actually an easy
process. The materials come in kits from art supply stores. All you do is
paint your design with the milky white adhesive size (I sometimes draw

my symbol in pencil first, then paint over it). When the white size dries and turns clear, take a little bit of the gold leaf tissue and lay it over the surface. First brush it into contact with the size, then burnish with a soft cloth. The leaf will adhere only where you painted the size. Finish with a clear protective coat and you have a beautiful Journey Stone to give as a gift. Wrap it in a leaf or flower petal and tie it with a piece of raffia to give it away.

RAINBOW DREAMING STAFF

Wrapping and binding—as you will see in this
exercise—helps us to ceremonially bring together two
energies or to bind an energy into an object.

SOMETIMES what people need in their lives is joyous, unbounded energy. A "rainbow dreaming staff" (or wand, or branch—you can customize the size to fit your vision) is both a symbol of and a container for ebullient energy. It uses the method of wrapping to bind an intention firmly into an artifact.

To begin with, you will need to select a stout branch or stick. For a staff, look for something five to six feet tall. For a wand, find something shorter and thinner. You can do this with commercially milled dowels instead of sticks, but I don't think they hold the same level of energy. I like irregularly shaped pieces of wood because of the personality they convey. I also try to avoid cutting live wood when I can help it. If you live in the country, finding downed branches will present no problem. In more developed areas, check what your neighbors put out for yard waste pick-up. Clean your stick and remove any loose bark. Trim off any branches or protrusions that need to go.

Next, gather wrapping material. Some options to consider are:

- Brightly colored string
- Yarns in different colors

- Heavy thread, if the wand is small and light
- Cloth ribbon (from a fabric store, not the ribbon used for wrapping gifts)
- Dyed raffia (found at craft stores)
- Colorful fabric scraps cut into long thin pieces (1 inch wide)
- Felt cut into thin strips ($\frac{1}{4}$ to $\frac{1}{2}$ inch wide)
- Copper or gold wire or cord with a metallic finish of various thickness as an accent.

Consider working with scraps of string or thread pulled from frayed fabric ends. Rescue cloth scraps that people throw out. Find pieces of wrapping material that have stories behind them or come from exotic places. You can mix and incorporate all of the materials you find or stick with one thickness of wrapping for consistency.

Next gather scissors, white glue, a brush, your stick, and all your wrapping materials. Spend some time handling each of the wrappings you've found. Think about the kinds of energy that you would like to bind into the stick. Are there any colors or qualities of the wrappings that suggest those energies? Beginning at the bottom of your stick, paint a light coat of white glue to cover as much area as you think you can mindfully wrap before it begins to dry. I usually paint about ten inches at a time. Select a wrapping material and tie it on. Fix the intention you want to bind into the piece and begin wrapping as neatly and precisely as you can. Do this wrapping slowly, as if you were saying a prayer with each revolution.

When you reach the end of your scrap or when you decide to shift colors, tie on the next scrap with a square knot, leaving a dangling piece long enough to tie something on to the end. Continue to paint with the white glue and wrap until the entire staff is covered. You can wrap in one neat layer, or you can overwrap and bundle. If your staff is wrapped in fabric strips, consider overwrapping with colored string or ribbon. Finish the staff by tying small objects to the loose wrapping ends. Found objects, feathers, beads, bells, noisemakers, bits of other wrapping materials, or natural objects can further enhance the energies bound into the staff.

If the staff is for you or even if it's to be given as a gift, allow yourself the opportunity to dream with it first. This is like taking it for a test journey in the dreaming world. Set an intention to dream about the staff. Record what you remember about your dream and make it part of the gift you give.

DREAM FETISH

*Learning to make physical representations of the
energy we wish to manifest, as you will do in this
exercise, helps us be more effective in the world.*

THIS exercise brings together all the methods of altering to create a spirit vessel for the essence of a dream. A fetish is not merely a representation of a dream, it is the carefully crafted container for the essence of that dream. This is why in tribal cultures fetish objects are considered living beings.

Begin in your dreams. Incubate the following question by writing it down in your journal and repeating it to yourself before falling asleep: *What is my power?* Write your dream down the next morning. Repeat the process over several days looking for the strongest or most significant dream imagery. Select a dream to work from. Answer the following questions in your journal:

- What am I trying to do in the dream?
- What is the conflict or question in my dream?
- How do I respond to the conflict or answer the question?
- Where do I end up in the dream?

Don't analyze the meaning of the dream or judge your actions. Simply record your answers. You may find objects for this piece in four separate walks or in one long walk, but if you don't find what feels right to you, don't force it. This is what you are looking for:

1. Find a piece of a tree. It might be driftwood, a branch, a large piece of bark, or a cut slab. Try to avoid taking living wood. This is your map. It represents what you are trying to do in the dream. Select one end as the starting point of the dream and the other as the finishing point. Signify these points by carving, wrapping, or marking each end. Make sure you remember which is the beginning and which is the ending.

2. Select a found object or material to serve as the conflict or question that stands between you and your goal. Attach it somewhere on the branch.

3. Find one found object (stone, shell, nut, seedpod, etc.) to represent yourself in the dream and a second found object to represent your way of dealing with the conflict or answering the question. Decide how you will join the object representing your way of dealing with the conflict to the object representing you. Remember not to judge or evaluate that way of dealing with the dream conflict.

4. Bind the object representing yourself and your way of dealing with the dream conflict to the branch at whatever point you feel drawn to.

Feel free to use any materials you choose to do the binding, marking, carving, or combining. Incorporate materials that suggest the elements or feelings the dream contained. Embellish your fetish until it begins to take on its own personality. Hold the fetish you've made while you use your journal to answer the following questions. Write quickly and don't censor yourself.

- How am I like this piece of wood?
- How am I like the found object or material representing the conflict or question?

- How am I like the object representing me?
- How am I like the object representing my dream strategy for dealing with conflict?
- Where or what is the strength in each of these objects?

You may, at this point, be near to an answer to what your power is. Keep in mind that your power can be revealed in how you acted or in how others reacted to you in the dream. Your power can be in the things you learned or understood, even if you were not yet able to enact them.

The final step is to incubate another dream using your dream power fetish. This time, ask the fetish itself what your power is, as if it had the answer. Expect an answer. Sleep with the fetish on the left side of your bed. Record your dreams the next day. You now have the answer to this question.

A psychologist might say that you used active imagination, journaling, and introspection to tap into your psyche. A shaman would say that you carefully created a place for spirit to dwell in material form, and, in gratitude, that spirit helped you answer an important question.

It is important to remember that a fetish created for one person is not easily or appropriately transferred to another. I can make a fetish *for* you, but I cannot simply give you one I've made for myself. Also, fetish objects should be disposed of with the same care and intention that went into their creation. Ritually burn the elements, bury them, cast them into moving water, or carefully disassemble and return them to nature.

T he exercises described above use projects as a way of introducing ways of working. I selected these exercises because the end product was either an energetic and healing gift to give another or a useful tool for your own development a dream artist. But the exercises are also meant to set you on your own journey of creative discovery. You may find that painting or drawing directly on found objects is more satisfying than painting or drawing on any flat traditional surface. One of my grandmothers painted scenes on sand dollars and seashells. My other grandmother painted scenes in elaborately jeweled ostrich eggs. I know a woman who immerses porous stones in essential oils. Even after being cleaned and sun-dried, they still give off a wonderful scent when warmed in the hands. Permanent inks, natural dyes, and fabric paints are good for marking. Wood-burning tools are an easy way to get symbols and patterns onto found wood pieces. Pieces can be marked with words or simple phrases. Images can be applied to objects with decoupage solution.

You might be drawn to wrapping. The artist Christo has wrapped buildings, bridges, and even whole sections of rugged seashore. His works are epic in scale, but temporary. I like the look of wrapped things, but even more I find there is something deeply moving in the gesture of wrapping. Wrapping, coiling, and covering things is a kind of meditation for me. Buddhists use mala beads to pray, Catholics use the rosary, but my devotional practice is in my art. Consider creating gift bundles of found stones and natural objects wrapped in a beautiful piece of fabric. A high school student of mine returned from a weekend on the Outer Banks of North Carolina with a scallop shell for me. It was filled with tiny stones, shells, and bones she had collected. It was wrapped in a tiny bundle and made a simple but beautiful gift. Consider what energy might be enhanced by wrapping an object in handmade rice fiber paper with a glue solution to mold the paper close to the shape of the object it covers.

For some people carving is both mystery and revelation. It's the whole journey condensed into one artifact. More than likely, however, you will end up at the strategy of combining. You will begin by mixing several techniques, but you will progress to the point where you are combining as a way of altering, teetering on the verge of making.

And making is where we move now.

Practicing Making:
The Art of Transformation

THE ART OF MAKING is a drawing together of skills. Making combines finding, arranging, and altering in the creation of a new artifact or image. Those who make, transforming raw materials into works of living things of spirit and energy with a skill that seems nothing less than magical, may draw, paint, craft in mixed media, sculpt, or model. Making often requires a greater commitment of time and personal energy, but beyond that there is nothing that restricts anyone from making as an expression of creative consciousness.

Creating a spirit vessel from raw materials, whether it's an image or an object, is such a large subject that addressing it in a single book would be difficult. The range of media, the plethora of techniques, the variety of possible projects is immense. For our purposes, however, it may help to remember what it is that makes the work of a dream artist different.

First of all, a dream artist's work is part of a sacred creative cycle. The refined vibration of spirit is slowed down enough to take form on the physical plane, then is accelerated through ceremony to carry us back into the dreaming. In practice this means that dream states and nonordinary reality are used as source and resource for the creative process. Ceremony is part of a dream artist's creative work. Materials, objects, images and their relationship to one another are considered energetically, for the spirit they contain and the potential they have for holding spirit. Finally, a dream artist brings a heightened level of intention to his or her work. If you are living some or all of these principles in your creative practice, your choice of media, the techniques you use, even the particular projects you choose will serve you, your community, and the planet admirably.

Before taking on a new project, especially when you are creating spirit vessels from raw materials, it is important to set an intention. How do I want my work to affect me, my community, or the planet? Do I want this piece to be healing—to bring wholeness? Do I want it to be empowering—to increase a capacity? Do I want it to be instructive—to reveal truth and illuminate vision? Do I want it to enchant—to bring magic and soul balance?

Sometimes a piece of art, if done with intention, with spirit guidance, with rigor, and with discipline can accomplish all four goals. "Soul painting" is such a project and if I had to select one exercise, one example of making, to reveal its potential, it would be this.

SOUL PAINTING

To begin from a void of blank paper and create an image always changes you. Once you have done this exercise, you will have no doubt that you are a dream artist.

I dream I'm standing beside a beautiful old Victorian country house. There is a path from the back of the house down to a boathouse on a lake. A door opens and an old woman emerges walking slowly and unsteadily. She wears a yellow frilly dress and a straw hat with flowers and a veil. I can't see her face, but I can tell that she is very old. I also feel that she was once very beautiful and is still elegant and handsome in her old age. She is escorted patiently by a young man. He walks her down the steps and slowly down the path to the boathouse. They pass me as if I am a ghost—without acknowledging me. I know, without being told, that she is going to have her soul portrait made.

The scene shifts to a memorial service being held in a library or bookstore. Everyone is whispering and the questions I hear are "Has she passed on?" and "Will she be alright?" They are both confusing questions for what I understand to be a memorial service for the old woman I had just seen. I'm able to tell everyone I meet that yes, she will be fine because she had her soul portrait painted.

I woke from this dream thinking about what a soul portrait might look like. I had the feeling that it was a summation of a life, but that it didn't necessarily signal the end of a life, only a transition. I couldn't get it out of my mind, and I began experimenting with the idea of doing soul paintings in my classes and workshops. I researched the idea further through shamanic journeys and dreamwork. This is what I learned about soul painting.

⁂ Soul Painting Requirements

- Time: This process can take several weeks. I think it actually helps to spread it out over a month or two. Soul painting is something you should do during a time of transition when you have the liberty and the space to be introspective.
- Floor space: You need to be able to spread a 3-foot by 6-foot painting surface out on the floor and still walk around it. You needn't leave it all the time, but you will want to leave it to dry between painting sessions.
- Help: You will need an assistant for one task—tracing an outline of your body.
- Surface: You can paint on anything you can find that is large enough. You'll need at least 3 by 6 feet of surface. White or brown craft paper that comes in big rolls will work. Stretched or unstretched canvas will also work. You can paint on plywood, paneling, or refrigerator cardboard. The two factors to consider are permanence (how long do you want it to last?) and fear (how intimidating is it to work on professional materials?). If you are painting on canvas, you will need to gesso it (paint it with a special white paste found in art supply stores). If you are painting on plywood or paneling, you should seal both sides with a base color of acrylic or latex paint.
- Paints: If you are painting on paper or cardboard, use tempera paints. They're less expensive, they clean up with water, and they dry fast. If you're painting on more permanent surfaces, you might want to paint with acrylics. They appear a bit brighter and the colors can appear richer after they dry due to the fact that

---

OFFICIAL SOUL PAINTING DISCLAIMER

D*oing a soul painting is like living your life; it can be deeply rewarding, but some days it will be agonizing. You will be painting over
good stuff. You'll go through remorse and regret for how your painting
looked before you messed it up. The good news is that if you faithfully follow my directions, you can blame the ruin of your masterpiece on me. You
may love your finished product. You may learn something essential about
yourself and your soul from your finished product. These experiences may,
however, be mutually exclusive. Just remember to breathe.*

---

they dry with a semi-gloss finish (tempera paints dry to a chalky finish). Acrylics also come premixed in more colors. Generally speaking, it doesn't work well to mix the two types paints. Watercolors would be way too expensive for a project like this, and they don't offer the ability to layer. Oil paints work, but they're much messier. Unless you're already painting in oils and are convinced you must paint your soul portrait in oils, avoid them for this project.

- Brushes: Some fat ones, some skinny ones, some tiny ones for details.
- Other materials: crayons, pencils, colored markers, little bottles of dimensional fabric paints, glitter, rhinestones, white glue, stencils, a compass or circles to trace, scissors.

⁂ The 10 Steps of Soul Painting

Step 1. Lay your painting surface out on the floor. Light candles. Light incense. Put on relaxing music. Take your shoes off. Wear something form fitting, or wear as little clothing as your modesty will allow. Lay down on the paper on your back. Think about the silhouette you create. Stretch. Relax onto the surface. When you are ready, ask a sympathetic friend to trace your body outline carefully in pencil. Ask them to do this slowly. Imagine your boundaries being marked in this slow delineation. Sit up and examine your outline. If it's irregular in ways that have nothing to do with your own shape, redraw it. Fix parts of the drawing if you want to. When you are pleased, finalize the outline in pen. With a pencil, draw a small circle with a compass (2 to 3 inches across) at the crown of the head, the forehead, the throat, the heart, the solar plexus, just below the navel, and in the genital area. Draw five larger circles (5 to 6 inches across) anywhere outside of the body outline.

Step 2. Lie on the floor next to your outline. Using colored pencils, crayons, markers, or other drawing media, map the following events from the life of your physical body. Go back as far as you can remember. Draw little pictures, use your own symbols, write words, draw lines and borders, make notes and date things if you'd like to.

- Where have you been wounded or injured?
- Where have illnesses manifested in your body?
- Where are you ticklish?
- Where do you feel it when you know something is true?
- How many times has your heart been broken?
- Where does anger hide in your body?
- Where does joy emerge from in your body?
- What five places does sexual energy pass through when you're aroused? Number them in order.
- Where do you hide disappointment in your body?
- Where are you most old?
- Where are you still young?
- What places on your body are off-limits?
- What path does creative energy take in your body from seed to expression?
- What part or parts of your body has someone ever complimented?
- Which compliment pleases you most?

Step 3. Go back through your dream journal. Note any dreams that specifically involved your body or body parts. This might include dreams of being naked, dreams of being injured or attacked, erotic dreams, dreams of bodily processes, dreams of extraordinary physical achievement or restricted physical capacity, or even dreams where you were aware of a certain part of your body. Add these dreams as pictures, annotations, or symbols in places that feel relevant.

Step 4. Trying to ignore what you might or might not know about chakras, look at each of the seven small circles and write the first word that pops into your mind inside each circle.

Step 5. In the large circles outside the body outline, write, draw, or create a symbol to represent the five greatest achievements of your life to date. Draw a line from the achievement to the part of your body most responsible for that achievement.

Step 6. Add the following information in whatever form feels right. Remember that the form this takes is up to you. It may be very specific and very textual or it may be very abstract. If you want to add additional information or answer questions I haven't asked, trust your intuition.

- What have you longed for that you haven't received?
- Whom do you love?
- Who loves you?
- To what have you given birth?
- What are your most embarrassing secrets? (As soon as you write them out, color over them to hide them. All that matters is that they're there.)
- How do you imagine your death?
- What lasting thing will you leave behind?

Step 7. Now it's time to explore inner space. Find some time when you won't be disturbed. Put on your favorite trance-inducing music. Dim the lights. Lay down on your body outline, close your eyes, breathe slowly and deeply, and make the following journey. Slowly tense and relax your feet, calves, thighs, buttocks, abdomen, chest, hands, forearms, upper arms, shoulders, neck, and face.

Feel your body getting heavy and sinking into the ground beneath you. Feel yourself floating up out of your body. Float up through the ceiling, through the roof, up into the sky. Float higher and higher. Turn and look down. Beneath you is a primal landscape. Where your body once was is now grass-covered mound. Return to this mound and experience how big it is and how high. There may be trees growing out of it. There may be fallen stone and shrubbery. Look for an ancient entrance to this mound. It may be in the foot, the belly, the hand, or the head. It will be different for everyone. Find your entrance and descend into the mound. What you discover is an ancient temple complex within the space that was once your body. Explore this space. What do you see?

When you are ready, return to your physical body, remembering how to access this space for future visits. Record your journey in words and pictures on or around your body outline.

Step 8. Once you're familiar with accessing this body temple, I'd like you to return there on different journeys on different days with the following objectives.

1. Find a guide and ask that you be shown the patterns your energy body makes. Don't worry about whether there are enough of them or they match what you already know about energy bodies. You are mapping how your aura or nonphysical body glows or radiates. Return and draw these patterns as outlines.

2. Investigate the places within the temple that correspond to places in your body that are in pain or are diseased. What can you learn from the inside? Is there any work you can do from the inside? Record what you discover.

3. Ask your guide to show you the soul painting of you that hangs in the temple. This is the optimal you—the best you that you could ever be. This is the blueprint from which your soul is trying to direct your life on earth. How different is it from your sense of who you are? What can you do to grow into this inner soul portrait?

Step 9. Now it's time to paint. At first it will be exhilarating, then it can be frustrating. If you stay with the painting, you'll move past that and reach the point where it will be illuminating. I actually have very few instructions at this point. Just start painting. Paint every square inch of surface with some color of paint (yes, I consider white and black colors). You can paint within the lines you've drawn or ignore them. You can elaborate on the pictures and symbols you've drawn or paint as if they weren't there. You can paint neatly and precisely or wild and sloppy. Just paint. Let the information you've recorded and the notes you've made guide and influence you, but feel free to move in new directions. Mix colors on the surface. Paint with your fingers and toes if you want to. Paint with abandon. Paint to exhaustion. Stop. Rest. Take a day off—take two. Then come back and paint some more. Pay attention to the shapes emerging from your surface. What words or images lie under those layers of paint. What forms are bubbling to the surface. Elaborate on these new forms. As you paint, vision-shift to see the energetic pattern of the things you are painting. Look with x-ray vision beneath the surface of the paint. Journey back into the temple as necessary. Keep breathing.

Step 10. Repeat Step 9 until you reach that moment of illumination or understanding. You'll know when it happens. Through this process, pieces of your soul will seem to be returning to you. Things you had forgotten will resurface. Narrow your focus. Paint detail now. Add found objects and other materials to your painting. Hang it up. Step back from it. Don't judge the painting. Instead, review the process.

Being a dream artist is not just a formula for making art. Dream artists share certain concerns, but they are not defined by just one characteristic, rather, by four: the source of their imagery, the expressive form their imagery takes, their level of energetic sensitivity to materials, and their progress on the path of the dream artist.

They tend to use deep interior space—the dreaming—as their source, but they may tap into it in different ways. Some will mine the imagery of their night dreams. Others will explore the dream landscape through conscious techniques. Still others will access nonordinary reality in waking moments of flow, concentration, or reverie. Some dream artists use all three methods. As you explore this path, you'll choose the methods most useful to your practice.

The expressive form dream artists' imagery and artifacts take differs as well. Most dream artists use some combination of finding, altering, arranging, and/or making. These archetypal ways of thinking about manifesting dreams are flexible and inclusive enough to cross a variety of media. Your work may start out *looking* like another artist's work or the work of a specific culture. But, if you are true to the dreaming, your work will begin to take on an appearance that reflects the unique nature of its spirit.

Dream artists tend to value the energetic component of their work. This is not to say that they don't care what their work looks like, but their primary concern is what a piece means and what it is intended to do. They make art that has purpose. Shamanic dream art might be a map, a marker, a tool, a charm, or a teaching, but it is not mere decoration.

Finally, dream artists are defined, as are we all, by the point on the path at which they find themselves. Not everyone fully embraces each of these defining characteristics at once.

W e've explored the sacred creative cycle from spirit into matter, but to complete the cycle we have to examine how the art we make can, through communal and ceremonial work, carry us back into the realm of spirit.

The gift of this chapter is

connection.

Ceremony and creating healing artwork on behalf of others

weaves you into the fabric of a community of spirit. The

suggestions and exercises in this chapter will help you explore

your capacity to give gifts within a sacred container of

ceremony.

chapter 9

Healing Gifts:
Art and *Ceremony*

How does this rebirth of art and healing manifest itself in the outer world?
First, now there are artists, musicians, and dancers making healing art
purposely. A large body of work of this type is accumulating. This art heals by
freeing the artist's own healing energy and resonating their body, mind, and
spirit. Next, the artist can make a piece of art to heal another person. The
artist can do it specifically for one person or for a group of people. This is
transpersonal healing. It connects one to another; it is an art of
interconnection. The third type of art heals the world. The artist makes a piece
that works with the energy of a whole system, whether it be a neighborhood, an
ecosystem, or the planet itself. This art can be ceremonial, environmental,
performance, or static. It involves the community. It involves energy and
movement. It is truly shamanic; it balances the world.

—MICHAEL SAMUELS, M.D. AND MARY ROCKWOOD LANE, R.N., M.S.N.
Creative Healing: How to Heal Yourself by Tapping Your Hidden Creativity

The creative arts in healing movement that Samuels and Lane describe in their book, *Creative Healing,* is the work of dream artists. It's not art therapy in the traditional sense, though it is affecting and has been influenced by the practice of art therapy. It's more closely aligned with the emerging spirit-mind-body paradigm in medicine, and its power and promise is something that you—as a dream artist—have the ability to bring to your community and to those you love.

Hailed as a kind of discovery, this awareness that the mental and spiritual vitality of an individual is as important a factor in overcoming disease and injury as is the repair of the physical system is really more of a rediscovery. This wisdom has always been with us, but until recently it was deliberately suppressed by a mechanistic medical model into which it did not fit. Now, physicians like Larry Dossey are openly exploring the power of prayer and faith on healing. And well-known doctors and authors like Herbert Benson, Dean Ornish, and John Kabat Zinn advocate the mind-relaxing practice of meditation, while Jeanne Achterberg writes about the power of visualization and internal imagery to affect healing in the body. The placebo effect, a patient's belief in the efficacy of a doctor or a treatment, once seen as an anomalous by-product of scientific drug testing, is now a significant area of study in its own right. This is shamanic wisdom. Though it has been threatened by the cultural empiricism of a mechanistic worldview, it has never completely gone away. Its renaissance today takes many forms—therapeutic touch, bioenergetic healing, reiki, breathwork, ecstatic dance, plant spirit medicine, sound healing, contemporary shamanic counseling, and a long list of practices that have come to be known as alternative or complementary medicine.

Though no one has yet described the exact mechanism by which creative expression triggers a healing response, we do have some ideas. Imagery, whether it's the imagery we create, observe, or imagine, seems to affect our autonomic nervous system. If that imagery is positive and affirming, the messages sent by our nervous system induce a relaxation response in the body. Hormones shift to a healing mode. Blood flow and immune system response is enhanced. Neurotransmitters and endorphins that reduce pain are released in the body. In addition, when one focuses on creative expression, there is a sense of being carried away. Priorities shift, hope and affirmative life values are brought to the foreground of consciousness. Healing imagery is released and one feels newly empowered. Perhaps the best explanation, however, comes from an artist. In *Creative Healing,* Samuels and Lane quote the artist Gordon Onslow Ford. "And when we pray, when we travel inward and see, we can bring back traces of pure spirit. These footprints are art. Art is the voice of the spirit. And when the spirit is freed, when the spirit is seen and heard, the inner healer is released."

Our western, rational, linear culture has made great advances in technology and science, but the cost has been the sacrifice of our connection to the magic and soul and beauty of the dreaming consciousness. As shamans, as dream artists, we have the ability to restore balance, to heal this rift between waking and dreaming, the rational and the irrational, magic and science. To do this, we begin the work of healing ourselves. The dream artist has the capability to heal or shift energy through his or her artwork. If you've been practicing the exercises in this book or using them to influence your own artistic practice, you've probably already begun to experience these things. But it's also possible to heal and affect the energy systems of others.

In the last chapter I described an exercise called "soul painting." This work is a kind of personal creative soul recovery. And, while it is a highly effective process for personal growth and empowerment, it is also possible to do soul paintings for others. There are differences, of course, in how the work is done. In a soul painting done for another person, there is much more reliance on intuitive and spirit guidance, and much less dependence on personal history. Much more emphasis is also placed on the appearance of the finished product. When soul painting for myself, the look of the actual painting is less important because I have the transforming memory of the process. When I soul paint for another, I must consider aesthetics as a kind of point of access for the viewer. Just as I would want to do my best work for spirit, hoping to seduce it into taking up residence within an object or image, I take care to do the best work I can for others. For the surface value of a piece of art can either encourage or discourage the viewer from entering into the artist's world.

The shaman or dream artist can also heal and empower others

through the artifacts she or he creates. This capacity to heal should not be confused with a capacity to cure. Healing is moving toward wholeness. It can occur even in the final stages of a fatal disease. Healing can also occur on different levels. Sometimes a simple gesture—a gift stone or healing image—can help someone through a difficult period of mourning or grief. It can energize someone to carry on his or her own quest. It can have an effect out of all proportion to its size—like the butterfly of chaos theory that flaps its wings in Nepal and causes a tropical storm in Guatemala. Working with others to help them to create imagery from their own dreams can empower them to access their own healing energy. It's possible that dream images and artifacts may carry energy patterns that heal directly. They may also work on others by helping them repattern their images of themselves.

I once dreamed for a woman who had come to me with a problem.

I'm at a carnival watching a man handle snakes. He tries to get people in the audience to hold the snakes. Some do, some don't; but he fixes his gaze on me. He slides his jacket sleeve up to show me a beautiful rainbow-colored snake wrapped around his wrist like a bracelet. He asks if I will take the snake and wear it myself. He says that it will only bite me once, but that then we will be inseparable. I feel that there is power or advantage to taking this snake energy, but I'm still unsure.

I woke with the issue unresolved. I knew from this dream that I needed to give this woman a material way to choose to bring new energy into her life. I sometimes facilitate the process of someone creating his or her own dream artifact, but since it was my dream, I chose to create it for her. I selected an appropriate branch, carved it, sanded, painted, and finished it. I did these things in a deliberate and attentive way. I invited the power and the spirit of the dream serpent into the carved artifact. This was a descent—a slowing of the energetic vibration of spirit to the point where I could birth it into the world. I was literally teasing and seducing spirit into material form. In presenting it to her, I offered her the same choice with which I'd been presented in my dream—to accept or refuse the new energy. She thought about it seriously, then chose to pick up the painted snake. It is to this day a material reminder of the spiritual change she invited into her life in that moment.

As a dream artist, you may feel no desire to support the healing of an individual, a community, or the world. You may feel that transforming yourself is enough of a task, and you may be right. The healing power we release on our own behalf changes us. And, if we do nothing more than allow ourselves to become balanced and whole, we can still affect the world. If we are empowered, we inspire others to seek their own power. If we are at peace, peace follows us like an enveloping bubble. I've heard people say that if you want to change the world, you should change yourself. I would rephrase this slightly to add that it doesn't matter whether you want it or not: If you change yourself, you *will* change the world.

If you do feel called to give to others through your work as a dream artist, however, there are some aspects of healing through art that are important to understand. We must always be certain to work with the guidance of our higher heart, from a place of detached compassion. We must learn the value and importance of story. We need to know how and when it is appropriate to give and when it is not. Finally, we must understand the role of ceremony in the process of healing.

Healing Art from the Heart

ONE OF THE MOST important elements of healing work is clarity and intention. As dream artists, we work to connect with higher guidance. Through our dreams, our visions, our altered states of consciousness, we try to see more clearly. But it's on the material plane that we do our work, and we must be responsible for the images, artifacts, and energy we send out. To work with and for others, we must be both compassionate and detached from outcomes. Maintaining this balance means that we are less likely to be drained of our own precious energy. Detachment also helps us avoid ego inflation. We must be certain that we are not exercising our capacity to access the wisdom and healing images of the dreaming realm for our own glory.

One of the frustrations we all experience is being around someone who is living through trials, challenges, or difficulties and feeling as though we are powerless to help. We might have made suggestions or offered to help in material ways, but either the suggestions are ignored or the help feels somehow inconsequential. When there seems to be a clear path to the alleviation of suffering and a person is unable to take that path, I try to step back and understand that this may be an experience this person needs to have. Whether an experience is a physical illness or an emotional crisis, it may carry some important lesson. Attempting to intervene in such events—to solve them or "make them better"—is usually pointless, if not counter productive. Even when we do attempt to intervene and heal, there is a generally held belief among those who heal through energetic or spiritual work that one needs, at the very least, the permission of the person one is attempting to heal. Even allopathic medicine acknowledges that if patients don't cooperate with their treatment—if in their hearts they don't want to be healed—the treatment will fail. Or, if it succeeds, it will merely give way to a new disease or condition.

So, as dream artists, what are we to do?

I think we must do what we are called or drawn to do. We must give help where we can without expecting that that help will change the situation. This is what it means to be detached from an outcome. As dream artists, the help we can offer may take the form of healing and empowering art, but we must still work from the perspective of compassionate detachment. This means that when we are setting the intentions by which we work—energetically charging and filling our pieces—those intentions must originate with our higher heart and seek to support—rather than interfere with—that person's experience.

ACCESSING YOUR HEALING HEART

*What follows is a description of one way to follow your
heart in the creation of healing artwork for others. You
may adapt these techniques or use some part of them
in conjunction with your own practice. There are three
parts to this process: a meditation to access your
healing heart, a shamanic journey to receive guidance
from your artist mentor, and a ceremony to consecrate
or empower the piece of art you create.*

Healing Heart Meditation

THIS meditation is ideal preparation for work intended as a healing gift
for another. Find some time where you can sit quietly for fifteen to
twenty minutes. Sitting on the floor is best, but you can sit upright in a
chair if both feet are flat on the ground. Bring with you a candle and a
photograph of the person for whom you will be working. If you don't
have a photograph, a personal object of theirs will do. If neither is available, you will have to form a strong picture of this person in your mind.
Sit in a comfortable position with the candle and photograph in front of
you. Light your candle and begin long slow, deep, breaths originating
from your belly. Gaze at the photograph (or object). Soften your focus,
but don't shut your eyes. Relax your body. Identify places of tension. Direct your awareness to that part of your body, and release the tension.

*Visualize your crown (the top of your head) opening up to a beam
of pink light. This is the power of your healing heart. This is your
connection to the source of spirit. It is a kind of higher heart. Visualize a second beam of blue light being drawn up through the
soles of your feet and the perineum. This is the energy of physical
manifestation. It is the power to do. Feel these two beams of light
mixing into a sparkling violet mist inside you. It may tingle as it
circulates through and fills your body. After you've experienced*

this for a few moments, draw this energy into your heart area. Concentrate it there. Then expand it out around you like a bubble. Push out the borders of this violet bubble until the candle and the photograph (object) are contained within it. Feel the connection between the subject of your meditation and the healing heart energy channeled through your own heart. Hold this sensation.

Now ask this healing heart energy what this person needs to support him or her on the path to healing. This is not the same as asking that someone's symptoms go away, but rather has to do with asking that they have the kind of energy they need if they choose to heal. The guidance you receive at this point may be an image or it may come in words. It may also be just a feeling. Hold onto whatever guidance or impressions you receive, even if it seems contradictory or doesn't make much sense. If the image seems to be outside of the bubble you've created, draw it inside. Sit with this image a few moments longer, then begin to draw the bubble back to you. Feel the energy build inside your body as you draw in this healing heart field. After a few minutes, close off the energy coming in through your feet and perineum and close your crown. You should feel calm and relaxed and ready to apply the energy you have channeled.

✿ Healing Art Quest

IN many of the heroic journey tales, the hero sets out not for personal gain but to heal the king or rescue the princess. Because we tend to view everything in psychological terms, we see these stories today as symbolic of personal healing journeys. While I don't discount this interpretation, it is useful to remember that many heroic journeys are quests for magical healing artifacts.

The shamanic journey itself is such a quest. While it is possible to journey out of curiosity, I find it is always much more effective to journey with a strong purpose. It's as if the spirits know when you are just visiting, and when you are on a mission. To complete this second step in the creative healing process, follow the directions for a shamanic journey in chapter 5—this time journeying with the purpose of discovering a healing image or artifact.

When you met your artist-mentor earlier in the book, you found him or her in the upper or lower world. This is where you should return now. Once you are in the dreaming, remember to call your power animal to you. You should see it right away. Ask your power animal to take you to your artist-mentor. Pay particular attention to what you experience on the journey to your artist-mentor. Your power animal can often give you invaluable guidance about where you are in relation to the person for whom you are asking to work.

When you are with your artist-mentor, ask how you might best create a spirit vessel to manifest the healing energy that was revealed to you in your meditation. If you already have an idea for a painting, ask for specific imagery or a new technique of applying paint. If you intend to model with clay, you might ask for information about glazing or what symbols to inscribe in the piece. If you're going to create a shrine, you might inquire about materials and arrangement. Watch and listen to what is revealed.

Spend as much time with your artist-mentor as you need. Ask to be shown anything that will help to make your work be more effective. Ask for any instructions that might pertain to the specific creation of an artifact or image. When you hear the callback, thank your artist-mentor, excuse yourself, and ask your power animal to return you to your opening back to the waking world. Return to your body and spend a few moments recalling the experience. Log your experience in your notebook.

Now you should have the information you need to work. Use the healing heart energy you tapped into together with the guidance you received from the shamanic journey, but don't feel constrained by either. Ultimately you are responsible for what you manifest, so do the best work you can in each moment. Sometimes what I create looks exactly like what I saw in the dreaming; other times my visions are only inspiration, not a blueprint. Once you've finished creating the healing artwork, the third step in this process of working from the healing heart is to consecrate the piece.

❦ A Ceremony for Consecration

AFTER you've finished a piece of art, whether that work emerges through the process of finding, arranging, altering, or making, it needs to be dedicated to its purpose. This, for me, is the time of formally inviting a certain spirit of energy to take up residence in a piece. For me, this process begins when I'm doing finishing work. When I paint final details or seal and polish a piece, I do it with the conscious intention of drawing spirit into the piece. If I'm arranging, it might be the act of holding each object for a moment before placing it a final position. This begins to set the intention. To complete it, do the following.

Gather a candle, a stone (about the size of flattened baseball) or quartz crystal, some sacred herbs (sage, cedar, sweet grass, or copal) and a small dish or incense burner, some rainwater or spring water, and some relaxing music. Sit in a relaxed meditative pose as described in the healing heart meditation above. Place the object you've created in front of you. Place the candle in front of you on the right. Place the stone in front of you on the left.

In this ceremony, we are reactivating and honoring the energy we accessed in the healing heart meditation described before. To symbolically activate the healing heart energy you received through your crown, light the candle. Light a bit of the sacred herb you've chosen and offer the smoke to the piece of art you've created. You are not smudging the piece, merely sending smoke in its direction. To activate the material energy of creation that you drew up through the soles of your feet and perineum, offer a few drops of water to the stone (representing the earth beneath your feet). You need not go through the process of opening channels for this energy and visualizing it coming into your body. All you need to do is recall the sensation of being filled with the violet mist of these blending energies. Once you have that sensation again, pick up the piece and hold it in your right hand. If you cannot pick the piece up, direct your right palm toward the object. Send the healing heart power you experienced in the initial meditation into the piece through your right hand. Be specific about what kind of energy or spirit you are sending, and for whom this energy is intended.

As you send this energy, you should experience a tingling in your palm or fingertips. When you've sent enough, the tingling will cease. When this happens, set the object down or direct your palm away from the piece. Turn your palm back toward your own navel. This channels any remaining energy back into your own body.

The piece of art you now have—energetically inspired, spiritually guided, and consecrated or dedicated to a sacred purpose—is now ready to give to the person for whom it was made. But before making this gift, you should consider two more elements: the power that comes from sharing the story of the piece, and the actual giving of the gift.

The Importance of Story

CONSIDER THE differences in these three examples.

Story #1. You're walking along thinking about your material needs. Perhaps you're wishing for a bit more prosperity in your life, or maybe you're in serious financial need. Suddenly your eye catches a bright shiny copper penny on the sidewalk. Though it's only a penny and hardly the answer to your prayers, you stop and pick it up.

Story #2. You've been depressed about money matters, worried about how you will make ends meet. You think you've managed to keep this to yourself, so you're surprised when a little hand, perhaps it's your child, or grandchild, or the child of a friend, offers you a new clean penny as a silent gift.

Story #3. You share your concerns about money with an aunt who, though retired now, was a very successful businesswoman in her day. She tells you how she was in exactly your position early in life. She shares being down to absolutely her last penny. She tells you the story of what she discovered that helped her gain control of her financial life. The story has meaning for you, and you feel as if something has been exchanged between the two of you. As you start to leave, she takes a jewelry box from her dresser and opens it. She hands you an old penny wrapped in a faded piece of newsprint. "This is that penny," she says. "The last one I had."

In each example, you end up with a penny in a meaningful way. In each case, it is a kind of symbolic gift. But which of these three pennies do you suppose might seem the most precious? Which would you be most likely to hold onto and cherish? Which will stay with you longest? Probably it will be the third penny. Not because it's worth any more in a material sense, and not because the other pennies are lesser gifts, but because the story and context provided with the third penny have connected you to it in a much more substantial manner.

The healing impact of images and artifacts is dramatically increased by conveying meaning through story along with the gift. I learned this in a very practical manner with the artwork I did as a transition between what I learned in art school and the work I do today. Under the guise of being archaeological artifacts from the collection of the Irrational Geographic Society, my wife and I exhibited and sold work influenced by my dreams and my journeys. When we displayed the pieces, they always had explanatory text that accompanied them. The text provided anthropological background, "the story" of the piece, of the kind one would find in a museum display. I found that when I sold a piece, the person purchasing it always wanted the text as well. Whether they were giving the items as gifts or keeping them for themselves, the stories were important to them.

~~~~~

TELLING THE STORY OF
AN IMAGE OR ARTIFACT

With this exercise, learn to add power to a gift or object
by placing it in context through story.

F OR this exercise we will assume that you have found, arranged, altered, or made some image or artifact. You might have intentionally done this work for someone, or you might have simply done the work and now are planning to give it as a gift to someone. You can do this process for any image or artifact, whether you intend to give it away or not, but it's a nice motivation to imagine this work actually going to someone.

The first step is to gather information. You may use all three methods for accessing guidance: vision-shifting, dreaming, and shamanic journeying. In addition to a title or a descriptive phrase for the piece, there are three types of information you may want to include with a gift you give:

- Inspiration: How the piece came to be.
- Purpose: Why you are making a gift of it.
- Instructions: How it is meant to be used.

Use your journal to write about what inspired the work that you did. If the image or artifact came from a dream, try distilling the dream down to its most important points. The inspiration for a handmade artist's book might have been something like this.

I dream I'm walking through my grandmother's house. I'm drawn to the room with the high four-poster bed. In the room a child in pajamas is sleepily eyeing the bed. I remember that when I was young I was not tall enough to get up on the bed without help. I lift the child into the bed. She hands me a little book she is carrying, and I think she wants me to read to her. But when I open the book I realize it's blank, and I'm going to have to make the story up myself.

If the dream is too personal or specific, try recasting the dream as a fairy tale or myth. This gives you some distance from the material while still holding onto the magical quality of the dream.

Once in a far off kingdom, a spell had been cast upon a young princess. She was forced to wander from room to room in her great castle, never finding a comfortable bed in which to sleep. Her royal family and all the members of the court and all the servants were sleeping a charmed sleep from which they could not awaken, while the princess was without sleep. When a young prince helped the princess find a place to sleep, she gave him a magical book in which the things he would write would all come true.

The inspiration for a piece might have come from a shamanic journey in which an artifact or image was shown to you. It might have been inspired by something you saw in waking life—perhaps your attention was called to an image or artifact in a moment of vision-shifting. Whatever it was that inspired you to create, try to share this in a short paragraph. Not only will it deepen the connection between you, the object, and the person to whom it is being given, but it will also help you, as a dream artist, to track your own sources of inspiration.

The second piece of information you might want to provide is linked to the story or inspiration behind the image or artifact and is the purpose of the gift—why are you making this gift to this person? This is where you bind the gift to the recipient. You can make this an extension of your writing about the inspiration for the piece. For example, continuing on from the dream described above, you might add:

I realized when I woke from this dream that what I had to make for you was a blank book for your stories. For years, I've been entertained and touched by your gift as a storyteller, and I think you should write them down in a special place. I wanted to create a beautiful home for your stories.

Another variation might be:

The book the princess gave to the prince was one much like this. The gift of the book was the realization that the prince had the power to write his own ending to the story of his life. This is also the gift I'm giving to you—the power to retell your own story.

This piece of information is really the heart of the gift. It's a statement of the intention, energy, or spirit behind the artifact or image. This is what you are wishing for or sending to another person. Through the purpose, you convey the healing potential or capacity. You define what qualities reside in the piece. This short paragraph connects the gift and the story behind the gift to the person to whom you are giving it.

The final piece of information you may want to include is instructional—how the piece is to be used. This will not always be necessary. An image may need no instructions. The use of a particular tool, such as a journal, might seem so obvious that instructions are not necessary. But instructions can be more than just how-to information. This is a chance to offer advice or provide inspiration as well. An image, for instance, might be used for meditation. Simple instructions on how to meditate with the painting might be included with it. The instructions that accompany an artist's book might playfully encourage the recipient to write.

Instructions:

1. *To keep the magic alive in the book, you must write something in it every day, even if it's only a word or sentence.*

2. *If you can't write something, drawing something will also keep the power in the book. If you can't draw, paste in cut-out words and images.*

3. *If you write about a life event as though it were a myth or fairy tale and give it a happy ending, or at least an ending that signals the growth or development of the hero, this book will shift your relationship to and perception of that event in a positive way.*

Push yourself a little to imagine possible instructions to accompany your gift. It helps to imagine the healing possibilities behind the images and artifacts you have created. If you are at a loss as to what instructions you should give, do a shamanic journey to your artist mentor or to the upper world to seek guidance. This is often how I come to better understand the work I've done.

The next step is to title the piece. You may already have a title, but if not, try to come up with a title that is descriptive or suggestive of the spirit of the piece. A fun practice is to title pieces as they might be titled in a magical museum of anthropology or archaeology. A hand-thrown clay pitcher for a newlywed couple might become a "Ceremonial Fertility Vessel." A careful arrangement of stones on an antique woven cloth might be titled "Stone Shrine for Remembrance."

The final step is to transfer this information onto a card to accompany the gift. It's fine to present the gift with an oral explanation of its title, inspiration, purpose, and instructions, but always include the card as well. Think of the times that you've received gifts. It's often an emotionally charged moment, which can make it difficult to remember specific details. It is a gift in itself to acknowledge this and provide a reference to which a person can return in quieter moments. Story gives us context and context connects us to the world and to each other.

Select a nice blank card on rich-feeling stock or design your own. Print out your card on a computer, if you have one, using script or decorative type. Make a trip to a quality art supply store and look at their selection of handmade exotic papers. These sheets, when cut down to size, make wonderful gift cards. Consider writing with metallic or colored inks. Draw decorative borders or design elements. Make the card as special as the gift itself.

While I always recommend including a card with the story behind the piece, it isn't always necessary to wrap your gift. But wrapping does add to the ceremonial nature of the exchange. If you decide to wrap the gift, look for unusual materials with which to work. Fabric scraps (which can be reused), leaves and petals for small objects, handmade papers, tissue paper, brown wrapping paper stamped with colorful symbols, or any hand-painted or hand-drawn wrapping paper makes a good covering.

Consider decorating the outside of your package with found objects, such as shells, feathers, pebbles, seeds, pressed flowers and leaves, colorful wire, or string. If the wrapping you choose in some way reflects the gift, so much the better. Now you are ready for the third and final step in the creative healing process: the ceremony.

Art and Healing Ceremonies

The shaman is indispensable in any ceremony that concerns the experiences of the human soul.

—MIRCEA ELIADE

Shamanism: Archaic Techniques of Ecstasy

WHILE IN THE process of completing this book, the tragic school shootings in Littleton, Colorado, occurred. The ArtQuest high school students I worked with at the time wanted to talk about it. We sat in a circle on the floor of the art studio and took turns sharing our feelings. Though this event had occurred halfway across the continent, they were genuinely disturbed. The feeling that was repeated most was helplessness. The students were saddened by the event, and felt a distinct connection. I suppose it was easy for them to imagine something similar happening in their schools. I asked if they would like to have a ceremony to mark the event. I explained that we might send our best energy out in support of those whose lives were lost and those who survived, and they were eager to try.

One thing I have learned about ceremony is that its power increases in direct proportion to how much of ourselves we put into it. Ceremonies that are prepared for us and presented to us can have an impact upon us if we are drawn in through the performance, but the ceremonies we are intimately involved in creating affect us most deeply.

Keeping this in mind, I divided the students into groups of finders and arrangers. The finders would gather special objects, flowers, stones, and other raw materials. The arrangers would clear a space in a wooded area near our studio and construct a shrine at the base of a tree. The shrine was decorated with natural objects to symbolize our intentions. With this work done, we gathered some distance away from the shrine and sat in a circle. Each of the students had brought a short stick and a drum to the circle. They had also brought simple offering gifts they had constructed by hand or written.

After opening our circle and dedicating it to the spirits of those most directly affected by the school violence in Colorado, we began drumming. One at a time, when the feeling seemed right, each student stood up and was escorted to the shrine by an attendant. Along the way they passed a student who was tending a small fire. In turn, each student's stick of wood was added to the fire with a thought or prayer. Then the students were led to the shrine, where they had the opportunity to spend a few quiet moments before leaving their offering gift and being escorted back to the circle.

When everyone had taken a turn, we closed our circle and walked quietly to the shrine to see what it looked like after the offerings had been added. One student read a poem he had left. Other students made quiet comments. In the middle of this solemn moment, a tiny mole popped out of the center of the shrine and scurried about, before disappearing under some leaves. Everyone laughed, and the laughter was a kind of release in itself.

The following day we discussed the ceremony, and the general impression was that the feeling of helplessness and dread had lifted. We all felt as if we had done something, as if we had somehow contributed to the rebalancing of the world.

SIMPLE GIFTING CEREMONIES

When gifts are exchanged ceremonially, their power
and effectiveness increase significantly, as you'll see in
this exercise.

WHETHER you realize it or not, you've already created simple ceremonies. You've probably participated in gift-giving ceremonies. The Christmas mornings of my childhood had very specific ceremonial aspects. We were not allowed to simply tear open our gifts. My father sat by the tree and carefully presented each of us with gifts. He monitored the flow to ensure that no one finished unwrapping too far ahead of anyone else. We were supposed to share what we had opened and thank the person from whom it came. You may already have a good idea of what goes into creating a good gifting ceremony. In fact, though I could prescribe ceremonies for you, the best ceremonies will be the ones that you create or modify for the situations you encounter. What follows is not intended to be a set of careful instructions, but rather some suggestions for creating your own ceremonies. If they seem appropriate, use elements and aspects of these three ceremonies.

Individual Gift Ceremony

MODELED after the Japanese tea ceremony, this way of giving a gift works best when you wish to give a private gift to an individual. Though you can give the gift with other witnesses present, this is really a ceremony between two people.

Select a private, quiet place to hold your ceremony. This may be outdoors or indoors. Trust your intuition. If it feels like the right place, it probably is. Invite the person to whom you wish to present your gift. Make sure you arrive early to prepare the space. Burn some sage to cleanse the area and some sweet grass, cedar, or lavender to draw in refined energy. Define the altar or transitional space you will share with your guest. You can do this by laying a cloth square on the floor in front of you, or on a low tabletop. Make sure that the elements of earth, wind, fire, and water are honored. Light a candle. Have fresh flowers. Even if your gift is wrapped, consider wrapping it again in a cloth with a ribbon tie. Have your gift at hand. Make sure that you have comfortable cushions for you and your guest to sit on. Put on some soft meditative music, and relax for a few moments before your guest arrives. Use this time to do some deep breathing and to vision-shift your awareness.

When your guest arrives, greet him or her warmly. Look your guest in the eye. Speak softly. You needn't be overly solemn or humorless, but you should convey, through your voice, attitude, posture, and demeanor that this is an important moment. Sit opposite your guest and, if appropriate, share a cup of tea or a glass of wine. Ask your guest about his or her day or recent experiences. Really listen to the answers. If you've begun to see auras or energetic patterns around people, pay attention to these as you speak. When the time feels right, explain why you invited your guest. Tell the story of your gift. Give it context.

Finally, present your gift. Unwrap it slowly from the cloth bundle and formally pass it to your guest. Sit quietly as it is opened. Don't try to judge whether your guest "really likes" your gift. Know that you are giving a gift from the heart. Accept praise or thanks graciously, and avoid the tendency to dismiss your work or your efforts. Be proud of the gift you've created. Answer questions and be open to discussion that may arise from the gift.

❃ Birth Gift Ceremony

WHEN my niece was six months old, I conducted a "birth gift ceremony" for our extended family. I prepared the space in advance as described above, making sure there were cushions for everyone. I set up a central altar and asked each family member to bring photographs of ancestors, photographs of family members unable to be in attendance, and a gift symbolic of each person's individual connection to spirit.

I began the ceremony by having everyone enter the sacred space. They crossed a threshold of the four elements, represented by a stone for earth, a candle for fire, a bowl of water for water, and some incense smoke for air. After taking our places, we took turns placing our ancestor photographs on the altar. We did this to spiritually connect my niece to the family she would never be able to know. Then we added photographs of family members who could not be present. Many of them had also sent letters to be read, so we shared these as well. Then we welcomed the four elements, and each individual was asked to welcome his or her concept of spirit.

Next we took turns giving our gifts. The purpose of these gifts was to pass along to my niece the spiritual strength that her elders and family had been able to find. Some people brought natural objects that they had bound together, others brought personally meaningful objects from their own past. My mother provided a beautiful Red Cross volunteer's pin from her youth, explaining that she felt closest to spirit when she was in service. My brother-in-law's brother brought a bundle of natural objects that symbolized his connection to spirit—nature. My wife brought a gift of trees planted in my niece's name to represent her love for growing things.

We shared dreams we had incubated on my niece's behalf and did a guided visualization to see into her future. The ceremony did not take longer than an hour and we learned something of my niece's gifts and reason for choosing to be born. My sister commented later that if we had not done the ceremony, her daughter would still have had the same tendencies and mission, but recognizing these things formally gave all of us a chance to support her growth and development.

A Give-Away Ceremony

THE American Indians of the Pacific Northwest have the tradition of potlatch—the most powerful individual or family is the one who can and does give away the most. While I wouldn't win many converts by advocating that we give away everything we own, we can hold to the spirit of this event by ceremonially giving away something that has been personally meaningful.

A wonderful way to facilitate gift-giving among a group of friends is to host a give-away ceremony. The idea behind the ceremony is to select a personally meaningful gift—something that has had spiritual significance for you or been a source of strength, healing, empowerment, or positive memories. Each person wraps a gift and brings it to a gathering of friends. All the gifts are placed on an open table. The youngest person at the gathering goes first and selects any gift. That gift is unwrapped and the giver explains the meaning and the story behind the gift. Next it is the giver's turn to choose a gift. This cycle continues until all the gifts have been chosen.

The most amazing thing about this ceremony is that in all the times I've facilitated or participated in them, I've never failed to experience wonderful and meaningful synchronicities. It's as if the right gift almost always finds its way to the right person. I've seen an antique cosmetic compact end up in the hands of an aesthetician. I've seen a page of carefully hand-lettered lyrics from a Bob Marley song end up in the hands of a young student from Jamaica who aspires to be a poet. I myself, selecting the very last gift on a table, received a Swiss Army pocketknife just days after losing one I had carried for years.

This give-away ceremony has the added benefit of weaving a group of people together more profoundly.

Notes on Giving

Having discovered the power of making healing art for others, there is a tendency to want to always share these healing gifts. It's a natural urge that grows genuinely from our desire to help others and to share the joy we feel when we create. But sometimes, even with the best of intentions, this gesture can be misinterpreted on the part of others. Here are some of the stumbling blocks you may encounter:

- Your gift may be seen as conflicting with someone's current belief system. If a recipient absolutely does not believe in the healing power of artifacts or images, it does not mean that he or she will be unaffected by it. But it's often best to downplay that aspect of the gift rather than try to impose a new worldview on someone already in a time of crisis.
- Look carefully at your own motives. Even if you feel that the gift

you are giving is self-serving, it doesn't mean you cannot give it. It does mean that you should spend some time in meditation and reflection. Be certain that you are aware of your motivations and not blind to them. If you can hold that awareness and still give the gift, you will find ways to circumvent the aspects that are self-serving.

- Some people do not accept gifts well. The giving and receiving of gifts binds people into community and relationship, and this binding makes some people suspicious and uncomfortable. They are somehow uneasy with being in relationship. When giving to someone like this, it is best to do it remotely. Wrap a gift and leave it behind without a lot of fuss, or allow a third party to deliver it.

With the exception of the example I just cited, I generally think gifting works best with some sense of ceremony. A gift given in ceremony has even more power. This power comes from a richer context and a stronger emotional connection. One word of caution, however. You need to weigh your own motives carefully when deciding to impose a ceremony on others. Sometimes a public ceremony is appropriate. Other times a quiet exchange between the dream artist and the recipient would be best. Also, while asking permission to gift someone with a healing object or image is not absolutely necessary in advance, sometimes it can help alleviate misunderstandings.

For some people, accepting gifts graciously is very hard to do. We sometimes develop an aversion to being indebted or in relationship to anyone. We cannot change others, but we can work to accept the assistance and the gifts of others in a spirit of good faith and in acknowledgment of the healing power of sacred relationship. This is no small task. There is a great deal of cultural conditioning that runs counter to this way of being. But learning to live in balance and in sacred relationship is the true challenge of the shaman and dream artist alike.

The gift of this chapter is

integration.

When you begin to practice the exercises I've described in this

book on a regular basis, the dream artist inside you—your

creative soul—will become a part of your waking life.

chapter 10

Shape-Shifting: *Living* and Practicing as a *Dream Artist*

So why does the world need more dream artists? I've stated my belief that we owe it to ourselves to explore our own creativity and our own paths into the dreaming—that we do our own creative soul recovery—but I think there is another reason that is equally important.

Each of us needs to creatively express the animating spirit of our lives, but the need for regular contact with the dreaming states of consciousness is no less important. Without it we cannot see pattern, or connection, or our deep relationship to the world. We become deaf to the song of our soul. We begin to live out of balance. When our lives were defined by village and tribe, we had regular access to a shaman—someone fluent in the language of dreams, someone with direct access to the dreaming. Now, unless we seek out a therapist or counselor of a particular school of thought, no one facilitates our dreamwork. No one helps us re-imagine the world.

Most of us live cut off from the wisdom of the dreaming world and the joy of creative expression. Even if we feel a calling in this direction, there are few shaman artists to whom we can turn for information and inspiration. We are left to seek guidance from artists who teach us techniques for manipulating materials without addressing spirit. Or we turn to spiritual advisors who are sometimes ambivalent about their own creative energies or, worse, are dismissive of anything existing on the material plane.

The remedy for this is the path of the dream artist.

Becoming a dream artist is a kind of shape-shifting. You will change. You can't help but change. You will find that the ordinary world of a year, a month, a week, a day, or even a moment ago has become a world that's alive and interconnected. A dream artist's worldview is that we all live suspended in a kind of web or weave—linked to the stones, the plants, the animals, the people, and the spirits around us by invisible threads. There are no coincidences, only connections we cannot yet perceive. By entering into the realm of spirit through dreams and trance journeys, we perceive both the pattern and the connecting strands of our lives. Culture and personality may shape what's perceived or how it's expressed, but as a dream artist you will experience a heightened level of energetic awareness—a knowing beyond time and space.

Sometimes this shape-shift occurs suddenly and dramatically, other times the change is slow and subtle. The secret, if there is a secret, to shape-shifting into a dream artist lies with your intention and your will. If you wait until you're certain you are a dream artist to begin living as one, you may never make the shift. If you begin living as a dream artist first, changing how you view the world and altering what you expect from it, you will wake up one morning with the realization that you are fully connected to your creative soul once again—that you are a dream artist.

Living as a Dream Artist

ONCE A WEEK I meet with a group of brave explorers who share and work with each other's dreams. I had set myself the task of dreaming a way to help each of them find his or her dream artist inside. This is the dream I had.

I arrive at the warehouse loft space where I usually meet my dream-sharing group. It is the same and yet much larger, with rooms separated by gauzy curtains. I'm feeling some anxiety because I think I'm supposed to have prepared something—some activity to help my group discover their dream artists. The first person I encounter, my friend David, is playing with a deck of tarot cards. I think he's telling the fortune of the young woman seated opposite him, but as I watch I realize he's doing card tricks. He is giddy with his own ability to know the card the woman picks. I ask him how he does it, and he says he has no idea. He does a few tricks for me and is correct every time. He laughs and plays with the cards.

I wander off with the woman who had been sitting opposite the magician. She asks if I find what she is wearing sexy. She's dressed in a sarong like an Indian princess. I tell her that I find it very sexy, and she smiles and drifts off.

I next encounter an artist friend from my dream-sharing group. She is moving slowly, doing something that looks like tai chi. Every time she gracefully lifts and places each foot, she leaves a rainbow-colored footprint. I can see no paint on the soles of her feet, and I'm about to ask her how she does this, but she holds her finger up to her lips to silence me.

As I move on, I again encounter the woman who asked me about her attire. Again she asks me if I think what she's wearing is sexy. This time she's dressed like a gypsy. I tell her yes, and she giggles and moves along.

I meet a third member of my dream-sharing group sitting cross-legged on the floor before a bowl of burning incense. With the slightest of physical gestures, she causes the smoke to form animal shapes. When I compliment her, she is dismissive of her talent. "It's only smoke," she says. But just as quickly, she's drawn back into creating the shapes.

I move down a long passageway to the sound of bellowing roars. Again I meet the young woman in the changing costumes. This time she's wearing torn jeans and a t-shirt, but she still looks very sexy and I tell her so. She seems happy and follows me to the end of the hall.

The roars I had heard come from a man attacking a huge chunk of marble with a sledgehammer. He swings it around his head and smashes it into the stone with a great shout. Each chunk he removes reveals more of a statue. He's dripping with sweat but seems satisfied by his physical exertions. In another corner, a woman sits carefully making masks. She works in series, each mask a little more elaborate than the one before. The woman in torn jeans and a t-shirt stands close to me, and I'm aware of how sweet her perfume is. I think of how pleased I am that the members of my dream-sharing group have already discovered their dream-artists. It's as if I'm seeing their unfiltered creative souls.

Later, I shared this dream with my group. We discussed what it might mean both as a message to me and as a message to each of them. As I explained what I thought it might mean about each of them discovering their dream artists, heads nodded in agreement. For myself, I understood better that finding and recovering one's creative soul is a very individual process. Exercises and practice can help, but the most important thing is for each of us to find out how he or she best relates to the activity of physical creation. For some of us, like the magician, the engagement with art must be joyous and awe-inspiring. We must simply do the work and allow ourselves to be amazed at the outcome. For those of us who tend toward extremes, like the artist of the rainbow footprints, slowing down and finding balance and focus will help us connect with our creative souls. For those of us who evaluate and critique constantly, we must find way to be enchanted by the process of creating—to move beyond the space and time where we are used to making judgments. Some of us will engage in the work of art explosively—literally giving all our energy over to it. For others, the key will be patience and attention to detail. Finally, some of us will need to find the energy with which to power our creative work. For me, sexuality is a kind of raw generative force, and the young woman in the dream who was continually exploring the boundaries of her sexual energy was looking for the power with which to live her vision of being a dream artist.

To expand upon the meaning of the dream, I used a vision-shifting technique. I sat before my altar with a pen and paper. I lit a candle and some sweet grass, making sure to honor earth, wind, fire, and air. I relaxed my body and focused attention on my breath—gradually rolling my attention inward. When I felt that I had reached a state of relaxed awareness, I formed the question, "What words can I use to amplify the meaning of the dream for each of my friends?" As I formed an image of each of the members of my dream-sharing group, I allowed my hand to begin writing. I kept my eyes squinted to soften my focus, and allowed a minimal amount of my attention to be directed toward the page. The sentences that came from this exercise were brief but direct. I copied them out into my dream artist's journal.

Several hours before the next meeting of my dream-sharing group, I found myself in a gift store. I was not looking for anything in particular, but I had some time on my hands and I allowed myself to be drawn to this particular shop. Not knowing why I was there, I allowed myself to vision-shift for a moment to see what would draw my attention. Turning in a slow circle without focusing on any one thing, I found myself drawn to a series of greeting cards. I was amazed to find that another artist had put into images the very sentiments I had written down for the members of my group. One after another I found cards that perfectly reflected my observations.

I purchased the cards and used them to present these observations to the group. I also asked each person to pose in some stance that reflected how I had perceived him or her in the dream. I made photographs of each person and enlarged them many times with a simple black and white photocopier. I brought the images back and we created collages using magazine images, paints, markers, and other materials to embellish and illustrate our various dream artist personae.

This is what I mean by living as a dream artist. I live and work in the same world we all inhabit, but I try to do it as a dream artist. Sometimes I'm more successful; other times, I get distracted by the mundane business of life. When I'm most successful, I transform the mundane moments into the extraordinary and the enchanted. The secret to this kind of transformation is practice—steady consistent practice. As Arnold Mindell writes in his book, *The Shaman's Body: A New Shamanism for Transforming Health, Relationships, and the Community*, "I have seen in my practice how many shamanic abilities appear when you stop doubting the reality of the spirit. In this moment, something in you transforms, and you develop a deep attention, a steady focus on irrational events. This basic shamanic tool is attention to the dreaming process. When your inner life calls and you stop doubting, a personal transformation begins."

DREAM-SHIFTING

To make a change in your life, whether that means
living as a dream artist or some other change you wish
to manifest, you need to put energy behind the vision of
that change. This exercise will help you energize your
desire to shape-shift into a dream artist in your
waking life.

FOR this exercise, you will need a small stone that you can conveniently carry with you in a pocket or purse on a regular basis.

Find an image that represents the change you want to manifest.

This might be an image of yourself in a certain costume, decorated a certain way, or a picture with your face showing through a cut-out area. Set this image on your altar and study the image. Close and open your eyes until you can see it easily in your imagination. Ask your body how this image of your future makes you feel. If you feel energized, excited, happy, at peace, or even if you feel a little nervous, it's okay to proceed. However, if you find that you have a knot in your stomach, nausea, a sinking feeling, trouble breathing, a coughing spell, a spasm of pain, a headache, or a feeling of dread or panic, hold off on putting energy behind this transformation. Try a smaller step—something requiring a less dramatic shape-shift.

If your body clears the way for you to proceed, hold your stone in your right hand, activate your altar and relax into your own breath. Visualize a black void. Make it as inky or velvety a black as you can imagine. Now see a single star in the distance. Visualize your image of transformation. Bundle it in a ball of light energy and blow it out to the star. Watch it trail off to the star.

Now bring the star itself close to you. Allow it to be drawn into your own third eye (just above and between your eyebrows). Let the star's energy blaze inside your head, filling you with the light energy of your dream. Seven times in a row, explode the star inside your head and let it contract back into its star form. You might visualize this as some cosmologists imagine the universe—exploding out from a big bang, expanding in all directions, and then contracting to a singularity once again. With each explosion, feel the energy charging your very cells with the power to shape-shift into your new life.

Let the star drop down into your heart and repeat the process of expanding and contracting five times. Feel your body suffused with the power of the dream. Now drop the star to your navel area and repeat the process three times. After the third time, take the longest, slowest, deepest breath you can. As you inhale, draw in energy to power your transformation. Hold your breath for as long as is comfortable. Feel the energy surging and amplifying in your body. Hold your breath just beyond your comfort zone. Now bring the stone up to your mouth and exhale—blowing the energy of transformation into the stone.

Gently let the star rise up inside you. Send it out from your third eye. Put it back into the void. Remember that it contains the hologram of your transformation in the same way that the acorn contains all the information necessary to produce a mighty oak tree. Spend some time every day holding your dream-shifting stone. When things do start to shift for you, thank your stone.

ENCHANTED BIOGRAPHY

Reinventing your recent or distant past in this exercise
will add flexibility to your sense of perception.

LIVING as a dream artist means seeing yourself as a dream artist, but sometimes this can be difficult. After all, you're still working in the same job, you still struggle with the same daily issues, and you're still involved with the same people. It can be difficult to imagine change when so much seems to be remaining the same.

In *The Strong Eye of Shamanism: A Journey into the Caves of Consciousness*, Robert E. Ryan reminds us that ". . . The Navaho employ art, the art of sandpainting, to reconnect man with the plenitude of the creative source. In these sand paintings the various stages of the journey are recreated and placed in a meaningful mythic universe that the patient is himself expected to traverse under the medicine man's ritual guidance. It is within this framework that the heroes lead the soul to its source; that human consciousness finds its origin in the divine." To find our own origin in the divine we need art and story. One way of shifting our way of thinking about our lives is to practice the technique of enchanted biography.

Begin summarizing each day's events in your dream journal. Keep it short and succinct. Stick to the details of the day. Don't write more than a page, no matter how exciting your day was. At the end of the week, select one day and rewrite that day in the third person as if you were telling a fairy tale or myth. For example, my description of one of my days might read like this:

I woke up before dawn. My wife woke with me and prepared breakfast for me. She also gave me directions. I left while it was still dark and drove two hours to present a workshop. It was a long and tiring drive like so many others I make. I taught forty teachers how to use cameras to teach their children better. The power at the school went out and the air conditioning failed. We all got hot, but we finished the workshop and everyone expressed their gratitude. They gave me a check and I made the drive home. My wife was glad to see me return.

If I rewrote this as a fairy tale it might sound like this:

The hero arose in the silent darkness to slip away before the sleepy town roused itself. His true love prepared food to sustain him on his journey and gave him a magical map to speed his journey. He made the long trek through the misty morning, avoiding the demons and traps and finding his way with the help of the magical map. His final challenge lay in entering the ancient temple of knowledge and demonstrating his skills of envisioning and oration and his relationship with the great creative spirit. To further test his strength and commitment, the gods drained away all light and air from the temple to see if he could still work his magic. Having passed even this test, he was given a great treasure. He carried this home to share with his wife and community.

Even as I write this about my own experience, my perception of it shifts. My day, so like many other days, takes on a new meaning. Little things that I had forgotten or ignored in my original description—the early morning fog, the dim light of the room in which I was presenting—take on a new significance. What seemed like annoyances now seem like challenges and tests that I successfully negotiated. Even if I hadn't successfully negotiated them, they would now seem to be tests that I had the capacity to succeed at. As I write in this mode, I feel less like a victim and more empowered.

It might be enough to simply retell your experience in a style that allows for the possibility of magic, but you might also want to mark the experience in some way, especially if there seemed to be some lesson in it. As a dream artist, you can think about marking your day or honoring your experience in one of the four creative modes. As a finder, you might look for an image in a magazine that represents your experience. You could cut this out and add it to your journal. You might also select a stone, a shell, a piece of wood, a flower, or any found natural object to mark the observation of your day. As an arranger, you might work with a series of objects to create a small altar or shrine. This would probably be more meaningful for events that seem to have great significance in your life. As one who alters, you may choose to create a talisman that symbolizes your experience. As a maker, you might sketch, paint, carve, or model your experience. Remember that each of these modes can be used in their simplest or grandest form. Sketching with colored pencils in your journal or priming and painting a large canvas are simply different levels of engagement.

You won't do this every day, of course, but in the beginning of your transformation into a dream artist, it can be very useful. Eventually it will be second nature to think of the events in your life as elements in a myth or fairy tale. Soon, there will be no more coincidences, only messages you have yet to decode.

This process of retelling your recent experiences as myth or fairy tale can be extended to reviewing your whole life. Assume, as most fairy tales do, that there is a sense of destiny at work in your life. Retell your life story as if you were destined to become a shaman or dream artist. See in your personal tragedies the challenges that prepared you for the role you are assuming. When I've taken people through this process, they are always amazed that life events which once seemed random and meaningless now seem to fit into a grand design. In addition to your waking life, you can make fairy tales out of your dreams as well. This process often illuminates core or archetypal energies at work in your life.

But, however you use this technique, remember that you are consciously shape-shifting—restructuring the way you think about yourself, your relationships, your life story, and your world. You are becoming a dream artist.

--- ·⟋⟋⟋⟋· ---

JOURNEY STONES

Learning to live more in the moment opens you up to
direct communication from the unseen world on a
regular and continuing basis.

SHAPE-SHIFTING into a dream artist requires that you set aside time to engage in the "work of art," such as with the exercises in this book. It can also be greatly facilitated by studying with artists and shamanic teachers for intense periods of time like daylong, weekend, or longer retreats and workshops. As described above, reshaping and retelling your own stories can also facilitate shape-shifting. Eventually, however, for your shape-shift to be complete, you will need to stop becoming and begin being a dream artist. This is a perceptual shift that moves you into present time—into the moment. Instead of thinking about experiences as being magical after they've occurred, can you think about your life being magical right now, in this moment, as you read these words? Instead of setting aside and segregating time to be a dream artist, can you be a dream artist right here, right now?

While this exercise is similar to others you've read about (and I hope experienced) in this book, it's also an example of how being a dream artist might shape your day-to-day existence. And it's less of an exercise and more like the kind of task an apprentice might be given by a master, or that a hero or heroine might be challenged to accomplish.

To begin with, find a small bag or pouch that you can carry with you during the day. It should be large enough to hold several small stones. The actual size of the pouch you select will determine the size of the stones you will be looking for. The pouch can be of leather or cloth, but it is important that you are able to keep it with you. You can hang the pouch around your neck or tie it to a belt. You can keep the pouch in a pocket, a purse, a daypack, or a briefcase. Into the pouch, place some sage leaves, some shredded tobacco, or some cornmeal (not all three) to use as an exchange offering.

What you're looking for is a set of four stones to represent the four virtues that are most important to you. It's important that you spend a little time identifying these virtues yourself. I can tell you what mine are, but only as a guide, not as a prescription. The virtues I want to manifest in my life are wisdom, courage, compassion, and imagination. For me these virtues balance each other well. Without wisdom, knowledge is a trivial pursuit. Without the courage to stand by and practice what I believe, wisdom is impotent. Without compassion, my courage can become overbearing and manipulative. And, without imagination, I cannot change myself or my world. Think about these things for yourself. If you were beginning an epic quest that would test all your powers and abilities, what virtues would you want to have? If a child, student, or friend of yours was embarking on such a journey, what virtues would you like to tuck into his or her pack?

After you feel comfortable with your four virtues, set an intention to call four stones to you, each one containing the energy of one of the virtues you've identified. As you move through your day, these stones will be calling you. If you listen, if you keep your eyes open, you will find exactly the stones you need. This is where your ability to vision-shift becomes important. Can you attend to the business of your day, while simultaneously remaining open to the possibility of magic, of being called by stone?

Pay particular attention to your senses. Listen for animal sounds, or the sounds of sacred noisemakers like wind chimes, drums, rattles, or flutes. Are they directing your attention to something? Be aware of movement, sparkling light, or flashes of color in your peripheral vision. Soften your focus or squint your eyes. Practice looking through things. Be open to animal messengers crossing your path in physical form or as a picture. Might unusual smells be signaling something important? What about physical sensations, such as goose bumps, shivers, dizziness, or even tripping over something? Consider the possibility that you are being called.

Not only must you become aware of being called, but you must also allow yourself to answer. Stop the car to investigate something that is calling your attention. Deviate from the paved path or route you usually walk if some inner sense or outer sign activates your intuition. Give yourself the gift of time. Break your schedule. Take your watch off. Make having an encounter with spirit, with the luminous nature of the world, as high a priority as anything else you do.

As you find each stone, check it by holding it in your left hand and "listening" for what it might tell you. When you are certain it's the right stone, put it into your pouch. Leave an earth offering of the sacred food (sage, tobacco, or cornmeal). When you have the opportunity, clean your stones. If you feel called to mark them in some way, you may; otherwise, simply keep them together and with you for a period of time. Let their energetic fields mingle with your own.

After you've found your four journey stones, you may want to look for other stones for yourself or as gifts for others. Find stones with the energy of gifts or virtues you would like to give someone. Your intuition will tell you what gift that person could best use, and your intuition will tell you which stone contains that energy. These gifts might include inner calm, courage, guidance, direction, peace, happiness, love, compassion, etc. Try sleeping with each stone and incubating a dream about the virtue or energy of that stone.

If you want, you can mark each stone with a little symbol or image to signify the gift of that stone, as in the gift stones exercise in chapter 8, but this isn't necessary. Over the next several days, carry a different stone with you each day. Give the stone to someone who seems to need it. You needn't make a big deal out of giving it away, but try to do it in a quiet private moment. If it feels appropriate, you can relay the dream that went with the stone. Have no expectations about the effect the stone may have, but do have intention.

Be open to hearing the stories of those to whom you've gifted with the stones, but don't judge the effects of the stone on whether they are acknowledged.

I find that when I make simple gestures like this, the stories I hear back from people are wonderful. Sometimes people are just very grateful for this little gift. I'm sure that some people stare at this little pebble and think, "This is just a rock," but I know that some energy is entering their lives whether they accept it or not.

Through this relatively simple act of finding, combined with the power of the dreaming and an act of intention, you're experiencing living as a dream artist.

Shamans are not hermits or recluses. As a dream artist, you will not live in isolation. You will be part of a community. You may live at the edge of that community in some physical, emotional, or spiritual sense, but you are a part of it. You will hunt and gather for food and medicines in the same manner as your tribe or community. Like your shamanic ancestors from prehistory, you will develop sensitivities that help you live in harmony with, navigate in, and transform within the realm of spirit and energy. You may also find, however, that developing the gifts of attention, intuition, and intention can have an impact on the waking life you share with your community.

As you develop your ability to attend to materials in a sacred manner, you are developing your ability to pay attention to other elements of your life. You may find that all the inanimate objects around you take on a new glow and aura. Once you become aware of this quality, you will want to get rid of things that don't have this pleasing emanation and surround yourself with special things (and this doesn't mean expensive things, it means things that are energetically alive). You may begin to want fewer things—to limit yourself to those things you can regularly attend to. If you share a home with others, you will need to take this a bit more slowly. You might need to apply this principle to your own small private spaces first.

You will also find that your ability to attend to things in a sacred manner extends to people as well. Attention is the gift of the lover.

When you truly pay attention to someone with your whole heart, it improves communication and forges a bond that is difficult to betray. It's impossible to pay attention to more than one thing at a time. People who seem to be able to do it are actually shifting at a high rate of speed between the things to which they are giving their attention. We've all become adept at this constant attention shifting. It's how we watch television. It's how we manage businesses. It's how we interact with family and friends. The kind of attention you develop through a practice like meditation or shamanic attention is a powerful gift when you direct it at others. When was the last time you felt someone was freely giving you his or her full and undivided attention? How did it make you feel?

Developing your intuition—your extrasensory ways of knowing—can also be a benefit in your daily life. Intuition is the navigator's gift. There are, undoubtedly, certain situations in which decision making is hampered by insufficient information, but for most of the decisions we make on a daily basis, our problem is too much information. CEOs of major corporations have a wealth of information, market research, and expert opinion at their disposal when they need to make a decision, but in the end this doesn't make it any easier to choose one of several paths. Even the average person has access to huge amounts of information. What we need is not more information, but other ways of knowing.

Using intuition is more than simply guessing. Intuition adds internal or spiritual guidance to the information we gather through our physical senses. If your percentage of successful decisions is high, then intuition is probably at work. You are utilizing information to which everyone else has access, and then you are allowing your intuition to tell you what you're not supposed to be able to know. Even if your average of successful decisions is low, you may also be tapping your intuitive powers, but then rejecting them. Successful people, whether they admit it or not, always rely on intuition.

While attention and intuition are about being receptive and open to possibilities, intention is about being active—energetically active. Intention is the magician's gift. Just as intuition is more than just guessing, intention is more than just wishful thinking (though it's a great phrase, *wishful thinking*—shouldn't all thinking be wish-full?).

Intention is sending a thought form into the future. It's launching a rocket containing a possible outcome into some point in your future. If you send it with enough energy and guidance, it will arrive where you want, when you want it. Intention harnesses desire to imagination. You must both want an outcome and be able to imagine or see it clearly in your mind; but, of the two, imagination is the most potent. This is important to remember. Many people who seem to dwell on negative outcomes, fears, and anxieties actually draw those realities to themselves. It is as if the thought forms they send into their futures are all negative.

Developing intention requires an understanding of the power of ritual and repetition. These are the technologies that give power to our thought forms. Desire and imagination keep our thought forms on course, while ritual and repetition give them the energy they need to reach their point of fulfillment.

While each of the skills—attention, intuition, and intention—are useful in their own right, it is when they come together through some regular practice that they become powerful. Attention alone opens you up to a world of information, but without intuition, you have fewer options for decision making. When you rely on intuition without developing your ability to pay attention in a sacred way, you will not trust your choices. You will find yourself questioning and doubting and sometimes unable to distinguish between affirmative intuition and self-destructive behavior. Intention alone becomes a manipulative tool. You can use it to get what you want; but without attention and intuition, what you think you want might be the worst thing you could have.

The shamanic skills of attention, intuition, and intention are of equal importance. You may find that you are already adept at one or more of them. Some skills may come easier than others. The important thing to remember is that once you begin down this path, the things you will discover as you use attention, intuition, and intention will affect every aspect of your life.

As a dream artist, the images and artifacts you find, arrange, alter, and make can have real power. I had a friend who lived a full, rich life. In the years that I knew him, he never failed to make me laugh. When I sat up with him all night in the hospital while modern medicine helped him battle his cancer, my heart literally went out to him. I was drawn into the dreaming. As he labored to breathe, rumbling and moaning in pain and discomfort, this is what I saw.

I'm standing on a hill. The ground beneath my feet is vibrating as if a constant earthquake is churning deep below the surface. The sky is cloudy, and it feels as if it might rain. For some reason I don't know where to go or what to do. I remember that I'm here to help my friend, but I don't know what that means exactly. Suddenly an old man is next to me. He is shorter than I am, with bald head and farmer's coveralls. I ask this man how I can help and he points to the top of the hill. There is an old gnarled tree. It looks dead, but as we walk up to it, I see that there is some new growth on it. The old man says, "It'll last another season. Time enough." I notice that there are ornaments and photographs and various tools hanging from the tree. I put my hand on the tree. Though it is old, it makes me feel good to connect with it. I feel the rumble of the ground through the tree.

I returned from this journey where I had begun, with my hand on my friend's chest. True to the dream, he did come through the treatment and gained a little over a year of his life. I made the spirit tree I saw in my dream as a little altar for his hospital room. I cannot and would not claim that this piece affected his physical body, but it did touch his spirit body and in that, it had real power.

Of course, becoming a dream artist doesn't mean that one must disavow science and rational thought. Remember that the shaman or dream artist walks in two worlds—the material world and the dreaming world. In fact, upon close examination, cutting edge thought in the fields of physics, biology, and psychology seems more and more shamanic.

Physicist Fred Alan Wolf has explored the world of the shaman and the world of dreams in light of the description of the universe provided by quantum physics. He finds nothing contradictory in what shamans have claimed about the nature of reality and what scientists now believe is not only possible but also likely. Dean Radin, Ph.D., author of *The Conscious Universe: The Scientific Truth of Psychic Phenomena*, has turned the science of statistical verification toward a century's worth of experiments in psychic phenomena and finds compelling evidence for and proof of clairvoyance, telepathy, telekinesis, and other experiences commonly dismissed by those claiming to be rational and scientific. Chaos theory, superstring theory, and holographic modeling describe the universe in much the same way that shamans always have. These new models describe a place where energy, matter, time, and space are identical and interchangeable; a place where cause and effect is not so ordered and predictable; a place where the mere act of observing alters the outcome; and a place where space/time starts and stops and what is in between is neither space nor time.

This is the shamanic world, the world of nonordinary reality, the place of dreams. The science of quantum physics seems to validate it. Dream artists take the next step—exploring and utilizing this place between time and space, this dreaming world.

I dream I'm standing opposite a beautiful woman. There is a game board between us with elaborate and complex markings and playing pieces. I don't understand how the game is played, and worse, I don't think I am capable of understanding. It seems too difficult. I'm embarrassed that I don't understand the game, because I know I'm supposed to play it with the woman in the dream.

As I look up at her, she slowly begins to unbutton her dress, revealing her breasts slowly and erotically. Between her breasts there is an opening—a slit into which she reaches and removes her heart. It's not a bloody or violent act. Rather it's gentle and sensual. She places the heart down on the game board and suddenly it lights up. The board sparkles with gold and silver and crystalline forms. All at once I understand how the game is played. I know every aspect of the game as if I'd played it for years.

I woke from this dream with the simple but powerful understanding that acting from an open heart, putting heart into what I choose to do is the real key to playing the game of life. If I can leave you with nothing but this thought—this understanding—I will feel that the journey of writing this book has been worthwhile.

It feels important, as this book draws to a close, to add that being a dream artist is a journey—not a destination. I choose to describe what I do and teach and see in others as being the work of the dream artist rather than shamanic art for a specific reason. When one uses the term "shamanic art," it conjures up images that range from marvelous to painful. At the positive end of the spectrum one thinks of shamanic art as hand-carved walrus ivory soul catchers, or Navajo sand paintings, or brightly decorated Aboriginal maps of the dreaming, or beaded Lakota medicine pouches and Huichol string paintings. These are beautiful and authentic expressions of tribal cultures that happen to be shamanic. Sometimes I shiver when I walk through a museum with collections of tribal shamanic artifacts. I can feel the power that still resides in these objects and images. There is much we can learn from tribal shamanic artifacts, but I sometimes cringe when I see their forms, patterns, and designs copied by artists and shamanic practitioners as if the power resided in the surface qualities.

As dream artists we are contemporary shamanic practitioners. We are forging something distinct and unique while building on the knowledge and tradition of tribal shamanic practice. We need to understand the idea behind sacred tools such as medicine bags, soul catchers, and fetish objects, but then we must find our own expression of these forms. This may grow out of an exploration of personal ancestral heritage or from the guidance of the dreaming itself, but it must come if we are to be authentic.

Anthropologist Michael Harner's lasting contribution to contemporary shamanic practice was to strip away the culture-specific practices to what he called a core shamanism—the common practices that hold true for most shamanic cultures. I think the same thing must happen for dream artists. We must learn from tribal and cultural precedents, but we must go our own way. We will all have in our collections and among our tools significant pieces from different cultural traditions. I have two elk antler rattles made by an Inuit shaman-artist. I have a small hand-painted pot in the Aboriginal tradition. But I also have two ceramic rattles made by a contemporary artist, which owe their appearance more to her inner journeys than to any cultural appropriation. One of my favorite examples of a dream artist at work is the late Susan Seddon Boulet. Her paintings of shamans and spirits have graced calendars and book covers. They always seem to begin with a cultural tradition in mind, but what breathes life into them is that her vision is larger than any one culture. Her paintings are not about shamans or shamanism, they are shamans—spirits in a two-dimensional world, which reckon time at an infinitely slower pace.

Some dream artists are just beginning to explore the world of their own dreams. Their work may merely quote from the shamanic. They are being called through their artistic souls, but they have not yet answered. Other dream artists have journeyed into the dreaming and returned to tell us about their experience. Their work is reportage and illustration. They may not yet fully embrace the spirit behind their work, but they are on the path. Still others are living the life of the dream artist more fully. Some of these are dream artists who work only from their night dreams, or only from their waking dreams. If you embark on the path of the dream artist, you will discover your own best way of working just as have those who have gone before you.

It's important that you pursue this path of the dream artist, or not, as you are called. If you do, you will begin caring for your own soul. But with this journey there is both a spiral inwards—a journey into your own dreaming—and a spiral outward. With the inward spiral, you come to know your own power and hear the voice of your own creative soul. As you make the outward spiral, you will begin to care for the souls and dreams of others. As you invite magic and enchantment into your own life, you will be inviting these things into the lives of those around you. I hope you will take it upon yourself to encourage and empower others to exercise their creativity as dream artists. As a dream artist you can be both a healer and a teacher. You can help people find their power and you can make magic.

This is the challenge.

This is the journey.

I wish you good dreaming.

sources of music

Music and sound are very important to me. While it would be impractical to list my entire collection, I would like to recommend some recordings that I use in my workshops and find especially useful. In some cases the artists are a bit hard to find, so I've listed contact information.

Shamanic Journeying

THE best recordings for doing shamanic journeys are Michael Harner's series produced by the Foundation for Shamanic Studies. There were seven recordings in this series the last time I checked:

- *Solo and Double Drumming*
- *Didgeridoo*
- *Singing Chorus*
- *Tibetan Bowl*
- *Double Drumming*
- *Rattle*
- *Multiple Drumming*

My own favorites are *Multiple Drumming*, *Didgeridoo*, and *Rattle*, but this is a purely personal preference. You should find what works best for you. They are available by mail through the Foundation for Shamanic Studies, P.O. Box 1939, Mill Valley, CA 94942; (415) 380-8282.

Shamanic Movement

IF movement helps you enter a trance state, consider the work of Gabrielle Roth. Along with her group, The Mirrors, she has created a body of music that is designed to carry the dancer into an altered state of consciousness. Her recordings include:

- *Totem*
- *Luna*
- *Trance*
- *Waves*
- *Ritual*
- *Bones*
- *Initiation*

My favorites are *Totem, Luna*, and *Trance*. They are available by mail through Raven Recording, P.O. Box 2034, Red Bank, NJ 07701; (201) 642-1979.

For additional passionate percussion, I highly recommend David and Steve Gordon's *Sacred Spirit Drums*, available by mail through Sequoia Records, P.O. Box 280, Topanga, CA 90290; (800) 524-5513. I also recommend percussionist Mickey Hart's work with his group Planet Drum. His work is commonly available at most record stores.

Trance Music

THE following pieces are personal favorites of mine. These recordings never fail to take me into a trance state.

Craig Kohland and Chuck Jonkey record under the name Shaman's Dream Music. The two pieces I use most are *Breathing* and *Bindu*. Their music is a deeply relaxing blend of synthesizer and guitar mixed with natural recorded sound. Their work is available by mail through Shaman's Dream Music, 25604 Wildwood Drive, Calabasas, CA 91302.

Tanya Gerard and Rob Thomas record as Inlakesh. Their recording, *The Dreaming Gate*, is a sonic field trip in which the magic bus is didgeridoos, Tibetan horns, gamelan gongs, and a variety of rhythm instruments. They can be reached at P.O. Box 8237, Santa Fe, NM 87504; (505) 989-6642.

CHÖ is a beautiful blend of Steve Tibbet's guitar and the songs of Buddhist nuns from the Nagi Gompa Nunnery in Nepal. This is a rich hypnotic blend of sounds that is wonderful to listen to while working or meditating.

Cellist David Darling's recordings, *Eight String Religion* and *Dark Wood*, are both moving and evocative pieces that I return to again and again.

Healing Music

ONE of the best ways to build a collection of music for trance, healing, relaxation, or meditation is through The Relaxation Company's Acoustic Research Series. Each set of four CDs or audiocassettes contains four complete works by pioneers in the healing power of sound. It's hard for me to recommend just one set because each set has pieces I particularly like. But if I had to recommend just one for starting with, it would be *The Art and Science of Healing Music*, because of Will Seachnasaigh's recording, *Dreamings*, and Tom Kenyon's *Soma*.

bibliography

Abram, David. *The Spell of the Sensuous: Perception and Language in a More-than-Human World*. New York: Pantheon, 1996.

Allen, Pat B. *Art is a Way of Knowing: A Guide to Self-Knowledge and Spiritual Fulfillment through Creativity*. Boston: Shamabala, 1995.

Baring, Ann and Jules Cashford. *The Myth of the Goddess: Evolution of an Image*. New York: Arkana, 1993.

Belle, Maureen L. *Gaiamancy: Creating Harmonious Environments*. Greenbank, Wa.: White Doe Productions, 1999.

Coburn, Chuck. *Reality Is Just an Illusion: The World of Shamans, Ghosts, and Spirit Guides*. Saint Paul: Llewellyn Publications, 1999.

Cowan, Tom. *Shamanism as a Spiritual Practice for Daily Life*. Freedom, Ca.: The Crossing Press, 1996.

Cruden, Loren. *The Spirit of Place: A Workbook for Sacred Alignment*. Rochester, Vt.: Destiny Books, 1995.

Diaz, Adriana. *Freeing the Creative Spirit: Drawing on the Power of Art to Tap the Magic and Wisdom Within*. New York: HarperSanFrancisco, 1992.

Gold, Aviva, and Elena Oumano. *Painting from the Source: Awakening the Artist's Soul in Everyone*. New York: HarperPerennial, 1998.

Gore, Belinda. *Ecstatic Body Postures: An Alternate Reality Workbook*. Santa Fe: Bear & Company, 1995.

Guiley, Rosemary Ellen. *Dreamwork for the Soul: A Spiritual Guide to Dream Inter-pretation*. New York: Berkley Books, 1998.

Harner, Michael. *The Way of the Shaman*. New York: HarperSanFrancisco, 1980.

Heinze, Ruth-Inge. *Shamans of the Twentieth Century*. New York: Irvington Pub-lishers, 1991.

Hoffman, Kay. *The Trance Workbook: Understanding and Using the Power of Altered States*. New York: Sterling Publishing, 1998.

Ingerman, Sandra. *Soul Retrieval: Mending the Fragmented Self*. New York: HarperSanFrancisco, 1991.

Ingerman, Sandra. *Welcome Home: Following Your Soul's Journey Home*. New York: HarperSanFrancisco, 1993.

Jamal, Michele. *Deerdancer: The Shapeshifter Archetype in Story and Trance*. New York: Penguin Books, 1995.

Lake-Thom, Bobby. *Spirits of the Earth: A Guide to Native American Nature Sym-bols, Stories, and Ceremonies*. New York: Plume, 1997.

Lawlor, Robert. *Voices of the First Day: Awakening in the Aboriginal Dreamtime*. Rochester, Vt.: Inner Traditions, 1991.

Levy, Mark. *Technicians of Ecstasy: Shamanism and the Modern Artist*. Norfolk: Bramble Books, 1993.

McNiff, Shaun. *Earth Angels: Engaging the Sacred in Everyday Things*. Boston: Shambhala, 1995.

McNiff, Shaun. *Art as Medicine: Creating a Therapy of the Imagination*. Boston: Shambhala, 1992.

Mellick, Jill. *The Natural Artistry of Dreams: Creative Ways to Bring the Wisdom of Dreams to Waking Life*. Berkeley: Conari Press, 1996.

Mindell, Arnold. *The Shaman's Body: A New Shamanism for Transforming Health, Relationships, and the Community*. New York: HarperSanFrancisco, 1993.

Moss, Robert. *Conscious Dreaming: A Spiritual Path for Everyday Life*. New York: Three Rivers Press, 1996.

Moss, Robert. *Dreamgates: An Explorer's Guide to the Worlds of Soul, Imagination, and Life Beyond Death*. New York: Three Rivers Press, 1998.

Perkins, John. *Shapeshifting: Shamanic Techniques for Global and Personal Trans-formation*. Rochester, Vt.: Destiny Books, 1997.

Prechtel, Martin. *Secrets of the Talking Jaguar: A Mayan Shaman's Journey to the Heart of the Indigenous Soul*. New York: Jeremy P. Tarcher/Putman, 1998.

Radin, Dean. *The Conscious Universe: The Scientific Truth of Psychic Phenomena*. New York: HarperEdge, 1997.

Rael, Joseph. *Ceremonies of the Living Spirit*. Tulsa: Council Oak Books, 1998.

Ryan, Robert E. *The Strong Eye of Shamanism: A Journey Into the Caves of Consciousness*. Rochester, Vt.: Inner Traditions, 1999.

Samuels, Michael, and Mary Rockwood Lane. *Creative Healing: How to Heal Yourself by Tapping Your Hidden Creativity*. New York: HarperSanFrancisco, 1998.

Somé, Malidoma Patrice. *The Healing Wisdom of Africa: Finding Life Purpose Through Nature, Ritual, and Community*. New York: Jeremy P. Tarcher/Putnam, 1998.

Tonay, Veronica. *The Art of Dreaming: Unlock Your Dreams to Unlock Your Creativity*. Berkeley: Celestial Arts, 1995.

Wilcox, Joan Parisi. *Keepers of the Ancient Knowledge: The Mystical World of the Q'ero Indians of Peru*. Boston: Element, 1999.

Winsor, Janice. *Opening the Dream Door: Using Your Dreams for Spiritual and Psychic Development*. Carmel, Ca.: Merrill-West Publishing, 1998.

Wolf, Fred Alan. *The Dreaming Universe: A Mind-Expanding Journey Into the Realm Where Psyche and Physics Meet*. New York: Simon & Schuster, 1994.

Wolf, Fred Alan. *The Eagle's Quest: A Physicist Finds Scientific Truth at the Heart of the Shamanic World*. New York: Simon & Schuster, 1991.

about the author

Tom Crockett is a writer, an artist, a teacher, and a shamanic practitioner. He has a master of fine arts degree from the School of the Art Institute of Chicago and has continued his study of dreams, art, and indigenous shamanic traditions for over fifteen years. In addition to exhibiting his artwork in nationally recognized museums and galleries, he has taught both at the high school and university level. He is currently an education consultant to the Polaroid Corporation and develops curriculum materials for creative teaching and visual learning. He also directs an after-school, arts-based mentoring program in Norfolk, Virginia, called ArtQuest.

For information about subscribing to *Dream Artist Tribe: A Newsletter for Shamans, Artists, and Dreamers*, or for more information about Tom's Dream Artist Path workshops, he may be reached at Dream Artist Tribe, 1220 Manchester Avenue, Norfolk, VA 23508, or by email at *sayer@pilot.infi.net*.